Shakespeare's Rome
REPUBLIC AND EMPIRE

Shakespeare's Rome
REPUBLIC AND EMPIRE

Paul A. Cantor

CORNELL UNIVERSITY PRESS
ITHACA AND LONDON

First published 1976 by Cornell University Press.
Published in the United Kingdom by Cornell University Press Ltd., 2-4 Brook Street, London W1Y 1AA.

International Standard Book Number 0-8014-0967-5
Library of Congress Catalog Card Number 75-36522
Printed in the United States of America by York Composition Co.
Librarians: Library of Congress cataloging information appears on the last page of the book.

Contents

Preface   7
Acknowledgments   19
Introduction: Romanness in Shakespeare   21

Part One: *Coriolanus*

1. The Republican Regime   55
2. The City without a Ruler   78
3. The Man without a City   99

Part Two: *Antony and Cleopatra*

4. The Politics of Empire   127
5. The Liberation of Eros   155
6. Love and Tyranny   184

Notes   209
Index   227

5

Preface

i

This study of *Coriolanus* and *Antony and Cleopatra* is based on the assumption that Shakespeare's Roman plays may provide an opportunity to learn something about Rome as well as about Shakespeare. As innocuous as this assumption seems, it runs counter to the most common critical attitude toward the Roman plays. Ever since Ben Jonson, it has been fashionable to question Shakespeare's knowledge of Rome, and in some cases even to maintain that his Romans are merely Elizabethan Englishmen in disguise.[1] This view does not, however, seem to result from actual study of Shakespeare's Rome, but rather takes the form of a critical presupposition. For one reason or another, critics assume from the outset that Rome is at most of peripheral interest in Shakespeare's Roman plays. Shakespeare is concerned with universal human nature, one argument runs, and therefore is not interested in whether a given character is a Roman or an Englishman. In the classic formulation of Samuel Johnson's *Preface to Shakespeare:* "His story requires Romans . . . , but he thinks only on men. . . . A poet overlooks the casual distinctions of country and condition, as a painter, satisfied with the figure, neglects the drapery."[2] Other critics feel that as a poet Shakespeare cannot have been interested in so unpoetic a subject as politics, and therefore could not have directly concerned himself with so political a subject as Rome.[3] Another argument runs that Shakespeare as an

7

Elizabethan Englishman was simply too remote in time from
Rome to be able to understand it correctly,[4] and therefore any
investigation of his portrait of Rome would be of antiquarian
interest only.

Without attempting to criticize these positions at length,
one may point out that each in its own way begs the question.
Johnson may be right in saying that Shakespeare overlooks
"the casual distinctions of country and condition," but can
one be certain without investigation that all such distinctions
are merely casual? Only unprejudiced study of Shakespeare's
Roman plays can determine whether or not there is something
essentially Roman about his characters. As for the second
view, to come to the Roman plays with the assumption that
Shakespeare was uninterested in politics is to make a judgment
before examining the major piece of evidence on which that
judgment must be based. At first sight, Shakespeare's Roman
plays seem to deal with very political subjects; they are certainly the most political of his tragedies. Thus only in the
course of studying the Roman plays can one legitimately
come to any conclusion about Shakespeare's interest in politics. As for the third view, as a kind of self-fulfilling prophecy,
it has the defects of any historicist position. If we assume a
priori that Shakespeare was incapable of understanding Rome,
we will never read his Roman plays carefully enough to determine whether in fact he had any insights into Rome. It is
all too easy not to find something when one is convinced from
the start that nothing is there.

In short, the problem with making any theoretical presup-
positions as to what Shakespeare could or could not have
known about Rome is that it prejudices our reading of the
Roman plays in the direction of inattention to his actual portrayal of Rome. Only by admitting at the outset the possibility that something can be learned about Rome from Shakespeare's Roman plays will a critic study them with sufficient
care to discover whatever insights they may embody. I hope,

then, with this book to reopen the question of Shakespeare's knowledge and understanding of Rome, in the belief that investigating this subject reveals new dimensions to his achievement in the Roman plays.

Perhaps the decisive heuristic advantage to having provisional respect for Shakespeare's knowledge of Rome is that it imposes upon the critic himself the task of learning as much as possible about Rome. To give only one example of how lack of knowledge about Rome has led to difficulties, critics seem to disagree over the relatively simple question of what form of government is portrayed in *Coriolanus;* most call the Rome of *Coriolanus* an aristocracy, but some speak of Shakespeare's Rome as if it were instead a democracy.[5] If one considers only institutions like the Senate or the consulship in Shakespeare's Rome, the regime does appear to be based on an aristocratic principle, but if one looks at the tribunate and the plebeians' veto power, it appears based on a democratic principle. Critics who habitually make light of Shakespeare's interest in politics might attribute this apparent confusion to the playwright himself. Shakespeare, they could argue, simply portrayed Rome as an aristocracy at some points and a democracy at others, without caring about the contradiction, or perhaps without even being aware of it.

But it is not Shakespeare who is confused about the form of government in Republican Rome. If, as most discussions of the political aspects of *Coriolanus* seem to assume, only three possible forms of government exist (monarchy, aristocracy, and democracy),[6] classifying Shakespeare's Rome would indeed be difficult. But as writers in antiquity themselves pointed out, the Roman Republic cannot be understood on the model of one of the simple regimes. Political theorists have always considered the Roman Republic an example of a fourth form of government, the so-called mixed constitution or mixed regime,[7] which involves precisely the blend of aristocracy and democracy that Shakespeare portrays in *Coriolanus*. In this

case, Shakespeare's knowledge of Rome is evidently better
than that of many of his critics. The more one reads about
Rome, the more one is impressed by Shakespeare's grasp of
the essential nature of the Roman regime and the central issues
involved in Roman history. At the outset I can of course offer
this as only one reader's impression; I hope to document the
point in the course of discussing the Roman plays, showing,
for example, in Part One that understanding the working of
the mixed regime is essential to understanding the action of
Coriolanus.

ii

As important as it is in reading *Coriolanus* to have some
grasp of the details of the Republican regime, it is even more
important in approaching the Roman plays as a group to be
aware of the overall contrast between the Roman Republic
and the Roman Empire. For in studying Shakespeare's Rome,
we are actually confronted by two Romes with fundamentally different natures. We should be aware that the Empire,
which fell heir to the unparalleled military conquests of the
Republic, did not preserve the political principles that had
made those conquests possible, above all the Republic's concentration on encouraging martial valor in its citizens. The
Empire was, figuratively as well as literally, a gigantic holding
action, with the result that many of the special strengths and
virtues that had distinguished the Republican Romans disap-
peared, or at least began to wither, among the Imperial Romans. Throughout most of the history of the Republic, Roman
existence was basically civic in nature, since the city provided
the focus for the lives of its citizens. Once Rome began to extend its conquests beyond the borders of Italy, however, the
city itself began to lose its centrality in Roman life. Particularly important in undermining the primacy of the city
were the prolongation of military commands beyond the original limit of one year, which allowed generals to develop

private loyalties in their armies,[8] and the extension of Roman citizenship to all the peoples of Italy. Montesquieu writes of this second development:

After this, Rome was no longer a city whose people had but a single spirit, a single love of liberty, a single hatred of tyranny. . . . Once the peoples of Italy became its citizens, each city brought to Rome its genius, its particular interests, and its dependence on some great protector. The distracted city no longer formed a complete whole. And since citizens were such only by a kind of fiction, since they no longer had the same magistrates, the same walls, the same gods, the same temples, and the same graves, they no longer saw Rome with the same eyes, no longer had the same love of country, and Roman sentiments were no more.[9]

As we shall see, *Coriolanus* is set long before these developments took place, when the Roman spirit was still intact; *Antony and Cleopatra*, on the other hand, is set long after the process Montesquieu describes had run its course and the Roman spirit had been thoroughly corrupted.

One must bear in mind these differences between the Republic and the Empire in order to understand why being a Roman in the world of *Coriolanus* is quite different from being a Roman in the world of *Antony and Cleopatra*. *Coriolanus* portrays Rome very early in its history, when the city's territory did not extend much beyond its own walls, but *Antony and Cleopatra* takes up Rome's story at the point when its empire had reached its greatest extent. To live in a small republican city, struggling against hostile neighbors and just beginning to feel its strength, is obviously not the same as to live in a vast imperial realm, with no more worlds to conquer and hence with the peak of Roman achievement behind it. Shakespeare's sensitivity to the differences between the Republic and the Empire, which informs the setting, characterization, and action—even at times the imagery and style—of *Coriolanus* and *Antony and Cleopatra*, is the surest indication of how well he understood the phenomenon of Rome and Romanness.

For this reason I have organized this study around the contrast between the Republic and the Empire as portrayed in the last two Roman plays Shakespeare wrote.[10] It seemed to me significant that several years after writing *Julius Caesar*, which deals with the transition from the Republic to the Empire, and in which the issue of Republic versus Empire is the focal point of all the action and much of the dialogue, Shakespeare went on to write two more Roman plays, one dealing with the origins of the Republic and the other with the origins of the Empire. One can easily account for his writing *Antony and Cleopatra*, since it is the natural historical sequel to *Julius Caesar*, whose thread of action it does pick up and continue. On the other hand, Shakespeare's choice of the subject of Coriolanus has often puzzled readers, since this story has never been as famous as that of Julius Caesar or Antony and Cleopatra and has never attracted much attention from artists.[11] Other playwrights of Shakespeare's time took up the period in Roman history at the end of the Republic and the beginning of the Empire; what seems to be most characteristic of Shakespeare is the interest he shows in *Coriolanus* in the early days of the Republic.[12] In a discussion of *Coriolanus*, Harold Goddard offers the somewhat hesitant suggestion: "If its author had been historically minded, much of the play might be explained as an attempt to present the spirit of an early austere Rome."[13] Much less tentatively Geoffrey Bullough offers a similar explanation of Shakespeare's choice of Coriolanus as a subject:

What led Shakespeare to write this play on a comparatively minor and early figure in Roman history? By 1607 he had presented in *Julius Caesar* and *Antony and Cleopatra* two studies of Rome at the end of the Republic. He may have wished to show something of Rome in its beginnings. . . . He had only to glance into Livy and Florus or Plutarch to realize that Rome was not built in a day and that the story of Coriolanus illustrated its early state.[14]

The story of Coriolanus does take place during what amounted to the founding of the Roman Republic. Although the Republic is customarily dated from the expulsion of the Tarquin kings, its most characteristic institution was the tribunate, which gave the plebeians a share of power, and by introducing the popular element into Roman sovereignty gave the Republican regime its mixed character.[15] Since *Coriolanus* begins with the creation of the tribunate, and goes on to dramatize its precarious survival through a grave constitutional crisis, the play provides a portrait of the origins of republicanism in Rome.

One can hardly be sure of an artist's intentions merely from his choice of subject matter. The most one can say is that if Shakespeare had wanted to contrast the early days of the Republic with the early days of the Empire, he could not have chosen two better lives from Plutarch to dramatize than those of Coriolanus and Antony. Fortunately more evidence can be found in the texts of the plays that *Coriolanus* and *Antony and Cleopatra* can be profitably read as companion pieces, evidence which I hope to unfold in the course of my discussion. Time and again we find images, motifs, in some cases almost whole scenes from the two plays which work together to contrast the world of one with that of the other. For introductory purposes, I want only to suggest how the individual stories of Coriolanus and Antony illuminate each other. The two heroes embody different mixtures of heroic virtues and vices, and the vices of one serve to set off the virtues of the other. Whereas Antony wavers in command and lets his greatest opportunities escape him, Coriolanus displays a singlemindedness that borders on fanaticism. By the same token, whereas Coriolanus' arrogance eventually causes even the men for whom he has won great victories to banish him, Antony, with his generosity and human warmth, is able to win the love of even those whom he has led to defeat. If I have begun to sound like Plutarch in the comparisons with which he closes his pairs of biographies, it is a good reminder that Shakespeare

had before him in the *Parallel Lives* a model for using the
stories of individual men to develop a comparison between
different regimes, Greece and Rome in Plutarch's case. Anyone familiar with Plutarch's technique of pairing biographical
subjects would not reject out of hand the suggestion that
Shakespeare in dramatizing the stories of Coriolanus and Antony created his own parallel lives, highlighting the differences between the Roman Republic and the Roman Empire.

Consider, for example, the following passage from Plutarch's
comparison of Caius Martius Coriolanus and Alcibiades:

[Alcibiades] passed all others for winning men's good wills.
Whereas all Martius' noble acts and virtues, wanting that affabil-
ity, became hateful even to those that received benefit by them,
who could not abide his severity and self will, which causeth
desolation (as Plato saith) and men to be ill-followed or altogether forsaken. Contrariwise seeing Alcibiades had a trim entertainment and a very good grace with him, and could fashion
himself in all companies, it was no marvel if his well doing were
gloriously commended and himself much honored and beloved
of the people, considering that some faults he did were ofttimes
taken for matters of sport and toys of pleasure. And this was the
cause that though many times he did great hurt to the commonwealth, yet they did oft make him their general and trusted him
with the charge of the whole city. Where Martius, suing for an
office of honor that was due him for the sundry good services he
had done the state, was notwithstanding repulsed and put by.
Thus do we see that they to whom the one did hurt, had no
power to hate him, and th' other, that honored his virtue, had no
liking to love his person.[16]

It is striking how much Plutarch's Alcibiades sounds like
Shakespeare's Antony, and with the requisite changes of name,
this passage could serve to compare Coriolanus and Antony
as Shakespeare portrays them.[17] Perhaps Plutarch provides a
model of the sort of comparisons we ought to attempt in analyzing Shakespeare's characters. Without getting too deeply
involved in the question of Plutarch's influence on Shake-

speare, one can at least put forward the claim that the Coriolanus and Antony of the Roman plays are "representative men" in a Plutarchian sense. Each embodies the way of life characteristic of the regime under which he lives; each achieves the perfection of the virtues and the extreme of the vices characteristic of his era. Coriolanus is the exemplar of the austere, disciplined life of martial virtue practiced by the nobler citizens of the Republic. Though we can catch glimpses of this way of life in Antony, for him it has basically become a thing of the past (to be sure, not without regret on his part). Susceptible to the new influences abroad in the Empire, Antony exemplifies a new way of life for Romans, based on a rejection of old notions of nobility and an acceptance of indulgence of the senses, sometimes spiritualized into "immortal longings." As we shall see, Antony hopes to find in love the glory the old Romans found in war. Thus the heroes of *Coriolanus* and *Antony and Cleopatra* develop contrasting sides of human nature,[18] and a careful study of the Roman plays will show how this development is related to the different regimes under which the characters live. Even if one were only interested in trying to comprehend the individual careers of Coriolanus and Antony, one could not ignore the differences between the Republic and the Empire, for Shakespeare has grounded the stories of his heroes in very specific political and historical settings, which both contribute to the development of their characters and set the ethical terms of the decisions they must make. In studying the Roman plays we gradually become aware that Shakespeare could hardly have understood Romans without understanding Rome.

iii

I hope I have succeeded in giving a certain initial plausibility to the idea of looking for Shakespeare's understanding of Rome, and looking for it specifically in terms of the con-

trasted portrayals of the Republic and the Empire in *Coriolanus* and *Antony and Cleopatra*. The notion of Shakespeare's
Romes is the sort of critical hypothesis that can be established
in one, and only one, way: by illuminating in detail our reading of the Roman plays. Before turning to this task, I should
explain why I have not devoted a separate section to *Julius
Caesar*.[19] I had initially intended to give equal time to *Julius
Caesar*, but I found I had little to add to what has already been
written on the subject,[20] and what I did have to say was generally in conjunction with a point about either *Coriolanus* or
Antony and Cleopatra. Therefore I have integrated my discussion of *Julius Caesar* into my discussion of the other two
Roman plays. Although this organization may seem to slight
Julius Caesar, it gives coherence to my argument and makes
the contrast between the Republic and the Empire stand out
in sharper relief. I want to emphasize that I do believe that the
three Roman plays form a kind of historical trilogy, dramatizing the rise and fall of the Roman Republic, in a sense the
tragedy of Rome itself, in which the Republic is corrupted
and eventually destroyed by its very success in conquering
the world. In this drama *Julius Caesar* is not simply important
but quite literally central. Such an approach to the Roman
plays, first suggested to my knowledge by Harold Goddard,[21]
could be worked out in greater detail, and I have made some
tentative steps in that direction, particularly in Chapter 4,
section ii, and Chapter 6, section i. Regarding the Roman
plays as a trilogy does, however, raise certain difficulties, for
example, the problem of the continuity of the character of
Antony in *Julius Caesar* and *Antony and Cleopatra*. And
given the gap in time between the composition of *Julius
Caesar* and that of the other two Roman plays, one might
legitimately question whether the three plays were meant to
be read together. Not wanting to get involved in this sort of
controversy, I have confined myself to what I feel I can dem-
onstrate, namely that *Coriolanus* and *Antony and Cleopatra*

were written as companion pieces, a notion at least made plausible by their composition at approximately the same time. Finally, I want to explain why I have not attempted to discuss, as might have been expected, the question of what Shakespeare's contemporaries knew or thought about Rome. Certainly an interesting book could be written about Elizabethan views of Rome, but the point is the subject would require a whole book of its own. To try to cover so large a topic in an introductory chapter would require simplifications that might easily turn into distortions. The issue of the Elizabethan understanding of Rome is more complicated than may at first sight appear, especially since both growing imperial ambitions and nascent republican sentiments inevitably became bound up with the way the Elizabethans viewed Roman history. If one were to take into account writers as diverse as Edmund Spenser, Samuel Daniel, Fulke Greville, Thomas Lodge, George Chapman, Ben Jonson, Sir Walter Raleigh, and Sir Francis Bacon, one would be lucky just to reach Shakespeare in the space of a single volume. And in any case, the most comprehensive account of Elizabethan attitudes toward Rome could not substitute for a careful reading of Shakespeare's Roman plays, for one could never confidently ascribe to Shakespeare even a widespread view of Rome without first checking what he himself wrote on the subject. In point of fact, no single attitude toward Rome prevailed in the English Renaissance, for many of the great intellectual conflicts of the age had a way of focusing precisely on Rome as a point of dispute. One could, by citing different Elizabethan writers, ascribe to Shakespeare very different—even contradictory— views of Rome. Therefore I have avoided getting involved in substituting quotations from other writers for quotations from Shakespeare, especially when those other writers at times present difficulties of interpretation as great as those one encounters originally in Shakespeare. In the end I have relied on the assumption that the best authorities for learning what

Shakespeare thought about Rome are the texts of the plays he wrote about Rome,[22] and as elaborate as my argument may occasionally become, I have tried to keep it anchored at all times in the texts of the Roman plays.

Acknowledgments

Herschel Baker and Walter Kaiser of Harvard University first showed me the need for studying Shakespeare in the context of continental Renaissance literature and the classical tradition, and their patient criticism of the original version of this study guided me in the process of revising it. Among my other teachers at Harvard, I am especially indebted to Harvey C. Mansfield, Jr., whose knowledge of, and insights into, Renaissance and classical political philosophy I have been able to draw upon at every stage of my investigations into Shakespeare's view of Rome.

Of the many students with whom I have worked on the Roman plays, I would single out John C. Briggs, whose undergraduate honors thesis on *Antony and Cleopatra* I directed in 1970. This thesis forced me to rethink my view of the play, and much of my discussion in Chapter 4 is heavily indebted to it. Another unpublished essay that contributed significantly to my understanding of the Roman plays is "Shakespeare on Imperial Rome: A Political Interpretation of *Antony and Cleopatra*," by Paul H. Weaver, which first suggested to me the connection between love and tyranny in *Antony and Cleopatra*, and which, more generally, helped in my development of the contrast between the two Romes, Republic and Empire.

I wish to thank Scott McMillin of Cornell University, who

read the manuscript at two stages and was unusually perceptive and helpful in his comments.

For permission to quote from *The Riverside Shakespeare,* copyright © 1974, edited by G. Blakemore Evans, I want to thank the Houghton Mifflin Company.

Finally, I want to thank two friends, who, in their genuine interest in learning something about Rome and Shakespeare, have given me the opportunity to discuss my work as it progressed with exactly the kind of readers for whom I conceived this book. Douglas Hoffman has read the manuscript in all its various stages, and has been unfailing in his advice and encouragement. More importantly, it was in discussion with him that I began to formulate many of my basic ideas about Shakespeare's Rome. I did not meet Robert Krupp until that process had neared completion; nevertheless, in his own way he has helped to deepen my understanding of what I have referred to in the following pages as Romanness.

PAUL A. CANTOR

Lowell House
Harvard University

INTRODUCTION

Romanness in Shakespeare

i

The contrast between the worlds of *Coriolanus* and *Antony and Cleopatra* would be clear even in lists of stage props. The list for *Coriolanus* would obviously begin with swords, shields, helmets, and other tools of the warrior's trade. *Antony and Cleopatra* would call for its share of military equipment, too, but its more pressing demands would be upon a theater's resources of imitation fruit and bowls of wine. Anyone producing the play must be prepared to provision one major banquet (II.vii) and at least two minor ones (I.ii.12–13, IV.ii.9–10, 44–45). By comparison, though *Coriolanus* begins with talk of famine and an open rebellion for grain, and quickly passes on to an elaborate fable of the belly, the simple acts of eating and drinking never once occur on stage during the entire play. In this respect, as in many others, the contrast between *Coriolanus* and *Antony and Cleopatra* could not be greater. If one were to chart the frequency of eating and drinking in Shakespeare's works, these two plays would clearly stand at opposite poles.

To worry over whether or not dinner is served in a given play may seem pointless, but apparently trivial details of staging may be clues to important thematic concerns, especially if they fall into a clear pattern. A few lines from *Julius Caesar* are enough to show that in Shakespeare the act of drinking can have a dimension beyond the merely nutritional:

Brutus.   Give me a bowl of wine.
          In this I bury all unkindness, Cassius.   (*Drinks*)
Cassius.   My heart is thirsty for that noble pledge.
          Fill, Lucius, till the wine o'erswell the cup;
          I cannot drink too much of Brutus' love.   (*Drinks*)
                                        [IV.iii.158–62]

Cassius' "heart" is "thirsty," not his throat, and the act of drinking is emphatically an act of drinking together. The most elementary desires have always served as metaphors for the most elevated, so that speaking of love as a kind of hunger or thirst becomes quite natural. When Brutus and Cassius reach out for the bowl of wine they are metaphorically reaching out for each other's love. This symbolic connection between love and drinking wine is a relatively isolated example in *Julius Caesar*. When, in *Antony and Cleopatra*, the instances of eating and drinking begin to add up, clearly associated with the love affair of the main characters, they contribute to a pervasive erotic atmosphere that is a defining characteristic of the play.

By the same token, the exclusion of eating and drinking from *Coriolanus* helps build up its nonerotic, austere atmosphere. Wine is called for three times in *Coriolanus* (I.ix.92, IV.v.1, V.iii.203), but in each case none is served on stage, a conspicuous contrast to what happens on similar occasions in *Antony and Cleopatra*. There is one invitation to supper in *Coriolanus* (IV.ii.49–51), but it is abruptly refused ("I sup upon myself") in terms that signify rejection of the pleasures, not only of dining, but also of human fellowship. The one feast that is referred to in the play takes place among the Volsces in Antium, and it occurs offstage. In any event, the Volsces hardly have time to enjoy their meal before they must rush off to war:

You shall have the drum strook up this afternoon. 'Tis, as it were, a parcel of their feast, and to be executed ere they wipe their lips.
                                        [IV.v.214–17]

Such admittedly slight touches gradually reenforce each other until they create the image of a world in which men refrain from indulging their desires, either out of necessity or a sense of self-discipline. In view of how important a force sexual love generally is in Shakespeare's plays, we ought to be struck by how small a role it has in *Coriolanus*, if it has any role at all. We might even forget that there is one married couple in the play, Coriolanus and Virgilia, especially since their love is so emotionally restrained that it often must go without expression in words (II.i.175). In obvious contrast to *Antony and Cleopatra*, no great speeches of romantic love are delivered in *Coriolanus*. On the contrary, the most conventionally poetic lines in the play are called forth by the theme of chastity:

> The noble sister of Publicola,
> The moon of Rome, chaste as the icicle
> That's curdied by the frost from purest snow
> And hangs on Dian's temple—dear Valeria! [V.iii.64–67]

Valeria is clearly not the sort of woman whom the "holy priests" would bless "when she is riggish." For such a phenomenon, one must turn to the world of *Antony and Cleopatra*, in which Venus, not Diana, is the presiding deity, and in which the moon, "modest" and associated with chastity in *Coriolanus* (I.i.257), has become "visiting" or "fleeting" (IV.xv.68, V.ii.240) and associated with promiscuity.

It is unnecessary to catalogue all the references to eating and drinking in *Antony and Cleopatra*, or even the specific associations of food with sex, such as the imaging of Cleopatra as a "morsel" (I.v.31, III.xiii.116) or a "dish" (II.vi.126, V.ii.274).[1] It is, however, necessary to argue that this food imagery characterizes the whole world of *Antony and Cleopatra*, and not just a part of it. The contrast we have been developing between *Coriolanus* and *Antony and Cleopatra* in terms of austerity versus indulgence is generally thought to function within *Antony and Cleopatra* itself as part of an overall symbolic contrast between Rome and Egypt in the

play. In most formulations, Egypt is associated with images of
eating and drinking, while Rome is associated with images of
temperance and abstinence.[2] The difficulty with this understanding of the play is that it is untrue to the complexity of
the world of *Antony and Cleopatra*, which is composed not of
simple whites and blacks, but of gray areas that gradually
shade over into one another. To take only the most obvious
example, Act II, scene vii must be classed among the Roman
scenes, and yet it is also the most prominent banquet scene in
the play. To preserve the sharp symbolic contrast between
Rome and Egypt in *Antony and Cleopatra*, one would somehow have to consider this scene as Egyptian, which apparently is what Charney has in mind when he simply lists
Pompey's feast among examples of eating and drinking in
Egypt, without giving any justification for this rather problematic classification.[3] It is hard to see on what grounds Act II,
scene vii could pass as "Egyptian." Although no specific indi-
cations of locale are given in the Folio stage directions of
Antony and Cleopatra, the feast clearly takes place somewhere in Italy, and all the characters involved are Romans,
including the Triumvirs and Sextus Pompeius. There seems to
be no way to get around Act II, scene vii: if images of eating
and drinking characterize the Egypt of *Antony and Cleopatra*, they also figure in the portrait of its Rome. One cannot
discount as a minor exception the most lavish consumption of
food and drink that occurs in the entire play.

  In searching for evidence of Roman temperance in the text
of the play, critics have been able to cite only two passages
that begin to suggest a contrast among the Romans to Egyp-
tain indulgence in food and drink.[4] The first expresses Octavius' qualms about Pompey's banquet:

>   But I had rather fast from all, four days,
>   Than drink so much in one.   [II.vii.102–3]

Octavius does voice his distaste for drinking here, but the fact remains that he is by his own admission drunk when he does so (II.vii.98–99, 122–25). Our impression of how widespread indulgence has become in the world of *Antony and Cleopatra* can only be confirmed when we see even the usually abstinent Octavius caught up in the general round of drunkenness in Rome. The second passage commonly cited to establish Roman temperance in the play is Octavius' tribute to Antony's ability to fight against famine with patience (I.iv.55–71). But in this speech Octavius clearly is speaking in the past tense: Antony once was able to endure famine, but at the moment he is engaged in "lascivious wassails." The passage does not characterize the Rome of *Antony and Cleopatra*, but rather a Roman past that may have become only a memory in that world. As Janet Adelman writes: "The Roman virtues . . . in the play are distinctly in the past tense: we must look to Antony's own past and to the fathers of our modern Romans."[5] In other words, to find Roman austerity we must look to the Rome of the Republic. The austerity merely hinted at in *Antony and Cleopatra* appears as a major theme only in *Coriolanus*. Hence in order to understand *Antony and Cleopatra* fully one must go beyond the contrast between Rome and Egypt within the play and study the contrast between the whole world portrayed in *Antony and Cleopatra* and the whole world portrayed in *Coriolanus*. Only in light of this juxtaposition can the contrast between austerity and indulgence (somewhat fuzzy in the Rome and Egypt of *Antony and Cleopatra*) be revealed in all its sharpness.

Although one can trace meaningful contrasts between the Rome and Egypt of *Antony and Cleopatra*—for example, between the business of Rome and the idleness of Egypt[6]—taking these contrasts as absolute can become misleading, especially if it makes one neglect the extent to which the Romans of the play have become "Egyptianized" in their tastes. The Rome-Egypt contrasts are developed largely in the first half of the play, and start to become blurred toward its middle, as the

geographic scope of the action widens. The world of the play
is a cosmopolitan one, and the characters move from region to region with often startling speed.[7] Precisely because
of this free interchange between regions, distinctions like
Rome versus Egypt begin to lose their absoluteness. In point
of fact, the Rome and Egypt of the play are becoming assimi-
lated to each other as a result of their encounter and interac-
tion. The Romans display a marked curiosity about, and
knowledge of, the fabled "cookery" of Egypt (II.i.23–27,
II.ii.176–83, II.vi.63–65) and apparently have learned how to
stage an "Alexandrian feast" and dance "the Egyptian bac-
chanals" (II.vii.96, 104). Although Egyptians are rarely seen
acting like Romans in the play, when Cleopatra and her
women plan their suicides, they do take "the high Roman
fashion" (IV.xv.87) as their model, and, strange to say, as she
approaches death, Cleopatra seems to embrace a kind of Roman temperance toward food and drink (V.ii.49, 281–82).[8]

   Comparing the Romanizing of Egypt with the Egyptian-
izing of Rome, one would conclude that, although Rome
ostensibly conquered Egypt, Egypt is prevailing in what
would today be called the "peaceful cultural competition"
between the nations. That is, the Romans have gone much
further in adopting Egyptian styles of life than the Egyptians
have in adopting Roman. The model for the encounter of the
two nations seems to be the meeting of Antony and Cleopatra
at Cydnus. Antony comes to it as a victorious commander,
but the apparently powerless Cleopatra proves to be "a most
triumphant lady" (II.ii.184), and Antony leaves more the
conquered than the conqueror (II.ii.220–26). Generalizing
from Antony's case, one begins to suspect that in extending its
conquests into Asia, Rome, though a military victor, is in some
way overmastered by the forces it encounters there.

   In short, whatever real Romanness is left in the world of
Antony and Cleopatra is fast fading. Acting like a Roman may
still be talked of as a possibility (II.vi.8–23), but the talk remains just talk, sounding increasingly hollow as the play pro-

gresses and one searches in vain for some sign of the traditional Roman virtues *in practice*. If this sounds paradoxical for a so-called Roman play, the ambiguity of the designation *Roman* is at fault. *Roman* can simply refer to anyone born in Rome, or anything connected with Rome, but it also can be a term of distinction and as such refer to a very specific kind of man, characterized in part by temperance and austerity. Most of the characters from Rome we see in *Antony and Cleopatra* are Roman only in the first of these two senses, and when critics speak of Roman qualities in the play, they are talking of what is more absent than present in it, what is perhaps felt as a potentiality but not in fact seen as an actuality. Maurice Charney concedes: "Although the play develops a symbolic conflict between Egypt and Rome, the imagery of Egypt is set forth in much greater detail than that of Rome; perhaps the qualities of Egypt lend themselves more readily to metaphorical expression."[9] *Coriolanus* is sufficient evidence that Shakespeare was capable of giving metaphorical expression to Roman austerity, as Charney himself proves in his detailed discussion of the food and eating imagery in the play.[10] Perhaps, then, the difficulty of locating in *Antony and Cleopatra* what Charney calls the imagery of Rome should teach us something about the Rome of the play. Shakespeare could portray an austere Rome, but he knew that by the time at which *Antony and Cleopatra* takes place an austere Rome was a thing of the past. We must be awake to the possibility that, for Shakespeare, *Roman* as a term of distinction means primarily *Republican Roman*, and that with the death of the Republic, true Romanness in Shakespeare's view begins to die out also. This interpretation is supported by the despair voiced in *Julius Caesar* over the political fortunes of the Republic and the consequent threat of destruction to a noble way of life:

Cassius.   Age, thou art sham'd!
Rome, thou hast lost the breed of noble bloods!
When went there by an age since the great flood

But it was fam'd with more than with one man?
When could they say, till now, that talk'd of Rome
That her wide walks encompass'd but one man?
Now is it Rome indeed, and room enough,
When there is in it but one only man.   [I.ii.150–57]

Julius Caesar ends with the conviction that the race of noble
Romans is on the verge of extinction:

Titinius.   The sun of Rome is set. Our day is gone,
              Clouds, dews, and dangers come; our deeds are done!
                                                      [V.iii.63–64]

Cato.   Brave Titinius!
              Look whe'er he have not crown'd the dead Cassius!
Brutus.   Are yet two Romans living such as these?
              The last of all the Romans, fare thee well!
              It is impossible that ever Rome
              Should breed thy fellow.   [V.iii.96–101]

Undoubtedly an element of deathbed rhetoric can be detected
in these speeches, but they do suggest that something is happening to Rome as the Republic goes under, something that
will make it at least more difficult, if not impossible, to act like
a noble Roman in the Empire.

Octavius might be offered as the exemplar of the Romanness remaining in *Antony and Cleopatra*. Outwardly he may
be closer to the traditional Roman virtues than are other characters in the play, but inwardly he has none of the nobility
displayed by the Republican Romans in *Coriolanus* and *Julius
Caesar*. Although he hesitates to join in the merrymaking in
Imperial Rome, he has nothing positive to set against the
promptings of his desires, apparently restraining them merely
out of a sense of his own incapacity for indulging himself. It
is basic to Octavius' reluctance to drink, for example, that he
does not hold his liquor very well.[11] Whatever airs he may
put on in speaking of "our graver business" (II.vii.119), there
is nothing high-minded about his objections to indulgence. He

is not, as some maintain, a Stoic moralist condemning Epicurean self-gratification. All Octavius really objects to are the
bad consequences of indulgence (II.vii.122–25). In that sense
he would be difficult to distinguish from an Epicurean who
takes a long-term view of his pleasures, or what would today
be called a utilitarian.[12] In discussing Antony's faults with
Lepidus, Octavius is immediately willing to drop the moral
argument against him (I.iv.16–23), and never so much as
mentions duty, as a Stoic surely would under the circumstances. Anatomizing Antony's situation with the calculating
mind of a true utilitarian, Octavius first focuses on the physical consequence of the libertine life, and then alludes to the
political consequences of Antony's behavior:

> If he fill'd
> His vacancy with his voluptuousness,
> Full surfeits and the dryness of his bones
> Call on him for't. But to confound such time
> That drums him from his sport and speaks as loud
> As his own state and ours, 'tis to be chid—
> As we rate boys who, being mature in knowledge,
> Pawn their experience to their present pleasure,
> And so rebel to judgment. [I.iv.25–33]

The key phrase in this speech is "present pleasure." Presumably Octavius objects that Antony is sacrificing his long-term
and lasting interest to the whim of the moment. Such an argument is consistent with Epicureanism, once it has been tem-
pered by "experience," "judgment," and "mature knowledge."
Rather than representing a genuine alternative to the Epicurean way of life pursued by many of the characters in *Antony
and Cleopatra*, Octavius, then, only stands for a more prudent
conception of self-interest.

   Thus Octavius is not the standard by which Antony is most
properly measured. Certainly no one in the play, not Enobarbus or Scarus, not even Philo or Demetrius, ever expresses
a wish that Antony were more like Octavius. They only wish

that he were more like Antony, that is, the old Antony, the
Antony of the old Rome.[13] Antony is the only standard by
which Antony can be judged:

Philo.   Sir, sometimes when he is not Antony,
                 He comes too short of that great property
                 Which still should go with Antony.   [I.i.57–59]

Enobarbus.   I shall entreat him
                 To answer like himself. If Caesar move him,
                 Let Antony look over Caesar's head
                 And speak as loud as Mars.   [II.ii.3–6]

Canidius.   Had our general
                 Been what he knew himself, it had gone well.
                                                   [III.x.25–26]

Even Antony himself wants to be judged only by the standard
of his own past, as he tries to instruct Octavius:

        He makes me angry with him; for he seems
        Proud and disdainful, harping on what I am,
        Not what he knew I was.   [III.xiii.141–43]

In asking to be judged by the standard of his past, Antony is
asking to be judged by a standard of heroic virtue, not one of
efficient administration, such as Octavius provides. That is one
reason why it is illuminating to consider *Antony and Cleopatra* in conjunction with *Coriolanus*, for the standards of
personal valor and military leadership by which many of
Antony's followers judge him are far more evident in Coriolanus than Octavius. If one wants to understand the Roman
"temper" which Antony's heart "reneges" (I.i.6–8), one cannot do better than to turn to *Coriolanus*, with all its "scuffles"
and "great fights."

ii

We began by speaking of austerity as distinctively Roman,
and now have introduced heroic virtue as the standard of true
Romanness. It is important to grasp the connection between

austerity and heroic virtue in *Coriolanus*:[14] the hero scorns
death just the way he scorns food and drink. This attitude distinguishes the heroic or aristocratic austerity of a Coriolanus
from what one is tempted to call (somewhat anachronistically)
the utilitarian or bourgeois austerity of an Octavius. Octavius
will not indulge his desires because he is afraid of the result if
he does. Coriolanus' austerity, on the other hand, far from being the product of timidity, apparently stems from a heroic
urge to be above the need for food and drink, to prove himself
superior to ordinary humanity. In short, austerity can take
many forms, with very different meanings. If one merely considers the restraint of the desires, and not the purpose for
which they are restrained, one runs the risk of confusing the
fortitude of a hero with, for example, the asceticism of a
saint.[15] It is therefore necessary to analyze the distinctive force
at work in Roman austerity in *Coriolanus,* and for that purpose one can turn to the passage in which Menenius tries to
calm Volumnia after a quarrel with the tribunes:

> *Menenius.*   You have told them home,
>   And, by my troth, you have cause. You'll sup with
>   me?
> *Volumnia.*   Anger's my meat; I sup upon myself,
>   And so shall starve with feeding.   [IV.ii.48–51]

Menenius, who begins the play with the fable of the belly,
shows once again that he thinks of man as ruled by his stomach. If his appetite is satisfied, Menenius asks nothing further
of himself or the world, and therefore believes a good meal
can allay any passion. Volumnia is of a different temperament:
a good meal will not calm her because her anger makes her
indifferent to the demands of her body. The satisfaction she
seeks is not that of a full stomach, but rather something akin
to what an insulted man is looking for when he slaps someone
across the face with his glove and says: "I demand satisfaction." Her anger calls for revenge upon the tribunes, and to
gain her revenge she would willingly sacrifice her personal

pleasure and comfort, an attitude Menenius has a hard time comprehending.

The same opposition between anger and appetite is repeated later in the play. When Menenius is asked to try to convince Coriolanus to abandon his campaign against Rome, he is daunted by the fact that Cominius was refused an audience with his former comrade in arms. But he assures himself that the anger Coriolanus has shown is merely the result of bad diet:

> He was not taken well, he had not din'd:
> The veins unfill'd, our blood is cold, and then
> We pout upon the morning, are unapt
> To give or to forgive; but when we have stuff'd
> These pipes and these conveyances of our blood
> With wine and feeding, we have suppler souls
> Than in our priest-like fasts: therefore I'll watch him
> Till he be dieted to my request,
> And then I'll set upon him.   [V.i.50–58]

Coriolanus' refusal to see Cominius was obviously a product of his obsession for revenge on Rome, which makes him oblivious to all ordinary pleasures, including the companionship of an old friend. Menenius completely misinterprets all this, once again thinking that a good meal could calm the soul's anger, as if the passions of the soul were nothing but the feelings of the body.[16]

The austerity of Volumnia and Coriolanus, unlike that of Octavius, is not the result of prudential calculations to pursue some long-term self-interest. There is something in itself imprudent about their austerity, something suggesting that it too could be carried to extremes, much like eros, though of course to the opposite extremes, of "starving oneself" or "priest-like fasts." Volumnia and Coriolanus are not just restraining the force of eros, but are developing a wholly different side of human nature. The force they oppose to eros appears in its lowest form as a kind of anger, almost a childish testiness or peevishness (Menenius refers to it as "pouting upon the morning").

But we must recall that eros has its lower aspects, beginning
with the elementary forms of hunger and thirst. If eros can
have higher manifestations, reaching all the way up to a spiritualized form of love in *Antony and Cleopatra*, then the force
that opposes it may appear on more than one plane in *Coriolanus*. In *Antony and Cleopatra* eating and drinking are clearly
convivial activities, ways of bringing people together. By the
same token, the rejection of eating and drinking in *Coriolanus*
is explicitly associated with the rejection of human company
(Volumnia rejects Menenius' invitation to supper, Coriolanus
rejects both Cominius' and Menenius' pleas to see him). Both
Volumnia and Coriolanus want to stand alone, and their anger
is clearly rooted in a spirit of independence and self-reliance.
Since a longing always implies a need, a positive motive for
restraining eros in any form would be a will to become self-
sufficient. Volumnia and Coriolanus try to avoid being dependent in any way on other human beings, and Volumnia's
"I sup upon myself" is a way of saying "I don't need you or
your food, Menenius." What appear as purely negative acts,
the rejection of food and drink, are in fact assertions of self-
hood, and the force that opposes eros in *Coriolanus* is best
understood as a form of pride.

On first sight, the pride of characters like Volumnia and
Coriolanus would seem to have little to contribute to Rome as
a community. One might wonder how pride could be regarded as the preeminently Roman quality, when it is presented as an antisocial force, something working to keep men
apart rather than bringing them together as eros does. From
the viewpoint of the Roman citizens, the city is much better
off without the proud Coriolanus, at least according to the
tribune Sicinius:

> We hear not of him, neither need we fear him;
> His remedies are tame—the present peace
> And quietness of the people, which before
> Were in wild hurry. Here do we make his friends

> Blush that the world goes well, who rather had,
> Though they themselves did suffer by't, behold
> Dissentious numbers pest'ring the streets, than see
> Our tradesmen singing in their shops, and going
> About their functions friendly.   [IV.vi.1–9]

Coriolanus evidently is bad for trade in Rome, since his proud austerity interferes with the "friendly functioning" of the city. If his pride is to be viewed as *the* Roman trait, Sicinius thinks that Rome would do well to dispense with Romanness.

Sicinius' idyllic portrait of Roman tradesmen singing while they work must, however, be read ironically, because it occurs just after Coriolanus concludes his bargain with Aufidius for the destruction of the city. With increasing urgency it becomes evident in the course of Act IV, scene vi, that while the Romans are enjoying their daily pleasures, their whole existence is threatened to its foundations. The scene makes us aware of the distinction between public and private interest in Rome. The banishment of Coriolanus has served the private interest of most people in the city, making life easier for all but his family and close friends. But at the same time it has seriously hurt the public interest, for although the citizens are happy, the city itself is in mortal danger. This situation sounds at first paradoxical, but only as long as one conceives of the public interest as a mere sum of private interests. Clearly a new conception becomes necessary in times of war, when private interests must be sacrificed for the sake of the common good. In such circumstances Coriolanus' proud scorn for the promptings of eros would become an asset, not as Sicinius thinks a liability, to the community of Rome. Sicinius' account of the city omits at least one function, that of the warrior, and for the sake of war Rome would obviously require men like Coriolanus. Viewed from the perspective of the city, the opposition between appetite and anger, or eros and pride, appears in a new light. Because eros, with its concern for the pleasures and the welfare of the body, is inevitably bound up with the private interest, appealing to men's appetites is useless when asking them to serve their country in battle, even though Coriolanus scornfully attempts it (I.i.249-50). Although hunger may induce men to serve in the army, it cannot give them real courage in battle. A man governed by his self-interest will not jump at the opportunity of risking his life; from his standpoint, martial valor appears as "foolhardiness," as the conduct of Coriolanus' soldiers before the gates of Corioles amply demonstrates (I.iv.43-47). Pride, on the other hand, with its indifference to the demands of the body, is capable of rising above narrowly conceived self-interest and serving the public interest. By considering the needs of the city in wartime we begin to see the connection between austerity and heroic or martial virtue in Rome.

Observing Coriolanus command in wartime, we can see how his appeal to the pride of his men makes them willing to sacrifice their private interests for their city. He has remarkable success winning support for the fight with Aufidius and his Antiates:

> If any such be here
> (As it were sin to doubt) that love this painting
> Wherein you see me smear'd; if any fear
> [Lesser] his person than an ill report;
> If any think brave death outweighs bad life,
> And that his country's dearer than himself;
> Let him alone, or so many so minded,
> Wave thus to express his disposition,
> And follow Martius.
>> (*They all shout and wave their swords, take him up
>> in their arms, and cast up their caps.*)   [I.vi.67-75]

Coriolanus intuitively senses how to turn the very unattractiveness of his proposal into its chief selling point. He must make men who ordinarily fear for their lives love the sight of their own blood, and he can do so only by turning his proposal into a challenge. He makes his offer sound so unappetiz-

ing that accepting becomes a matter of honor. Even though
the plebeians are not dominated by a sense of honor as Coriolanus is, they are subject to the promptings of pride, if only
because they can experience shame. On the battlefield, Coriolanus creates a situation in which anyone who does not answer
his summons confesses himself a coward, in the presence of all
his fellow soldiers. The public character of the scene works to
Coriolanus' advantage, enabling him to use the pressure of
public opinion to overcome the Romans' atttachment to their
self-interest, and, in effect, shame them into acting like true
soldiers. Pride turns out to be the only force that can be
counted upon to make a man willing to die for his city. Men
take pride in causes, and Coriolanus sees to it that whatever
pride his soldiers have attaches them to the cause of Rome. In
a city constantly endangered by hostile neighbors and dominated by military affairs, he emerges in times of war as the
chief spokesman for the common good. His notion of the
common good may be narrow, and his zeal in upholding it
may turn him into a one-dimensional human being, with a
rather limited appeal. Nevertheless, given Rome's needs as a
city, his unquestioned heroism lifts him above the common
run of men, and earns him praise from even his bitterest enemies, as Cominius promises:

> the dull tribunes,
> That with the fusty plebeians hate thine honors,
> Shall say against their hearts, "We thank the gods
> Our Rome hath such a soldier." [I.ix.6–9]

However unattractive Coriolanus' austere and martial nature
may appear in peacetime, when it comes to war the citizens
who originally questioned his virtue suddenly find they want
him on their side.

Thus Roman austerity and martial virtue must be understood in the context of Rome. When all goes well, the city
supplies the motive for austerity, and warriors like Coriolanus

scorn their desires in the name of martial virtue, which they practice in the name of Rome. It is difficult to find one English word to cover this complex of austerity, pride, heroic virtue, and public service that constitutes Romanness in Shakespeare, in the way that the one word *eros* describes the force in *Antony and Cleopatra* that manifests itself in such diverse forms as hunger, thirst, sexual desire, and "immortal longings." Perhaps the best word to describe the side of human nature developed in a character like Coriolanus is *spiritedness*,[17] a term which has the advantage over alternatives like *heart* or *courage* of immediately calling to mind public spiritedness. The distinguishing characteristic of the Republican Romans in *Coriolanus*, and *Julius Caesar* as well, is that their spiritedness is ordinarily directed toward the service of the public. They display their devotion to their city repeatedly, whether they are talking to themselves or at a public forum, in moments of heated passion or studied reflection:

Brutus.   If it be aught toward the general good,
          Set honor in one eye and death i' th' other,
          And I will look on both indifferently.
                                    [*Julius Caesar*, I.ii.85–87]

Brutus.   I know no personal cause to spurn at him,
          But for the general.   [*Julius Caesar*, II.i.11–12]

Brutus.   Who is here so rude that would not be a Roman? . . .
          Who is here so vile that will not love his country? . . . As I
          slew my best lover for the good of Rome, I have the same
          dagger for myself, when it shall please my country to need my
          death.   [*Julius Caesar*, III.ii.30–33, 44–47]

Coriolanus.   I have done
            As you have done—that's what I can; induc'd
            As you have been—that's for my country.
                                    [I.ix.15–17]

Cominius.   I have been consul, and can show [for] Rome
            Her enemies' marks upon me. I do love
            My country's good with a respect more tender,

> More holy and profound, than mine own life,
> My dear wive's estimate, her womb's increase
> And treasure of my loins.   [III.iii.110–15]

This sense of serving a cause larger than oneself is the cornerstone of Romanness in the Republic. Among Shakespeare's Imperial Romans, by contrast, when Antony speaks of "the cause" (IV.viii.5–7), he only means that his soldiers should take his personal cause as their own.

Even if one were to discount the speeches of Brutus, Coriolanus, and Cominius as designed for rhetorical effect, it is still significant that each speaker feels his purposes require an appeal to the good of Rome. In *Antony and Cleopatra* not a single parallel can be found to any of these patriotic speeches from *Julius Caesar* or *Coriolanus*. Though many critics talk about Rome as a value in *Antony and Cleopatra*, the characters in the play are conspicuously silent on the subject. Not a word is spoken about the good of Rome in the course of the play: all one ever hears is the characters' concern for their relative positions in the pure power struggle in the Empire. Certainly one could draw too sharply the distinction between public spiritedness in the Republic and private interest in the Empire. Clearly there are characters in *Coriolanus* and *Julius Caesar* who try to cloak their personal greed or ambition under the pretense of public concern: one need only think of the tribunes in the former play or some of the conspirators in the latter. Furthermore, in both plays the characters are often bitterly divided over what constitutes the good of Rome, with the result that the public interest is endangered by dissension, conspiracy, and rebellion. By the same token, there may well be characters in *Antony and Cleopatra* who do have the interest of Rome as a whole at heart. Enobarbus might be offered as an example, although proving his concern from anything he actually says would be difficult. More to the point, the Triumvirs, Octavius in particular, do show some concern for achieving and preserving the peace and safety of their realm. But even with all these qualifications, the overall contrast between the worlds of *Coriolanus* and *Antony and Cleopatra* remains in force. At the very least public spiritedness is more prevalent and deep-rooted in the Republic than in the Empire. Ultimately, if Octavius cares about Rome, it is with the interest of a "landlord" (III.xiii.72) keeping an eye on the condition of the premises.

iii

The two forces we have been analyzing in the Roman plays, eros and spiritedness, are the theme of one of Julius Caesar's well-known speeches:

Caesar.   Let me have men about me that are fat,
          Sleek-headed men and such as sleep a-nights.
          Yond Cassius has a lean and hungry look,
          He thinks too much; such men are dangerous.
Antony.   Fear him not, Caesar, he's not dangerous,
          He is a noble Roman, and well given.
Caesar.   Would he were fatter! but I fear him not.
          Yet if my name were liable to fear,
          I do not know the man I should avoid
          So soon as that spare Cassius. He reads much,
          He is a great observer, and he looks
          Quite through the deeds of men. He loves no plays,
          As thou dost, Antony; he hears no music;
          Seldom he smiles, and smiles in such a sort
          As if he mock'd himself, and scorn'd his spirit
          That could be mov'd to smile at any thing.
          Such men as he be never at heart's ease
          While they behold a greater than themselves,
          And therefore are they very dangerous.
                                    [I.ii.192–210]

However pompously expressed, and however grotesque it may sound at first, Caesar's division of Romans into the categories "fat" and "lean" shows how well he understands the problem of ruling the city. He is aware of the connection between high and low in human nature, and starting from a

man's attitude toward food can tell something about his attitude toward politics. Caesar reads in Cassius' austerity, his
"lean and hungry look," a sign that he is not attracted by the
ordinary run of human pleasures. The negative traits in Cassius' character are clues for Caesar to something positive, the
Republican spirit that makes Cassius ambitious and fiercely
competitive, always observing his fellow citizens, on guard
against anyone achieving greater honors in the city. Caesar
analyzes Cassius by contrasting him, almost point for point,
with Antony, who apparently was on his way toward earning
a reputation for various forms of indulgence even before his
meeting with Cleopatra.[18]

Caesar's speech suggests in what way spiritedness is connected with a republican regime and eros with an imperial.
Deliberating about the type of man he would like to see prevail in the community, Caesar concludes that it would further
his own imperial ambitions to encourage eros and discourage
spiritedness. As Caesar himself indicates, Antony is the sort of
man with whom an Emperor could feel comfortable, since
most men dominated by eros find their satisfaction outside of
politics, and are content to be ruled by someone above them.
The "spare Cassius," on the other hand, does not indulge himself in food or plays and music the way Antony does, and
could not be placated by an imperial policy of bread and cir-
cuses. Caesar knows that Cassius is the sort of man he has to
fear, for someone who cannot rest easy as long as he beholds
anyone greater than himself is the inevitable enemy of an
imperial regime. For that very reason, men like Cassius provide a basis for a republican regime. In order to draw its citizens into public life, so that no one man can prevail over all
the others, a republican regime must foster spiritedness. By
considering together a passage from *Coriolanus* and one from
Antony and Cleopatra, we can get a preliminary idea of how
the different regimes work to bring out different sides of
human nature in their citizens.

But at this point someone might object that no evidence exists that Shakespeare was at all concerned about the political settings of his Roman plays. Shakespeare inevitably incorporated certain political details in the plays, the argument might run, because they were in his source, and required for simple narrative purposes, but none of this in any way proves that he was interested in an abstract problem like the difference between the Republic and the Empire, or even for that matter capable of comprehending it.[19] To counter this view one would have to show that Shakespeare went beyond Plutarch in creating the political settings of his Roman plays, and that he dwelt on political details for their own sake, lingering over them longer than simple narrative purposes would have required. These related points can be established by considering the passages we were about to analyze, the dialogue between the two tribunes that ends the first scene of *Coriolanus* and the brief scene that begins Act III of *Antony and Cleopatra*.[20] In these two passages, far from sounding like a poet blundering upon a theme for which he is temperamentally unsuited and intellectually unqualified, Shakespeare shows a sound understanding of political realities in Rome, an understanding expressed with a clarity of vision that reminds one of Machiavelli. The thoughts expressed in Act III, scene i, of *Antony and Cleopatra* are in fact so remarkably similar to those expressed in *Discourses on Livy*, Book I, chapter xxx, that after reading the two passages in succession, one finds it difficult to believe that Shakespeare was not acquainted in some form with Machiavelli's work.[21] Furthermore, both the passage in *Coriolanus* and the one in *Antony and Cleopatra* go well beyond anything Plutarch says about Rome. The dialogue between Sicinius and Brutus has no basis at all in Plutarch, and would appear to be entirely Shakespeare's addition to the story. The scene between Ventidius and another soldier is based upon an incident narrated by Plutarch, but Shakespeare has given it much more prominence, first by singling it out from among

the many events connected with Antony's Parthian campaigns
mentioned by Plutarch, second by dwelling upon it at greater
length than Plutarch does. Moreover, finding a straightforward narrative or dramatic reason for either the passage in
Coriolanus or the one in *Antony and Cleopatra* would be
hard. Neither passage directly advances the plot of its play;
both could be cut from stage productions without any loss of
continuity at all. Shakespeare stops the action in both plays
and turns the stage over to some hard-headed, practical men,
who unromantically assess their own and others' political
prospects. And most importantly, the two passages (as well as
the chapter in Machiavelli upon which one of them seems to
be based) focus directly on the contrast between the Republic
and the Empire.

At the end of the first scene of *Coriolanus*, just after the
patricians have decided upon the order of command for the
new wars with the Volsces, the two tribunes try to figure out
why the proud Coriolanus consented to a subordinate position:

Sicinius.   But I do wonder
His insolence can brook to be commanded
Under Cominius.
Brutus.   Fame, at the which he aims,
In whom already he's well grac'd, cannot
Better be held nor more attain'd than by
A place below the first; for what miscarries
Shall be the general's fault, though he perform
To th' utmost of a man, and giddy censure
Will then cry out of Martius, "O, if he
Had borne the business!"
Sicinius.   Besides, if things go well,
Opinion that so sticks on Martius shall
Of his demerits rob Cominius.
Brutus.   Come.
Half all Cominius' honors are to Martius,
Though Martius earn'd them not; and all his faults
To Martius shall be honors, though indeed
In aught he merit not.   [I.i.261–76]

The low-minded tribunes, assuming that everyone is as dupli-
citous as they themselves are, see very devious motives behind
Coriolanus' loyal acquiescence in the will of the Senate. Their
suspicions do, however, contain some truth, for Coriolanus
gets more honor out of the Volscian War than does the consul he serves under. But no one can object to this outcome,
since Coriolanus in fact accomplished more than Cominius did
in battle. What would be shameful would be for a commander
to get the glory for the accomplishments of his subordinates,
but according to the tribunes the Republic works on a kind of
merit system and, if it must err in one direction, it does so on
behalf of the man on the way up in the world. Because the
Republic gives the benefit of the doubt to the man out of
power and puts the burden of proof on the man in power, it
prevents its citizens from growing complacent and forces
them to compete with each other constantly to see who can
serve the city best. Subordinates hope to rise to positions of
authority by proving their courage and ability, while commanders must remain alert to opportunities for glory if they
are not to be eclipsed by men who serve under them. One
may conclude provisionally that the cornerstone of the Republic's encouragement of public spiritedness is the fact that
it gives the advantage to the man trying to earn political
honors and thus keeps bringing new men into the political life
of the city.

Turning now to *Antony and Cleopatra*, we find that exactly the opposite conditions prevail in the Empire. Act III,
scene i, offers the strange spectacle of a Roman captain deliberately refraining from pursuing a military victory to its
conclusion. The prospect of adding to Rome's dominion is
held out to Ventidius, but he declines, not for any strategic or
tactical reasons, but out of purely personal motives. He is
afraid of seeming too ambitious in Antony's eyes, for by adding to his own glory he would necessarily detract from his
superior's, and risk falling out of favor:

> I have done enough; a lower place, note well,
> May make too great an act. For hear this, Silius,
> Better to leave undone, than by our deed
> Acquire too high a fame when him we serve's away.
> Caesar and Antony have ever won
> More in their officer than person. Sossius,
> One of my place in Syria, his lieutenant,
> For quick accumulation of renown,
> Which he achiev'd by th' minute, lost his favor.[22]
> Who does i' th' wars more than his captain can
> Becomes his captain's captain; and ambition
> (The soldier's virtue) rather makes choice of loss
> Than gain which darkens him.
> I could do more to do Antonius good,
> But 'twoud offend him; and in his offense
> Should my performance perish.   [III.i.12–27]

Ventidius' reasoning reveals the fundamental difference between the Roman Empire and the Republic. Because in the
Empire a commander generally gets credit for his subordinates' accomplishments, the advantage is with those already in
power, and the temptation for a commander to rest on his
laurels is much greater than it is in the Republic. At the same
time, for men trying to make their fortunes in the world, the
inducement to perform heroic and glorious deeds for Rome is
much less. As Ventidius points out, the man who achieves a
great military victory may ruin his political chances by awak-
ening the jealousy and suspicion of his superiors. Preferment
in the Empire is achieved through maintaining the good
graces of one's commander, whatever the cost to Rome as a
whole. The Republic seeks to establish a harmony between
the interest of the individual and the interest of Rome, which
in turn creates salutary competition for honors among subordinates and commanders. As Ventidius' speech reveals, the Empire instead sets up a harmony between the interests of subordinates and commanders, with the result that the interest of
the individual and that of Rome no longer coincide. Ventidius

does not make the slightest reference to the good of Rome in considering whether to pursue his victory against the Parthians.

The Empire actually discourages public spiritedness by failing to provide legitimate paths for advancement to the top of the Imperial hierarchy. In the Empire there is room for only one man at the top at a time, as the course of action in *Antony and Cleopatra* amply demonstrates, and unlike the Republican consul, the Emperor does not quietly step down from office after a year's term. Due to the rapid turnover and orderly succession of the consulship, the Republic holds out to its citizens the prospect of attaining to the highest position in their countrymen's esteem. By contrast, citizens under the Empire cannot succeed to the Imperial throne by their own efforts on the basis of merit, but only by palace intrigue and treachery. An ambitious man in the Empire can honorably and reasonably expect to advance at most to one of the higher rungs on the Imperial ladder, and to accomplish that, the art of flattery will serve him better than the art of war. In contrast to the Republic, then, the Empire works to replace public loyalties with private, as is evident in the case of Ventidius, who clearly is not so much devoted to the cause of Rome as he is to the cause of Antony. But the transformation of the nature of politics in the Empire is not as important as the demotion of the whole sphere of the political itself. To an ambitious man in the Empire, the prospects for political advancement cannot look as great as they do in the Republic, and thus the whole matter of a career in politics inevitably seems less attractive. Ambition must be rewarded with honors and offices, or men will turn to sources of satisfaction other than public service. The comparative rigidity of political hierarchy in the Empire works to redirect the energies of men from public to private life. Once the world of politics loses its glory, the world of eros can take on a new glamor.

To judge by the examples of the tribunes and Ventidius, the Republican and Imperial Romans in Shakespeare view their worlds from quite different perspectives. When Ventidius looks at his world, he sees a long chain of command, with "captains" and "captain's captains," stretching all the way up to the "grand captain" himself (III.i.9), the Emperor Antony. In the Empire the relationship of subordinate and commander is relatively self-contained, making reference at most to some third party higher in the chain of command. There are only two terms in Ventidius' analysis of his situation: himself and Antony. But when the tribunes analyze Coriolanus' relationship to his commander Cominius, they immediately introduce a third term, what they variously describe as "giddy censure" and "opinion" (I.i.268, 271), alluding to the communal voice of Rome. The deeds of Coriolanus and Cominius will be evaluated by the people of Rome, who may not be the most objective and dispassionate of judges but who can at least be more impartial in any issue arising between Coriolanus and Cominius than the two themselves could be. The situation in the Republic can best be described by stating that the city is a third party in the affairs of its citizens. Consequently the Republican Romans are not as rigidly bound in a chain of command and subordination, because they all are ultimately subordinate to the city and can look beyond their immediate superiors to Rome.

The mediating role of the city is further evident in the fact that the Republican Romans in Shakespeare even stand in a different relation to their gods than the Imperial Romans do. When Coriolanus is threatening to destroy Rome, his mother Volumnia expresses her dilemma in terms of her situation with respect to the gods:

> Thou barr'st us
> Our prayers to the gods, which is a comfort

> That all but we enjoy. For how can we,
> Alas! how can we, for our country pray,
> Whereto we are bound, together with thy victory,
> Whereto we are bound? Alack, or we must lose
> The country, our dear nurse, or else thy person,
> Our comfort in the country. We must find
> An evident calamity, though we had
> Our wish which side should win.   [V.iii.104–13]

The corresponding passage in *Antony and Cleopatra* is Octavia's expression of her dilemma when her husband, Antony, threatens to make war with her brother, Octavius:

> A more unhappy lady,
> If this division chance, ne'er stood between,
> Praying for both parts.
> The good gods will mock me presently,
> When I shall pray, "O, bless my lord and husband!"
> Undo that prayer, by crying out as loud,
> "O, bless my brother!" Husband win, win brother,
> Prays, and destroys the prayer, no midway
> 'Twixt these extremes at all.   [III.iv.12–20]

These speeches are so similar that they are sometimes offered as evidence that *Coriolanus* and *Antony and Cleopatra* were written at approximately the same time.[23] Nevertheless, examining the specific terms of the speeches, one finds that Volumnia and Octavia are in fundamentally different situations. Volumnia is torn between love for her country and love for her son; Octavia is torn between love for her husband and love for her brother. A conflict between public and private loyalties has been replaced by a conflict between two private loyalties. Volumnia in effect views her problem as a conflict between her city gods and her family gods, whereas Octavia views hers as a conflict within her family gods. This difference is by no means trivial, because the first of these conflicts contains the principle of its own resolution, whereas the second does not.

Faced with her bond to her husband on one side and her

bond to her brother on the other, Octavius has no way to measure the value of one against the other. Volumnia, however, has always judged the worth of her son by the standard of his service to Rome (I.iii.1–25). Hence she continues the speech quoted above by searching for a way to reconcile the interests of the city and her son, but in the end resolves her dilemma in favor of the city, rejecting the notion that an enemy of Rome could truly be her son (V.iii.178–80). Her decision is that her city gods are higher than her family gods and must take precedence over them. But Octavia does not even mention the city in her prayers, and thus she is left with individual gods, who offer no principle of hierarchy among themselves. In such a situation, the only solution is for one god to prevail over another, an outcome reflected on the political level in *Antony and Cleopatra* by the gradual reduction of the claimants to the Imperial throne in Rome from three to one.

In general, Shakespeare shows the civic institutions of Republican Rome working to produce some kind of common good, however low, out of the many conflicting private goods in the city. The city serves as a mediator in the affairs of its citizens, and although its institutions never achieve perfect harmony, they generally succeed in preventing the community from falling apart entirely. One can observe this principle at work in the argument scenes in Act III of *Coriolanus*, during which party strife threatens to tear Rome to pieces. The surest way to restore calm is to remind the Romans of the interest of the community as a whole by raising the specter of the city in rubble:

> That is the way to lay the city flat,
> To bring the roof to the foundation,
> And bury all, which yet distinctly ranges,
> In heaps and piles of ruin.   [III.i.203–6]

In a play in which anger flares as much as it does in *Coriolanus*, we may be surprised at how successful the various characters are who try to act as mediators in disputes, starting with Menenius in the opening scene taming the rebellion of the plebeians with a "pretty tale," and ending with Volumnia in the last act persuading her son to abandon his campaign against Rome. These mediators do not succeed on the strength of their own eloquence alone: they all speak with the authority of Rome behind them. In *Antony and Cleopatra*, on the other hand, the characters who try to act as mediators, such as Lepidus or Octavia, fail completely in their efforts. The action of the play can be viewed as the progressive elimination of all the factors that might mediate in the disputes of Antony and Octavius, until the two stand facing each other across an unbridgeable gulf. Since none of the potential mediators can speak with the authority of the Roman community, the major characters are left to pursue what they conceive to be their private goods to the exclusion of all else. The situation in the Empire is truly an absence of mediation in the conflicts of men: "no midway / 'Twixt these extremes at all."

As Octavia's words suggest, there is something essentially "extreme" about the ways of life portrayed in *Antony and Cleopatra*, as if the characters were flying apart in different directions, with no central point to which they might relate their conduct. The characters tend to make absolute claims upon each other and infinite demands upon their world. Evidently the sprawling Roman Empire cannot bring the force of the public to bear in checking human desires and aspirations, thereby allowing "immortal longings" to awaken in its citizens, a dissatisfaction with the ordinary limits of human existence and a drive to "find out new heaven, new earth." By contrast, *Coriolanus* presents a far more down-to-earth world, a world firmly anchored in practical concerns like finding food to eat. In the close-knit community of the Roman Republic, the city is able to exert a much greater influence on its citizens, and as a result they have much narrower horizons, of vision and aspiration, because they see things as the city defines them. The fact that the city mediates in the affairs of its citizens means that it exerts a moderating influence on their lives. As Coriolanus fails to learn, in the Republic "the word is 'mildly'" (III.ii.142). Menenius expresses the Republican principle most clearly when he tells the hot-headed tribunes: "temp'rately proceed to what you would / Thus violently redress" (III.i.218–19). This emphasis on temperate procedures reflects the conventional character of life in the Republic, which contrasts with the increasingly unconventional cast to life in the Empire. In *Antony and Cleopatra* the characters are as likely to disregard Roman custom as to obey it, as shown in the case of Antony himself, who seems to relish doing what is least expected of him.

In conclusion, the fundamental opposition between *Coriolanus* and *Antony and Cleopatra* is implied in the opening scenes of the plays. *Coriolanus* begins in the everyday world of the city, *Antony and Cleopatra* in a lavish imperial court remote from the cares of daily life. In the first scene of *Coriolanus*, the most elementary of human desires—hunger—cries out for satisfaction, but it is unclear from the opening scene of *Antony and Cleopatra* what exactly its characters are hungry for. Antony speaks as if mere feeding were beneath him (I.i.35–36): his longings are evidently more complicated than those of ordinary men and so perhaps more difficult to fulfill. His concern is not with need but with pleasure, more specifically, with an endless succession of momentary pleasures (I.i.46–47). Whereas *Coriolanus* begins in an atmosphere of necessity and urgency, with Rome plagued by famine and open revolt, *Antony and Cleopatra* begins in an atmosphere of luxury and languor, with the hero dismissing news from Rome and idly wondering: "What sport to-night?" (I.i.47). All of this goes to suggest that the world of *Coriolanus* is somehow more basic than that of *Antony and Cleopatra*, if only because it involves simpler needs and desires and hence simpler choices in life.[24] *Coriolanus* reveals Rome in its pristine and uncorrupted state, with both the virtues and defects of its lack of sophistication. The Rome of *Antony and Cleopatra*, by contrast, is sophisticated to the point of decadence, a world in which the possibilities for living like a traditional Roman have been virtually played out, leaving a man like Antony to search out new pleasures to "sharpen" his jaded "appetite" (II.i.25).

In short, Romanness, the distinctively Roman way of life, is still fresh in *Coriolanus* but has gone stale in *Antony and Cleopatra*. Recall that in *Julius Caesar*, Titinius proclaims of Rome: "Our day is gone; . . . our deeds are done!" (V.iii.63–64), a sentiment echoed by Antony in the later play when he tells Eros: "The long day's task is done / And we must sleep" (IV.xiv.35–36). The mood of the "setting sun," sinking into night (*Julius Caesar*, V.iii.60–61), seems to dominate Imperial Rome in Shakespeare's portrayal. The characters in *Antony and Cleopatra* feel themselves to be latecomers on the Roman scene (III.xi.3–4), forced to "stand" "darkling" on "the varying shore o' th' world" (IV.xv.10–11). No one is more possessed by this feeling than Antony himself, particularly in his attitude toward Cleopatra:

> I found you as a morsel, cold upon
> Dead Caesar's trencher; nay, you were a fragment
> Of Cneius Pompey's—besides what hotter hours,
> Unregist'red in vulgar fame, you have
> Luxuriously pick'd out.   [III.xiii.116–20]

The image of the magic "Egyptian dish" Cleopatra reduced to stale meat conveys a sense of how the memory of the Roman past can poison Antony's enjoyment of the present, stripping his conquests of their glory. In his outburst to Cleopatra, Antony reveals that never far from his mind is the thought of his great predecessors, Pompey, and, above all, the "noblest man / That ever lived in the tide of times," Julius Caesar. Antony knows he cannot equal the achievements of such men in their own terms: indeed if Cleopatra is any indication, he is condemned to receive his conquests at third-hand from Pom-

pey and Caesar. His sensitivity in this regard would explain
why he apparently grows tense when the younger Pompey
reminds him that Caesar enjoyed Cleopatra first (II.vi.64–70).
Even Antony's house is "inherited" from Pompey, or rather
stolen from him, again a fact which the younger Pompey does
not let him forget (II.vi.26–27, II.vii.126–28). The Roman
past looms large in *Antony and Cleopatra*, and one cannot understand the play unless one shares with its characters a sense
of what Rome used to be and what it has become.[25]

For this reason, any attempt at understanding Shakespeare's
Rome must begin from *Coriolanus*. The order in which the
two plays were written is unimportant, if in Shakespeare's
finished portrayal the Rome of *Antony and Cleopatra* must be
viewed as developing out of the Rome of *Coriolanus*. As Antony and Cleopatra announce at their first appearance, their
conduct involves a conscious attempt to go beyond the limits
traditionally set on men in Rome (I.i.16–17). It is therefore
only logical to study those limits first, as they are portrayed in
Coriolanus. Even Antony's achievement in love is premised
on the prior existence of the values he rejects through love.
Antony could not be noble in love (I.i.36) if it had not once
been possible to be noble in politics in Rome. More generally,
Rome had to be built up, stone by stone, before Antony could
triumphantly call for it to melt and tumble down (I.i.33–34).
Antony eventually has his wish, when, unsure of himself and
of his role in life, trying to read the signs of his destiny in the
ever-changing clouds (IV.xiv.1–14), he is confronted by a
dreamlike pageant in which the substantial world of Rome,
the world of rocks, mountains, and trees, and even the
"tower'd citadel" itself, threatens to dissolve into one great
blur, as "indistinct / As water is in water." But before turning
to the dissolution of the Roman world in *Antony and Cleopatra*, we must first examine it in all its rocklike and stubborn
solidity in *Coriolanus*, where one may say of the ancient city
that is "yet distinctly ranges" (III.i.205).

PART ONE

Coriolanus

Now look for once at an aristocratic commonwealth . . . as an arrangement . . . for breeding: human beings are together there who are dependent on themselves and want their species to prevail, most often because they *have* to prevail or run the terrible risk of being exterminated. . . . The species needs itself as a species, as something that can prevail and make itself durable by virtue of its very hardness, uniformity, and simplicity of form, in a constant fight with its neighbors or with the oppressed who are rebellious or threaten rebellion. Manifold experience teaches them to which qualities above all they owe the fact that, despite all gods and men, they are still there, that they have always triumphed: these qualities they call virtues, these virtues alone they cultivate. They do this with hardness, indeed they want hardness; every aristocratic morality is intolerant—in the education of youth, in their arrangements for women, in their marriage customs, in the relations of old and young . . . —they consider intolerance itself a virtue, calling it "justice."

—Nietzsche, *Beyond Good and Evil*, sect. 262[1]

CHAPTER 1

The Republican Regime

i

We are introduced to the Republican regime in *Coriolanus* in a moment of crisis. Faced with open rebellion against their authority, the city's rulers must give an account of themselves:

> I tell you, friends, most charitable care
> Have the patricians of you. For your wants,
> Your suffering in this dearth, you may as well
> Strike at the heaven with your staves as lift them
> Against the Roman state, whose course will on
> The way it takes, cracking ten thousand curbs
> Of more strong link asunder than can ever
> Appear in your impediment. For the dearth,
> The gods, not the patricians, make it, and
> Your knees to them (not arms) must help. [I.i.65–74]

Menenius begins his defense of patrician rule sensibly, from our point of view, by assuring the plebeians that the Senate does care about them. We would expect him to continue with detailed evidence of the Senate's care, perhaps an explanation of the measures being taken to alleviate the famine in Rome, at least a declaration of the Senate's intention to do something about the problem. But Menenius says nothing of the kind, and the ease with which he dismisses the "wants" of the plebeians leaves us wondering in what way the Senate can care about them, especially if it claims to be unmoved by their "suffering in this dearth." In lines 67–72, Menenius creates a powerful image of the Senate's utter indifference to the demands of the plebeians. As he pictures it, the "Roman state" is not rooted in the soil of the Roman people, deriving its power from them, but is instead raised far above them, as high as the heavens, and seems to have a motive force of its own, sufficient to crush any number of its citizens who might get in its way. Whatever Menenius' notion of the state may be, it seems to fly in the face of all our ideas of the proper relation of a government to its people.

Given our bewilderment at his reasoning with the plebeians, we must question whether Menenius is talking about a "state" in our modern sense at all. In view of the way he speaks of the Roman gods, for example, he apparently knows nothing about our idea of "state" being clearly separate from "church," a distinction that reflects the modern belief in dimensions of life beyond the political. From our standpoint, we cannot help being struck by the way Menenius indiscriminately mixes religion and politics in his address to the plebeians. He identifies rebellion against the "Roman state" with impiety to the Roman gods, and moreover speaks as if the state and the gods were on the same level. This attitude is common among Shakespeare's Romans, who repeatedly assume that the gods take a particular, almost proprietary, interest in their city's affairs (I.vi.6–9, III.i.288–92, IV.vi.36). In reproaching the tribunes for their part in banishing Coriolanus, Menenius finally equates respect for the gods with civic justice:

Sicinius.   The gods be good unto us!
Menenius.   No, in such a case the gods will not be good unto us.
  When we banish'd him, we respected not them; and, he returning to break our necks, they respect not us.   [V.iv.30–34]

To Menenius, the gods themselves are apparently political beings who treat the specifically political actions of their worshipers as signs of respect or disrespect, and reward or punish them accordingly. The connection made in Rome between injustice and impiety clearly heightens what is at stake in the

politics of the city, heightens the "Roman state" itself, in
Menenius' metaphor, until it seems to encompass even the sky.
Taken in all seriousness, Menenius' image of the plebeians
lifting their staves skyward would lead to the assertion that
the horizon of Rome and the horizon of heaven are coexten-
sive, or, to put it differently, in Shakespeare's Rome even the
gods are in some sense included within the precincts of the
city. Clearly this aspiration to totality on the part of the Roman community goes beyond the claims of the modern state
as we conceive it.

Examining the status of the gods in *Coriolanus*, then, one
realizes that the play does not portray a state in the modern
sense, but rather a city in the ancient sense, a polis.[1] The
clearest indication of this fact is the presence of a civic religion in Shakespeare's Rome, but there are other important
ways in which the community portrayed in *Coriolanus* differs
from a modern state, and we must bear them in mind to avoid
analyzing the play with concepts foreign to its subject matter.
For example, with our notion of representative government,
we think that rulers should reflect the values or opinions of
those they rule, more generally that a government should take
its character from the society out of which it arises. But in the
classical understanding of the polis, the regime (*politeia*) has
a formative role, and is itself the primary factor in shaping or
giving character to the community it rules.[2] Some such notion
of rule is necessary to make sense out of Menenius' two-fold
claim that the Senate can care for the plebeians and at the
same time disregard their wants. He must believe that the
patricians understand what is in the interest of the plebeians
better than the plebeians themselves do, but he leaves it to the
less politic and more outspoken Coriolanus to give a direct
statement of the patrician position to the plebeians:

> your affections are
> A sick man's appetite, who desires most that
> Which would increase his evil. [I.i.177–79]

Because Coriolanus believes the plebeians are utterly incapable
of comprehending political realities in Rome (I.i.190–96), he
feels the Senate should treat them like children, restraining
their desires against their will:

> Let them not lick
> The sweet which is their poison.   [III.i.156–57]

Clearly, for Coriolanus, ruling does not involve representing
the will of those ruled but in fact opposing it. We may find
this view distasteful, but we must make an effort to understand it in order to avoid simply remaking Shakespeare's
Rome in our minds on the model of a modern state. Perhaps
what is most needed at the start of any study of *Coriolanus* is
a frank admission of how alien the political world presented
in the play is to us.

The most important point to glean from the statements by
Menenius and Coriolanus concerning rule in Rome is that an
authoritative idea of the good prevails in the city, a notion of
what the good life for man is that is actively supported by the
regime.[3] This point becomes explicit in the elaborate oration
Cominius delivers in praise of Coriolanus before the assembled
citizenry of Rome, a speech which reveals the one trait the
city encourages above all others:

> It is held
> That valor is the chiefest virtue, and
> Most dignifies the haver; if it be,
> The man I speak of cannot in the world
> Be singly counterpois'd.   [II.ii.83–87]

This speech is carefully phrased to stress that Cominius is expressing one city's opinion ("It is held," "If it be . . ."). Another city might well hold justice, for example, or piety to be
the "chiefest virtue," in which case Coriolanus would not be
regarded as the highest human type. But in Rome he is the
man everyone looks up to, and as such becomes the authoritative type in the city, *the* model for imitation. The admiration

Rome bestows upon him is the city's way of directing its citizens (above all, its youth) to the cultivation of martial virtue. As Cominius points out, in the heat of battle, Coriolanus can "by his rare example" make even "the coward / Turn terror into sport" (II.ii.104–5).

As one reads on in Cominius' speech, and finds Coriolanus called "a thing of blood" (l.109) and then "a planet" (l. 114), one might begin to feel that in his concern that "the deeds of Coriolanus . . . not be utter'd feebly" (ll.82–83), Cominius is getting carried away with his own rhetoric. There is unquestionably something hyperbolic about Cominius' speech. But that is just the point: Rome's praise of its military heroes *is* one-sided and exaggerated. The city does not, and could not, honor all forms of human excellence equally, but has instead singled out the courageous warrior for public esteem. Cominius' speech culminates in a direct tribute to Coriolanus' spiritedness and his consequent indifference to the demands of his body:

> then straight his doubled spirit
> Requick'ned what in flesh was fatigate,
> And to the battle came he, where he did
> Run reeking o'er the lives of men, as if
> 'Twere a perpetual spoil; and till we call'd
> Both field and city ours, he never stood
> To ease his breast with panting.   [II.ii.116–22]

Cominius' speech gives some idea of why spiritedness prevails among the Republican Romans in *Coriolanus*. Rome deliberately fosters the opinion that the best way of life is that of the public-spirited warrior. When he praises Coriolanus, Cominius is not speaking simply for himself but for the whole Roman community (II.ii.49–51). The style of his oration—the complicated syntax, the elevated diction and epic similes, the amplitude with which he expresses himself—serves to lift his speech above the level of merely private utterance.[4] He talks with the dignity and measured pace of a man who knows

that he has a solemn public duty to perform and fears that he
may not be equal to the task (ll.82, 103). But as he rises to
the occasion, one can picture his listeners nodding in agreement with his weighty statements of his grave theme. The
scene has a ritual quality to it, a celebration of communal
values through the praise bestowed upon one great exemplar
of them.

But Rome's support for public spiritedness is not merely a
matter of speeches. The sum of the honors heaped upon the
military victor in the first two acts of *Coriolanus* shows how
great a premium the Republic places upon martial valor. Caius
Martius is offered a tenth of the spoils of battle (I.ix.31–36),
awarded the "war's garland" (l.60), given the consul's own
"noble steed" (l.61), and finally receives the name of Coriolanus (ll.62–66) as a perpetual memorial to his victory. The
honors Coriolanus receives on the battlefield are, however,
only the prelude to even greater honors showered upon him
when he returns to Rome. The whole city turns out to welcome the hero home, as he celebrates what came to be known
as a Roman triumph. Soon we learn that the Senate wishes to
make him consul, and although he never achieves the office, in
the ordinary course of Roman events a man with his record
surely would (II.i.221–22). For men who display public
spiritedness, Rome has positions of authority to offer, reward-
ing their passion for honor, not only with speeches, garlands,
and triumphs, but also with public offices. As we have already
seen, the Republic's ability to make room at the top for its
ambitious and spirited men enables the regime to draw its
citizens into political life.

The Rome of *Coriolanus* is, then, lavish with the honors it
bestows upon public service, but so far the only form of service we have seen acknowledged in the city is military. This
situation is all very well for the patricians, who are trained in
warfare almost from birth (I.iii.5–15), but what of the plebeians, who cannot expect to perform the wonders in battle

that a Coriolanus can? Unless the patricians have a monopoly
on spiritedness, the Roman regime apparently has to deal
somehow with the ambitious among the plebeians to keep
them attached to the cause of the city, too. The answer to this
problem in Republican Rome turns out to be the tribunate,
which serves more or less the same function for the plebeians
that the consulship does for the patricians. *Coriolanus* opens
with the creation of the tribunate, and when one considers
how peculiar a response to the uprising this is—it is twice referred to in the play as "strange" (I.i.210, 221)—one begins to
suspect the purpose of the institution. The plebeians demand
grain and instead get the right to elect five officers. Evidently
the patricians are more concerned about the political ambitions of the leaders of the rebellion than about the desires of
the plebeian class as a whole. As is evident from the opening
scene, the plebeians must be actively led in revolt. The man
labeled "First Citizen" is necessary to incite the mob, to direct
its fury, and to counter any objections, whether from his own
ranks (the Second Citizen) or from the opposition (Menenius). His aggressiveness stamps him as the spirited member of
the plebeian party, and the patricians apparently realize that
they must direct their efforts at placating such men. Simply
to give the grain to the plebeians might satisfy their desires for
the moment, but it would also increase the authority of the
inciters of the rebellion without at all satisfying their personal
ambition. The creation of the tribunate, on the other hand,
while it does nothing about the demands of the people at large,
does appeal to the real movers of the uprising by giving them
an office of their own to which they can aspire. Perhaps
Shakespeare had in mind the wry comment in North's Plutarch on the filling of the newly created positions: "So Junius
Brutus and Sicinius Vellutus were the first Tribunes of the
People that were chosen, who had only been the causers and
procurers of this sedition."[5] In an ironic twist, the most revolutionary of Romans become the leading spokesmen for con-

servatism once they are given a stake in the status quo. Shortly
after they have secured a change in the existing order themselves, the tribunes begin to insist on the "old prerogative"
(III.iii.17) and speak in favor of "all season'd office" in Rome
(III.iii.64), while attacking Coriolanus as a "traitorous inno-
vator / A foe to th' public weal" (III.i.174–75). By creating
the tribunate the city has won new defenders for itself from
the ranks of its bitterest enemies.[6]

Shakespeare developed the two tribunes into important
characters from the barest hints in Plutarch, revealing a sound
grasp of the active role the plebeians played in the politics of
Rome. Shown basking in the affection and admiration of their
fellow plebeians (IV.vi.20–25), Sicinius and Brutus evidently
take great pride in their newly found position in the community. Like many of the patricians, the tribunes want to be
honored and are willing to do public service to attain distinction. What makes them appear a good deal less impressive
than a Coriolanus is a certain pettiness, a lack of grandeur in
their goals. With their narrower perspective, they take the
day-to-day affairs of the city more seriously than Menenius
thinks fit, in part because they are concerned about appearing
important in the eyes of their fellow plebeians:

You are ambitious for poor knaves' caps and legs. You wear out a
good wholesome forenoon in hearing a cause between an orange-
wife and a forset-seller, and then rejourn the controversy of
threepence to a second day of audience.   [II.i.68–72]

Menenius is making fun of the tribunes' exaggerated conception of their own role in the city, which leads them to mimic
the demeanor of graver magistrates in Rome. From the standpoint of a patrician concerned with the fate of the city as a
whole, a "controversy of threepence" will inevitably appear
trivial and somewhat comic. Perhaps Rome is fortunate, however, that somebody is willing to take an interest in such matters, even if the result is to leave them "the more entangled"

(l. 77). Since the tribunes are ambitious only "for poor knaves' caps and legs," they are content with their somewhat limited office in the city. As a consequence, the Roman Republic can offer an active political life to both plebeians and patricians, involving its citizens in activities that give their public spiritedness a chance to develop.

While the city is working to cultivate spiritedness, it also is striving to keep the force of eros in check, to channel it in "legitimate" directions. Love occurs in *Coriolanus* only in the context of marriage, that is, in a lawful form over which the city can maintain control. The marriage of Coriolanus and Virgilia illustrates the austere Roman ideal of love, a partnership in which the clear subordination of the wife's interest to the husband's reflects the more basic subordination of the love as a whole to the good of the city. Virgilia must be content to stay at home while her husband goes off to war (I.iii.71–75): her love must not in any way interfere with the needs of Rome. Moreover, the restraint of eros in Republican Rome is evident from the play's emphasis on marital fidelity. Virgilia is compared to Penelope (I.iii.82), the model of that virtue, and her husband is no less faithful to his marriage vows:

> Now, by the jealous queen of heaven, that kiss
> I carried from thee, dear; and my true lip
> Hath virgin'd it e'er since.   [V.iii.46–48]

Finally, two scenes in *Coriolanus* showing three generations of Romans together in one family unit (I.iii and V.iii), indicate the purpose of love and marriage in Rome. The family is the institution by means of which Rome can use even the force of eros for the good of the city, by directing it toward the goal of generation. In the Roman Republic, generation is presented as a matter of framing warriors (V.iii.62–63), and therefore as an extension of the city's own goal of encouraging spiritedness. The model of motherhood in *Coriolanus* seems to be Hecuba suckling Hector (I.iii.40–41), and what

Coriolanus took in at his mother's breasts was the same "valiantness" (III.ii.129) that is held to be the "chiefest virtue" in Rome. One would think that the realm of love, marriage, and the family would be a source of private interest even in the Roman Republic, but at least at first sight the city seems able to make eros serve spiritedness, and thus in turn the common good.

ii

In its effort to restrain eros, the Roman regime cannot simply allow the spiritedness it calls forth to go unchecked. With its single-minded concern for doing what is noble, spiritedness can often lead men to act irrationally, without regard for their own welfare or safety. As is said of Coriolanus:

> His nature is too noble for the world; . . .
> What his breast forges, that his tongue must vent,
> And, being angry, does forget that ever
> He heard the name of death.   [III.i.254, 257–59]

In particular, because Coriolanus cannot imagine how anyone could fail to live, as he does, strictly according to the dictates of honor, he becomes incapable of appreciating the importance of eros in human life. He enters the first scene asking "What's the matter?" as if the motive for the uprising were something mysterious. He seems genuinely puzzled that the plebeians could be so worried about merely filling their bellies and staying alive:

> They said they were an-hungry; sigh'd forth proverbs—
> That hunger broke stone walls, that dogs must eat,
> That meat was made for mouths, that the gods sent not
> Corn for the rich men only. With these shreds
> They vented their complainings.   [I.i.205–9]

Because the proverbs of the plebeians all embody the practical wisdom of self-preservation, they are no more than "shreds" to Coriolanus in his whole-hearted concern for the noble life. In his attitude we witness how Roman austerity can get out of hand: he would rather see the plebeians starve than risk giving encouragement to their appetite by any official recognition of the fact that men need to eat. Certainly some of the claims of eros are legitimate, even from the standpoint of a noble and warlike city. If men stopped eating altogether, they would soon be too weak to fight, and universal chastity would leave Rome without any warriors at all in one generation. For Rome to suppress eros entirely would, in fact, be impossible, but the city does not even try to make all its citizens into spirited men. As Shakespeare portrays Rome in *Coriolanus*, the city seems content with a compromise, a blend of spirited and appetitive[7] men in the community. Rome fundamentally supports the spiritedness in men, but at the same time it makes important concessions to eros, in effect using the force of eros to moderate the extreme claims of spiritedness. This compromise is reflected in the political organization of Rome, the division of the city into patrician and plebeian parties.

One might at first be tempted to make a simple formula, and identify the plebeians as the party of eros in Rome and the patricians as the party of spiritedness. But although the division of the city into patricians and plebeians is not irrelevant to the division into spirited and appetitive men, the two divisions do not exactly correspond. We have just seen that the tribunate was necessary in Rome to accommodate the spirited men among the plebeians. By the same token, a glance at Menenius confirms the presence of appetitive men in the patrician party, even in the early days of the Republic. Thinking in terms of food comes naturally to him (II.i.55–57, V.iv.17–18),[8] and when he sets out to define his own character, he immediately makes reference to his appetite:

I am known to be a humorous patrician, and one that loves a cup of hot wine with not a drop of allaying Tiber in't. [II.i.47–49]

Apparently each party in Rome includes both appetitive and
spirited men, though in different proportions. In the opening
scene of *Coriolanus* the appetitive nature of both parties is
emphasized, since Shakespeare focuses on food as the issue in
the plebeians' rebellion. In Plutarch's version, the original revolt is occasioned by the Senate's support of the city's usurers,
and the issue of the scarcity of grain does not come up until
after Coriolanus' battles with the Volsces. Shakespeare pushes
the issue of usury into the background (I.i.81–82) and brings
the issue of grain to the fore. The appetitive character of the
plebeians is stressed as soon as Coriolanus enters and begins
speaking of their "sick man's appetite" (I.i.178) and predict-
ing that, left to themselves, they will "feed on one another"
(I.i.188). And with Menenius as the initial spokesman for the
patrician party, the first image of the Senate we get is, somewhat surprisingly, a belly. To be sure, Menenius is able to
make his analogy work to his advantage, but he may at the
same time be unwittingly revealing much about himself and
his fellow patricians by the way he chooses to portray their
role in the city.[9] Less dazzled by Menenius' rhetoric than the
naive plebeians are, we come away from his speech remember-
ing his original characterization of the Senate as stomach of
Rome: "idle and unactive / Still cupboarding the viand"
(I.i.99–100). At first sight in *Coriolanus*, we can find no more
difference between a patrician and a plebeian than between a
full and an empty stomach.

And yet this difference need not be insignificant or trivial,
for it suggests why patricians and plebeians might develop
along different lines in the city. With their bellies crying out
for satisfaction, the plebeians find it hard to rise above the
level of appetite, whereas the patricians, "still cupboarding the
viand," can afford to scorn their bellies. These distinctions are
rooted in the fact that the patricians are rich and the plebeians
poor, a division in effect legislated by the city, since the laws
play a large role in determining how wealth is distributed

among men. The First Citizen raises this point when he replies to Menenius' claim that the Senate cares for the plebeians
"like fathers":

Care for us? True, indeed! They ne'er car'd for us yet. Suffer us
to famish, and their storehouses cramm'd with grain; make edicts
for usury, to support usurers; repeal daily any wholesome act
establish'd against the rich, and provide more piercing statutes
daily to chain up and restrain the poor. [I.i.79–85]

The laws can favor either the poor at the expense of the rich
or the rich at the expense of the poor. Shakespeare, following
Plutarch,[10] shows that Roman legislation fosters inequality of
wealth, making the rich richer and the poor poorer. The
point is not simply that the patricians are wealthy but that
they hold their wealth by privilege, a privilege which helps
explain why they are more likely to develop spiritedness than
the plebeians.

The privileged status of the patricians relieves them of the
need to worry about money. Since they are born to wealth,
they do not have to work to accumulate it, and, with the laws
supporting them, they hold their wealth securely. Acting with
noble contempt for money is obviously easier for someone
who has never truly faced the prospect of being poor. In the
case of Brutus in *Julius Caesar*, we can see clearly that a man
can maintain his noble indifference to wealth only so long as
he does not have to concern himself about its acquisition. In
his quarrel with Cassius, Brutus can still speak of money as
"vile trash" (IV.iii.74), but he also implies that without
money he could not act with noble liberality to his friends
(ll.79–82). He falls into the contradiction of condemning
Cassius for taking "base bribes" (IV.iii.24) and then demanding a share of the booty because he himself "can raise no
money by vile means" (IV.iii.71), and yet needs it to pay his
legions. In Act IV, scene iii, of *Julius Caesar* we get a glimpse
of what happens to Roman nobility once the patrician privi-

lege of wealth is taken away: it begins to look hollow, as hollow as an empty cashbox. The lesson to be learned from Brutus is that Roman nobility depends on an adequate supply of "means," since men must be relieved of certain low concerns if they are to devote themselves to the concerns thought high by the city. The Roman patricians are given the luxury of developing their spiritedness, and therefore have an obligation to do so. By contrast, Rome leaves the plebeians poor to maintain the pressure of necessity on them, keeping their desires simple and their sights low, focused on the basics of life. As long as the plebeians have to worry about merely staying alive, they will find it hard to give attention to grand public matters or to develop ambition for political life. Hence their poverty works against the development of public-spirited men in their class.[11]

Nevertheless, being born to wealth in Rome cannot guarantee that any given patrician will become a spirited man, and by the same token the poverty of the plebeians cannot prevent the emergence of spiritedness among them. All one can say is that the distribution of wealth and privilege in Rome favors the growth of spiritedness among the patricians and works against it among the plebeians. One might wonder why Rome does not organize itself into a party of spirited men and a party of appetitive men. To be rational, the city ought to classify its citizens according to their natures rather than the chance circumstances of their birth. But if Rome were to divide along the lines of natural, as opposed to conventional, distinctions, it would become two different cities, with nothing in common and no means of communication between them. A party composed entirely of men like Coriolanus would be utterly indifferent to the concerns of the appetitive men in the community, perhaps altogether incapable of understanding them, but in any case too proud to make any compromises with those who did not share their single-minded concern for nobility. On the other hand, a party composed

entirely of appetitive men would lack the spiritedness necessary to stand up and fight for their rights in the city. The
plebeians in *Coriolanus* need more than hunger to impel them
to rebellion; they need some of the irrational willingness to
risk their lives that only spiritedness can give them. They
must become so morally indignant at their treatment at the
hands of the patricians that they "are all resolv'd rather to die
than famish" (I.i.4–5). When contemplating the prospect of
unmixed parties in Rome, one ought to bear in mind that the
scheme in Plato's *Republic* for dividing the best city into arti-
sans and warriors according to their natures requires the
supervision of a third class of wise rulers. But no such authority is raised above both patricians and plebeians in Shakespeare's Rome, a point made obliquely but tellingly by the
fable of the belly. It certainly is, at least on first thought, puzzling to find the Senate compared to the belly, and not the
head or the heart.[12] Menenius' fable suggests what is absent
from Rome, a guiding mind in the city. Checking the list of
civic functions provided by the First Citizen's attempt to turn
Menenius' tale against him, one finds the city well supplied
with soldiers, steeds, and trumpeters (I.i.116–17), but one
searches in vain for the precise location of "the kingly crowned
head, the vigilant eye, / The counsellor heart" (I.i.115–16).[13]
In the absence of a separate class embodying these functions
to oversee the division of the city, Rome is forced to leave the
composition of each party at least in part to chance, and to
allow in each a blending of appetitive and spirited men.

In assessing the effect of the mixed parties in Rome, one
realizes first that the appetitive men in the patrician class serve
to moderate its spiritedness. They themselves can make their
fellow patricians aware of the claims of eros, and also are the
means of communicating with the plebeians. However in-
effectual he may be at times, Menenius, the appetitive man in
the patrician party, is on the whole the most important mediating factor in the disputes of Rome. He can speak to both

the plebeians and Coriolanus because he shares an appetitive nature with the one and patrician status with the other. Similarly, the spirited men in the plebeian party are needed to speak up for the rights of their class in the city. The spiritedness of the tribunes acts in the service of the eros of their fellow plebeians. Even though they may have their own goals foremost in mind, the tribunes do serve as "the people's mouths," giving voice to the hunger of Rome and working to make the patricians consider it as a factor in their calculations. Significantly, Menenius and the tribunes often appear together (II.i.1–96, IV.vi.10–79, V.iv), and any real communication that takes place between the two parties in Rome is the result of their exchanges (consider especially III.i.263–334). The net effect of the mixed composition of the Roman parties is to check the potentially extreme spiritedness of the patricians. First the appetitive men within the patrician class work to restrain the immoderate pride of some of their party. If the patricians cannot control one of their number, the power of the tribunes comes into play, as shown in the rejection of Coriolanus as consul and his eventual banishment. The Roman parties must be understood to function as a classic example of a system of check and balances.

As Shakespeare portrays Rome in *Coriolanus*, the Senate basically rules the city. It deliberates and decides on the most important foreign and domestic matters, such as declaring war or distributing grain. The Senate also chooses the two consuls, the highest officers of the Republic and commanders of its armies. But the Senate's rule is by no means absolute, since through their tribunes the plebeians have a veto power over anything it proposes (III.i.144–46). The Senate is therefore forced to take the interest of the plebeians into account in its deliberations. It must pass laws that are acceptable to the whole city, and not just to the patrician class. Furthermore, the Senate can only nominate men for the consulship; the plebeians must ratify its choices. A patrician who wants to be-

come consul must be willing to make concessions to the plebeians. As the case of Coriolanus shows, no man who holds
the plebeians in total contempt can become consul, or at least
no man who is willing to show his contempt openly. "The
price" of the consulship is, as Coriolanus learns, "to ask it
kindly" (II.iii.75). The plebeians, who are chiefly characterized in terms of their appetite, see to it that not even the
noblest Roman can disregard the needs of the body completely. The patrician who makes no allowance for the eros of
the plebeians is banished from the city.[14]

iii

In its attempt to balance political forces in the community,
the Republic threatens to go from one extreme to another.
The power given to the plebeians to check immoderate spiritedness among the patricians could itself get out of hand. The
plebeians could block all laws and keep the consulship vacant
if they were willing to veto everything the Senate proposed.
One might well wonder if anything checks the plebeians'
power to bring the city to a standstill. Shakespeare is in fact
careful to portray those aspects of the plebeians' character and
situation which prevent them from abusing their power. First,
the plebeians have only just acquired their political rights in
Coriolanus and do not hold them securely. Even the tribunes
are unaccustomed to exercising their authority and use it with
restraint, as shown by their caution after the banishment of
Coriolanus:

Sicinius. Bid them all home, he's gone; and we'll no further.
         The nobility are vexed, whom we see have sided
         In his behalf.
Brutus.   Now we have shown our power,
         Let us seem humbler after it is done
         Than when it was a-doing. [IV.ii.1–5]

If the patricians are pushed too far by the tribunes, they might rescind the power recently granted the plebeians (IV.iii.21–24), a consideration which inhibits Sicinius and Brutus.

The ordinary citizens of Rome are even more circumspect than the tribunes in asserting themselves in the community. At least some of them possess a healthy sense of their own inadequacy to rule themselves. When the First Citizen charges Coriolanus with calling the people "the many-headed multitude," the Third Citizen goes to his enemy's defense:

We have been call'd so of many, not that our heads are some brown, some black, some abram, some bald, but that our wits are so diversely color'd; and truly I think if all our wits were to issue out of one skull, they would fly east, west, north, south, and their consent of one direct way should be at once to all the points a' th' compass.   [II.iii.16–24]

Although flatterers of the people are at work in the Rome of *Coriolanus* (II.ii.7–8, 24–27), they have not yet succeeded in convincing the ordinary citizens that they are equal to the patricians in virtue and wisdom. On the contrary, the plebeians still look up to the patricians and admire them for the services they have performed for the city (I.i.30–31, II.iii.132–33). The fact that the plebeians are ashamed to appear ungrateful to men who have aided Rome is the most important reason why they hesitate to use their veto against Coriolanus:

We have power in ourselves to do it, but it is a power we have no power to do; for if he show us his wounds and tell us his deeds, we are to put our tongues into those wounds and speak for them; so, if he tell us his noble deeds, we must also tell him our noble acceptance of them. Ingratitude is monstrous, and for the multitude to be ingrateful were to make a monster of the multitude; of which being members, should bring ourselves to be monstrous members.   [II.iii.4–13]

This concern for appearing noble in the eyes of their superiors makes the plebeians come close to allowing their avowed and inveterate enemy, Coriolanus, to become consul.

Even the electoral procedures of Republican Rome are

contrived to make the plebeians' sense of shame work to the patricians' advantage. There is no secret ballot in *Coriolanus:* the people have to "give their voices" openly, and in a direct confrontation are embarrassed to use their veto on a candidate for consul. To make matters more difficult for the easily intimidated plebeians, they have to approach the candidate "by ones, by twos, and by threes" (II.iii.41–43). Like Swift's Lilliputians, the only strength they have is in numbers (II.i.34–38); one at a time they are no match for the giant Coriolanus. He surely exaggerates when he says that the plebeians stand "still, and wonder" whenever a patrician merely gets up "to speak of peace or war" (III.ii.11–13), but Coriolanus is able to bring them to a halt, even at the height of their collective rage, simply by reminding them: "There's some among you have beheld me fighting" (III.i.223). Having served in the wars, the plebeians may well suspect that Coriolanus' boast—"On fair ground / I could beat forty of them" (III.i.241–42)—is not an empty one, and they will not risk angering him when they have to meet him face-to-face.

Finally, in trying to keep the plebeians in their place, the patricians are able to enlist the Roman gods on their side. Coriolanus' scornful question to the rebels in the opening scene contains an ambiguity:

> What's the matter,
> That in these several places of the city
> You cry against the noble Senate, who,
> (Under the gods) keep you in awe, which else
> Would feed on one another? [I.i.179–83]

One might well ask, Who is "under the gods" here, the Senate or the plebeians, and of whom are the plebeians "in awe," the gods or the Senate? Undoubtedly Coriolanus wants to say that the Senate, in obedience to the gods, keeps the plebeians pious, but the same lines without much twisting could indicate that by means of the gods the Senate keeps the plebeians in awe of itself. We have already noted Menenius' manipulation of the plebeians' piety to maintain their allegiance to Rome. The plebeians are characterized by a religious awe that can be readily directed toward the city's gods or a patrician who has achieved godlike deeds, such as Coriolanus:

> I have seen the dumb men throng to see him, and
> The blind to hear him speak. [II.i.262–63]

If a single patrician can call forth this sort of worship from the plebeians, the party as a whole should be able to maintain control of the city. In fact, the real danger to the Republic stems, not from plebeian disrespect for nobility, but from the readiness with which the plebeians are willing to fall down before the military heroes of the city. A commander willing to court the favor of the plebeians could use their support as leverage against his fellow patricians and make himself sole master of Rome, thus ending aristocratic equality in the city. Coriolanus does not take advantage of the credit his military victories give him with the plebeians, but his story suggests that Rome is waiting like "mellow fruit" (IV.vi.100) to fall into the hands of the first general willing to strive with any and all means for mastership in the city.

That general turns out to be Julius Caesar, who is not inhibited by those considerations of honor which restrain Coriolanus from exploiting his reputation with the plebeians. The difference between the two is indicated by the fact that Caesar is willing to put himself on display before the plebeians:

> If the tag-rag people did not clap him and hiss him, according as he pleas'd and displeas'd them, as they use to do the players in the theatre, I am no true man. [I.ii.258–61]

Evidently not sharing Coriolanus' shame at acting a part in Rome,[15] Caesar is able to win the plebeians over to his side, defeat all his rivals among the patricians, and bring the Republican era in Rome to its close. By considering what finally destroys the Republic in *Julius Caesar*, one becomes aware of

what in the deepest sense makes it work in *Coriolanus*. The
Republican regime depends on a very delicate (though remarkably durable) balance between the parties in the city.
Patrician and plebeian must understand that they do have a
certain common interest, but they must at the same time keep
their distance from each other. In speaking of Coriolanus,
Menenius reveals exactly what the Republican regime requires:

> He loves your people,
> But tie him not to be their bedfellow.   [II.ii.64–65]

Some degree of respect and regard is needed between the hostile
parties in Rome, but it must stop short of real fraternizing with
the enemy, for any alliance of patricians and plebeians would
upset the balance of power on which the Republic is based. The
Republic can survive only if its citizens do not break ranks
once they have divided up along party lines, and above all,
only if the patricians maintain their class solidarity. The
Republic seems finally dependent on the class prejudices of its
citizens, the fact that the plebeians do not trust the patricians,
and the patricians quite simply cannot stand the smell of the
plebeians. Once the plebeians begin following a powerful
patrician against the advice of their own tribunes (*Julius
Caesar*, I.i), or, more importantly, once the patricians cease
to quarrel among themselves but take their disputes to the
plebeians for arbitration (*Julius Caesar*, III.ii), the Republic
is doomed.

The corruption of the plebeians in *Julius Caesar*[16] confirms
the point that the Republican regime can function only as
long as the people realize their unfitness for rule and are willing to defer to the Senate's government, though not to submit
to it docilely. This is the paradox of the Republican regime:
the plebeians must accept the Senate's right to rule, and yet
dispute bitterly the way it rules, as they do in the opening
scene of *Coriolanus*. Coriolanus' characterization of the ple-

beians as "such as cannot rule / Nor ever will be ruled"
(III.i.40–41) reveals, not as he thinks their defect, but their
virtue in the context of the Roman regime. With continual
tension between the parties in Rome, no one man can gain
control of the whole city. Only if individual patricians are
unable to use the plebeian party for their personal purposes
can the people of Rome be safely entrusted with as much constitutional authority as the Republic gives them. Under the
proper conditions, the plebeians' share in the regime serves to
prevent the spiritedness of the city's warriors from running
counter to the ordinary necessities of life, without at the same
time redirecting Rome from the noble goal of martial glory to
the mere satisfaction of the body's appetites.

   To understand the durability of the party loyalties on which
the durability of the Republic rests, one must refer back to
the unique character of the ancient city, of the power of a
narrow-horizoned, tradition-bound community to mold its
citizens. For example, to see through his party loyalty Coriolanus would have to understand that in a very real sense he has
more in common with Sicinius than with Menenius, that sharing a spirited nature with the one is in some ways more significant than sharing a party label with the other. But that
recognition would require Coriolanus to overcome his almost
physical revulsion at all things plebeian, and to unlearn
everything his breeding and training have taught him about
what is praiseworthy. He would have to understand what is
naturally, rather than conventionally, worth valuing. But the
city has a way of making the conventional look like the
natural, as is evident in Act II, scene i, when Menenius and
the two tribunes vainly try to break through their party opinions in order to understand each other's viewpoints.

   According to Sicinius, the people hate Coriolanus because
"Nature teaches beasts to know their friends" (II.i.6). Of
course, for the plebeians to hate Coriolanus is in part natural,
but their reaction to him is also in part the conventional re-

sponse of their class to anyone of the opposite rank in the city. That is just the point: the plebeians' opinions are formed of one part nature, one part convention, but they cannot distinguish the two components in their minds.[17] Sicinius states his attitude toward Coriolanus, not as one man's opinion, not even as a party slogan, but as a universal truth of nature. Clearly Rome wants its citizens to believe that what it teaches them is the same as what nature teaches, for this will make their beliefs more fixed. Judging by the exchange between Menenius and the tribunes (II.i.7–12), each party in Rome thinks its position can be defended by appealing to natural analogies, and as we listen to patrician and plebeian argue back and forth, apparently in all seriousness, over whether Coriolanus is best understood on the model of a "lamb" or a "bear," we realize how childishly stubborn partisanship in Rome can become. Perhaps Shakespeare is suggesting that party opinion in Rome is ultimately on the level of beast fables, that is, morally edifying lessons told in a form which even children can understand and remember. In studying the Republican regime, we finally come back to the point we started from, that there is an authoritative idea of the good in the city, and Rome tries to teach its citizens, as a parent tries to teach his children, what to value in life. Only now we see that Rome teaches two different lessons, in a sense contradictory, in a sense complementary, one to the plebeians (I.i.206–8) involving concern for self-preservation, and one to the patricians (IV.i.4–11) involving scorn for mere life and respect for nobility. Out of these two lessons, and the parties with which they are linked, the Roman Republic seeks to give a balanced representation to the different sides of human nature in the city.

CHAPTER 2

The City without a Ruler

i

The Republican regime succeeds admirably in turning out the warriors it wants; more important, it manages to control their spiritedness in the service of the city. But there is one obvious exception to this rule—the Coriolanus who goes over to Rome's enemies. And, paradoxically, it is the very regime designed to keep men loyal to Rome that ends up making a traitor out of the city's greatest soldier. The Roman regime itself becomes the object of Coriolanus' indignation, finally turning him against his native land. For Coriolanus the divided rule in the Republic is not a means of harmonizing the competing claims of eros and spiritedness but rather a way of reducing the patricians to the level of the plebeians:

> You are plebeians,
> If they be senators; and they are no less,
> When, both your voices blended, the great'st taste
> Most palates theirs. They choose their magistrate,
> And such a one as he, who puts his "shall,"
> His popular "shall," against a graver bench
> Than ever frown'd in Greece. By Jove himself,
> It makes the consuls base; and my soul aches
> To know, when two authorities are up,
> Neither supreme, how soon confusion
> May enter 'twixt the gap of both, and take
> The one by th' other.   [III.i.101–2]

Refusing to accept divided rule in Rome, Coriolanus turns

traitor to the city that seemed to have such success in maintaining the loyalty of its citizens. Clearly one cannot claim to have understood the Roman regime until one has explained its failure in the case of Coriolanus.

In view of the intemperate manner in which Coriolanus expresses his anger at Rome, it is tempting to lay the blame for this failure entirely at his feet, and explain away his break with his native city on psychological or even psychiatric grounds. Many modern critics treat Coriolanus as a case of "maladjustment," painting a picture of an immature, awkward boy, given a man's role to play, but psychologically overdependent on his mother and unable to get along with others.[1] Any critic so-minded is of course free to look for psychiatric case studies in Shakespeare, and in any event a full interpretation of Coriolanus must take into account his relationship to his family and the defects of his upbringing. Nevertheless, to concentrate solely on the ways in which Coriolanus fails to adjust to the Roman community is to adopt the city's standards uncritically, as if there were no legitimate grounds for objecting to its regime and as if winning acceptance in Rome were the measure of human worth. But the fact is that Coriolanus' speeches in Act III, scene i, however passionately argued, do raise some serious questions about divided rule in Rome, and before digging beneath the surface of the play to find deep psychological motives for Coriolanus' behavior, one ought to study the reasons he himself gives for his actions. The narrowly psychiatric view of Coriolanus characteristically trivializes the meaning of his story by refusing to take seriously his quarrel with Rome and ignoring what he has to say in justification of his stance. By contrast, if one examines his arguments carefully, one finds that his break with the city raises as many doubts about Rome as it does about Coriolanus, thereby deepening our understanding of the political roots of his tragedy.

Coriolanus' first objection to the Republican regime con-

cerns its potential for instability. He sees that everything
hinges on the self-restraint of the plebeians, and does not believe that the Senate's policy is calculated to keep them from
misusing their authority. On the contrary, he thinks any concessions to the plebeians will only make them hungry for
more power:

> How shall this bosom multiplied digest
> The Senate's courtesy? Let deeds express
> What's like to be their words: "We did request it,
> We are the greater pole, and in true fear
> They gave us our demands." Thus we debase
> The nature of our seats and make the rabble
> Call our cares fears; which will in time
> Break ope the locks a' th' Senate, and bring in
> The crows to peck the eagles.   [III.i.131–39]

Coriolanus views Rome not as a mixture of aristocracy and
democracy, but rather as an aristocracy on its way to becoming a democracy. *Julius Caesar* shows that his fears concerning the role of the plebeians in the city are well grounded,[2]
but he underestimates the time it will take for the plebeians to
become corrupted. It is debatable whether one can regard a
regime that lasts several centuries as merely transitional. However, Coriolanus does not simply foresee trouble for Rome in
the future, but has a more important criticism of the mixed
regime that is already applicable in his own time. He thinks
that the need to compromise with the plebeians repeatedly
prevents the patricians from doing what is truly virtuous:

> This double worship,
> Where [one] part does disdain with cause, the other
> Insult without all reason; where gentry, title, wisdom,
> Cannot conclude but by the yea and no
> Of general ignorance—it must omit
> Real necessities, and give way the while
> To unstable lightness. Purpose so barr'd, it follows
> Nothing is done to purpose. . . .
> . . . Your dishonor

> Mangles true judgment, and bereaves the state
> Of that integrity which should becom't,
> Not having the power to do the good it would,
> For th' ill which doth control't.   [III.i.142–49, 157–61]

According to Coriolanus, the mixed regime cannot be wholly devoted to its "purpose," or fully "do the good it would." Rome is insufficiently devoted to the goal of producing warriors because of the concessions it makes to the plebeians. The key word in Coriolanus' speech is "integrity": in his view, Rome's fault is that it is not of one mind. While claiming to be committed to the pursuit of military glory, Rome at times rewards cowardice instead of punishing it (III.i.122–27). The indecisiveness of Rome is reflected in the ambiguity of the word *Roman* even in the Republic; does it refer to a special type of man, who has to be cultivated (the noble warrior), or does it simply refer to anyone who happens to come from the city of Rome?

Two different views are expressed in *Coriolanus* on what it is to be a Roman, a citizen of the Republic.[3] According to Sicinius and the plebeians, anyone living in Rome is a citizen of Rome:

Sicinius.   What is the city but the people?
All.   True,
> The people are the city.   [III.i.197–98]

For Coriolanus, on the other hand, *Roman* is a term of distinction, and only a warrior deserves to be called a citizen of Rome. The plebeians may customarily be considered Romans, but it takes more than merely being born within the city limits to make Coriolanus regard a man as a fellow citizen:

> I would they were barbarians, as they are,
> Though in Rome litter'd; not Romans, as they are not,
> Though calved i' th' porch o' th' Capitol!   [III.i.237–39][4]

Coriolanus' use of terms for animal procreation, *litter'd* and *calved*, reveals his point: the plebeians no more deserve to be called Romans than do the tame beasts who happen to be born every year within the city's walls. Coriolanus cannot accept the idea that a cowardly man could be a true son of Rome, and feels debased to share the name of Roman with plebeians (III.i.108, 135–36). He wants Rome to take an unequivocal stand in favor of the warrior type he himself represents, and, as Sicinius understands, will not be satisfied until the only Romans are men just like him (III.i.262–64). He wants one party to conquer the other once and for all and put an end to the divided regime in the city. For Coriolanus, the distinction between patricians and plebeians resembles the difference between two species of animals,[5] and therefore he thinks of the plebeians as slaves (I.i.199, I.v.7, IV.v.77). In view of the tradition of comparing Rome to Sparta,[6] one might formulate Coriolanus' wish for Rome this way: the relation of patrician to plebeian should be that of Spartan to helot, that is, of conqueror to conquered, or master to slave. Sparta was more successful than Rome in suppressing eros, with the result that *Spartan* is synonymous with *austere* in a way that *Roman* is not. More fully dedicated than Rome to the goal of encouraging martial valor, Sparta and its way of life would inevitably be more attractive to Coriolanus. If he had his way in Rome, he would reduce the number of citizens (by restricting citizenship to patricians and regarding the plebeians as slaves) and concentrate on making every citizen fully a Roman in his sense, namely a public-spirited warrior.

But to turn Rome into Sparta would require major changes in the city, above all some restraint of the acquisitiveness of the patricians. The basis of the Spartan regime was equality of landholdings among citizens, and contempt for moneymaking.[7] But as we have seen, Roman laws favor inequality of wealth and support, and in effect legitimate, usury. To bring about the changes Coriolanus wants in Rome, then, he would have to change the Roman laws, that is, become a legislator for his city. Indeed the central difference between Sparta and

Rome is that the one city had a legislator at its origin and the other did not. It is perhaps to suggest this point that Shakespeare, for no apparent reason and without following any source, introduces the name of the Spartan legislator into *Coriolanus*. Menenius tells the tribunes: "I cannot call you Lycurguses" (II.i.55), comparing them unfavorably with the celebrated founder of the Spartan regime, the framer of the city's laws and institutions.[8] Since one man designed it, the Spartan regime can be viewed as the product of reason. But as Shakespeare discreetly hints, no Lycurguses can be found in Rome, and the Roman regime is arrived at by chance.[9] Rome frames its institutions by a process of trial and error, adopting a law if it happens to work. The Roman regime continues to change in response to the difficulties the city encounters, until it achieves a kind of equilibrium. Rome's greatness thus ultimately depends on good luck in finding the right laws at the right time, and one's appreciation of the city must be qualified by an understanding of the role fortune plays in its success.[10]

The creation of the tribunate is a good illustration of this point. The way this sweeping reform in the Roman constitution is made on the spur of the moment is a paradigm of how haphazardly the city operates. The patricians are interested only in putting down the rebellion, and not in perfecting the Republican regime. As Coriolanus perceives, the tribunate is not created on the basis of anybody's opinion as to what is good for Rome as a whole in the long run, but rather because it seems to be necessary to the patricians at the moment:

> In a rebellion,
> When what's not meet, but what must be, was law,
> Then were they chosen; in a better hour,
> Let what is meet be said it must be meet,
> And throw their power i' th' dust. [III.i.166-70]

The plebeians never convince the patricians that the tribunate is in the public interest of Rome, but instead create a situation

h it seems to be in the private interests of each and
ۥtrician to give the other party a stake in the regime.
‿ a system of party conflict becomes the substitute for
the wisdom and foresight of a legislator like Lycurgus, who
has a purpose in mind in framing his laws and understands the
effect they will have. By contrast, the patricians act blindly in
granting the right of the tribunate: Coriolanus calls them "un-
wise" and "reckless" (III.i.91–92). They toss a bone to the
ambitious among the plebeians, without calculating the profound effect the existence of the tribunate will have on Rome
in the future.

Coriolanus' critique of the Republican regime uncovers a
possible defect in that regime: the absence of a legislator, not
simply at its founding, but throughout its history. Rome lacks
truly wise rulers, in the sense of men who have a comprehensive understanding of the common good, and no one in the
great city really knows why it is great. Recognizing Rome's
lack of a legislator in turn leads to an important question about
Coriolanus. If he wants a Spartan regime for his city, he will
have to become its legislator. Fortunately for him he seems in
some respects qualified for the role. He understands the existing Roman order at least as well as anyone else in the city,
despises the mixed regime, advances very specific ideas on
how to remake Rome, and, most importantly, seems to have
the power to become the founder of a new regime. The patricians are devoted to him, and after his victories against the
Volsces, the plebeians, too, are disposed to honor his authority:

> The nobles bended,
> As to Jove's statue, and the commons made
> A shower and thunder with their caps and shouts.
> I never saw the like. [II.i.265–68]

This is a rare moment in Roman history, as one man stands
above the party conflicts of the city like a god, worshiped by

both sides, seemingly able to do anything he wants with Rome. But Coriolanus lets the opportunity escape him and soon is rejected by both patricians and plebeians. Yet his banishment does not end his story. Once more he approaches his native city as a conquering hero, only this time he intends to conquer Rome. And once again he has control of both parties in his grasp:

> All places yield to him ere he sits down,
> And the nobility of Rome are his.
> The senators and patricians love him too;
> The tribunes are no soldiers, and their people
> Will be as rash in the repeal, as hasty
> To expel him thence. I think he'll be to Rome
> As is the aspray to the fish, who takes it
> By sovereignty of nature. [IV.vii.28–35]

There is a "sovereignty" in Coriolanus' nature: he strikes others as a kind of god, and men like to believe that their institutions have a divine, rather than a simply human, origin. If the Roman Republic is ever to be given a unified regime, Coriolanus would seem to be the man to do it, and yet none of his ideas for Rome are ever put into effect. The most puzzling problem about Coriolanus is, Why—with everything seemingly in his favor—does he fail to rule, and remake, his native city?

ii

Any consideration of Coriolanus as a ruler must begin from one fact: he has remarkable success as a leader in wartime but is a complete failure at leading in peacetime. When he leads the Romans against the Volsces, the Romans win; when he leads the Volsces against the Romans, the Volsces win. His individual powers of leadership appear to make the difference between victory and defeat in war.[11] He cannot simply be unfit for leadership in any ordinary sense, especially when he is able to convince even his one-time enemies to accept him as

a general. Somehow Coriolanus' inability to rule Rome must
be related to a difference between wartime and peacetime.
From what we have already seen, we know that he can appeal
to men's spiritedness and their concern for the common good,
but is openly contemptuous of their appetites and their concern for their private interests. For that reason, men will consent to his rule during wartime, when their spiritedness is
aroused and they clearly perceive a threat to the common
good, but not during peacetime, when they are more interested in following good providers than good protectors. Coriolanus' mistake is not realizing that men look for different
qualities in leaders in war and peace, as Aufidius understands
when he criticizes his rival's inability

> to be other than one thing, not moving
> From th' casque to th' cushion, but commanding peace
> Even with the same austerity and garb
> As he controll'd the war.   [IV.vii.42–45]

In trying to show her son how to adapt to peacetime politics and win the consulship, Volumnia, in contrast to Aufidius, bases her reasoning on an analogy between peace and
war:

> I have heard you say
> Honor and policy, like unsever'd friends,
> I' th' war do grow together; grant that, and tell me
> In peace what each of them by th' other lose
> That they combine not there. . . .
> If it be honor in your wars to seem
> The same you are not, which for your best ends,
> You adopt your policy, how is it less or worse,
> That it shall hold companionship in peace
> With honor, as in war, since that in both
> It stands in like request? . . .
> Now, this no more dishonors you at all
> Than to take in a town with gentle words,
> Which else would put you to your fortune and
> The hazard of much blood.   [III.ii.41–45, 46–51, 58–61]

Even though Coriolanus fails to answer his mother's argument, we must consider whether deceptions in peacetime
really are no different from deceptions in wartime. Aufidius
provides us with a clue when he counsels the Volsces "to
seem the same they are not" in war:

> Nor did you think it folly
> To keep your great pretenses veil'd till when
> They needs must show themselves.   [I.ii.19–21]

Aufidius reveals the distinctive aspect of military deceptions,
the fact that eventually "they needs must show themselves."
A war stratagem is in the end revealed to have been a stratagem, for with the victory of one side or the other, all deceptions come to light. The victor can afford to tell the van-
quished: "My retreat was just to draw you into an ambush,"
if the tactical details have not already become painfully obvious. None of this, however, is true of the stratagems of peacetime politics, where deceptions must be kept up forever. One
cannot sue for the consulship and then announce to the people: "I said I wanted to serve you, but now that I'm in office
I admit that was just a lie to get the post: in truth, I can't
stand the sight—or smell—of you." Volumnia talks as if, once
Coriolanus became consul, he could freely reveal his contempt for the plebeians (III.ii.20–23). But a consul must still
avoid antagonizing the tribunes, as long as they can veto any
action he takes in peacetime. Moreover, as the tribunes understand, a candidate for the consulship can be held to whatever
promises he makes to the people (II.iii.192–94), and thus cannot honorably repudiate the pledges of friendship he has
publicly given them.

The problem, then, for Coriolanus is that if he ever begins
to flatter the plebeians he can never stop, for in seeking their
voices he would grant their right to sit in judgment on him,
and in that sense, acknowledge their superiority. As Volumnia
unconsciously lets slip, to win power in Rome Coriolanus

must let himself "go, and be rul'd" (III.ii.90). A general does
not subject himself to his opponent by using a stratagem, since
his aim is to have his conquest openly acknowledged. By contrast, a victory in an election is not regarded as a defeat of the
electorate. Quite the opposite, it is viewed as the triumph of
their will: "The people have spoken." By accepting office,
Coriolanus would not conquer Rome but would instead surrender, as he sees it, to the plebeians. Volumnia tells her son
to treat the plebeians just as he would a foreign enemy, which
is of course what he really wants to do.[12] He might not mind
deceiving the plebeians in order to triumph over them, that is,
if he could stand up in the end and assert his superiority to
them openly. But that is exactly what Rome will not let him
do. It offers deception, not as a temporary tactic, but as a
permanent way of life. Instead of treating the plebeians as
foreigners, Coriolanus must regard them as fellow citizens if
he stands for office, and that runs counter to his deepest political convictions.

What Coriolanus senses is that the whole mixed regime of
Rome is one enormous deception, but it is a peacetime stratagem that does not work quite as the patricians think it does.
The patricians try to give the plebeians the semblance of
power without the substance, hoping that the tribunate will
make them believe they have a share in the ruling of Rome,
without actually interfering with the decisions the Senate
wants to make. The electoral procedures of Rome are a similar smokescreen for the Senate. It wants to be able to select
the men it thinks right for the consulship, and yet give the
people the impression that the ultimate decision was really
theirs. The Roman Senate thinks it has solved the political
problem of at one and the same time framing wise laws and
getting men to consent to them. The patricians believe the
constitutional powers of the people are a sham because they
have complete confidence in their own ability to manipulate
the politically naive plebeians in any direction they choose

(III.ii.72–89). The decisive error of the patricians is to under-
estimate the talents of the politically quite sophisticated tribunes, to forget that men like Sicinius and Brutus are at least
as skilled as they are in manipulating the plebeians. The tribunes are capable of using deception themselves; they can hide
their real power behind a smokescreen, too, making it seem,
for example, that the attack on Coriolanus was the people's
idea, rather than their own (II.iii.213–63). When they can
mobilize the people, the tribunes can neutralize the will of the
Senate, and transform their office from an empty title into a
genuine force in Rome. The requirement of obtaining the
agreement of the plebeians to the Senate's nomination of
Coriolanus results in Rome's banishing its true defender and
leaving itself a prey to its enemies (III.iii.127–33). The need
for consent here turns wisdom into folly. The patricians believe that the reality in Rome is that the Senate rules; the
people only appear to have a share in power. But what happens to Coriolanus shows that in politics, appearances are
sometimes the only reality. If ambitious men are given authority on paper, they will find a way to exercise it.

The problem of appearance and reality, which is raised in
one way or another in most of Shakespeare's plays, takes a
special form in *Coriolanus*. Politics is presented as a realm of
appearances, and that is why Coriolanus rejects it. He is no
hypocrite (III.i.255–57, III.iii.27–29), and cannot act a part
(II.ii.144–45, III.ii.14–16, 105–23, V.iii.40–41). As different as
he is from the Prince of Denmark, Coriolanus could say along
with Hamlet: "I know not 'seems.' " He is afraid that if he
does play a role, the appearance will become reality:

> I will not do't,
> Lest I surcease to honor mine own truth,
> And by my body's action teach my mind
> A most inherent baseness.   [III.ii.120–23]

Because Coriolanus disdains concerning himself with appearances, he shows no appreciation of the need for rhetoric. In wartime he is able to rouse his men to action with a stirring speech (I.vi.66–85), but he fully believes what he says in this speech: it just happens to be wholly appropriate in the particular circumstances. He does not see that different situations require different approaches, as shown by the fact that he gives essentially the same speech again in circumstances where it is no longer appropriate (III.i.149–57).[13] Above all, he is evidently insensitive to the distinction between a public and a private situation. Twice he discusses in public what should have been discussed only in private: when he tries to talk the patricians into abridging the plebeians' rights (III.i) and when he grants an audience to his mother, wife, and child among the Volsces (V.iii). In the first case, what he says is meant for the ears of his own party alone, not the plebeians, as his fellow patricians try to tell him (III.i.63, 74–75, 115, 139). In the second case, when Coriolanus is among the Volsces he makes a major issue out of not granting any private interviews to Romans (V.iii.6–8, 92–93), a resolve which works to his disadvantage when he has to deal with his family. Because the scene takes place in public, and the Volsces are witness to everything he says to his mother, Coriolanus has no room for maneuvering. If he had spoken to Volumnia in private, he might have been able to put a fairer face on his actions when he came to report the results to his new masters. Also the fact that he grants a public audience to Volumnia allows her to use the force of shame against him ("let us shame him with our knees," V.iii.169). His capitulation to her is due in part to his reluctance to appear like an ungrateful child in front of others. As he himself admits, he feels a need to appear better than "common sons" (V.iii.52).

In short, Coriolanus is unwilling or unable to admit that certain things should not be said in public. He shows signs of wanting his life to be like an open book, available for all to read, so that no one can think he feels constrained to hide anything from the world. But even though he seems concerned about always standing vindicated in the eyes of others (V.ii.92–93, V.iii.2–4), some things he wishes to conceal. In fact, he wants to keep private what from a political standpoint ought to be made public. He will not bare his wounds to the plebeians, even though it would further his political cause.[14] One aspect Shakespeare has added to the character of Coriolanus is an acute sense of personal shame: he is inhibited by a fear of standing naked before the plebeians (II.ii.137). In some sense, then, he must be concerned about appearances, at least about how he himself appears in public. He wants to appear just as he thinks fit and not to have to alter his appearance to suit anyone else's expectations. The essential point is for him to maintain control over how he appears, which would explain why he claims he will show his wounds only in private (II.iii.76–77, 108–9). "He said he had wounds, which he could show in private" (II.iii.166), that is to say, could show if he wanted to. In public appearances Coriolanus will not adapt his appearance to what the public wants, which is of course exactly the opposite of the way a political man would behave. Repeatedly in *Coriolanus* it is of the utmost importance whether a scene takes place in public or in private, that is, between men who have reason to conceal things from each other, or between men who can be free and open with each other. Coriolanus' inability to perceive what is called for in a public as opposed to a private situation is his chief disqualification for peacetime politics in Republican Rome.

iii

One final reason why Coriolanus intuitively recoils from politics leads to the central issue of the play. The necessities of politics force him to think about questions he would rather forget. In the course of her little political catechism, Volumnia tells him that at times his "honor" will require him to do things he normally regards as dishonorable:

> I would dissemble with my nature where
> My fortunes and my friends at stake requir'd
> I should do so in honor.   [III.ii.62–64]

This advice is, to say the least, disconcerting to Coriolanus. He would like to conduct himself by a simple rule in life: "Do what is honorable," but his mother and Menenius show him that what is honorable varies with different situations. That reasons of state can force a noble man to do base things is something Coriolanus finds it hard to accept:

> Must I
> With my base tongue give to my noble heart
> A lie that it must bear? Well, I will do't;
> Yet, were there but this single plot to lose,
> This mould of Martius, they to dust should grind it
> And throw't against the wind.   [III.ii.99–104]

Coriolanus wants his values to be absolute, so that he can follow them without question or doubt.[15] His mother, however, claims that he cannot unthinkingly obey the dictates of honor, as defined by Rome, because there are extreme cases in which a man can no longer afford the luxury of being noble:

> You are too absolute,
> Though therein you can never be too noble,
> But when extremities speak.   [III.ii.39–41]

Coriolanus learns that his code of honor cannot in all cases yield unambiguous and indisputable answers to the question, "What must I do?" because he will have to decide for himself when and where the command to act nobly applies. Moreover, the fact that what is honorable seems to depend on changing political conditions casts doubts on the status of honor itself. Coriolanus would like the laws of honor to resemble the laws of nature, equally valid at all times and at all places, but Volumnia reveals to him the conventional side to honor. The regime defines what is honorable, and therefore honor stands or falls with the regime.[16]

The demands of politics make Coriolanus aware of his dependence on the city of Rome, and as long as he prides himself on being self-reliant that awareness must grate on him.
He is so concerned about being indebted to anyone for anything that he finds it easy to forget the name of a man who
once helped him (I.ix.82–91),[17] and he never fails to point out
when he has accomplished something alone (I.vi.76, I.viii.7–9,
IV.i.29, V.vi.113–16). Coriolanus does seem to win battles
single-handedly, but the consulship, requiring as it does the
voices of the plebeians, is one goal he cannot achieve by himself. Considered in the abstract, the idea of serving Rome
strikes Coriolanus as a noble aim. But in standing for the
consulship, he is forced to see the city in concrete human
terms, to look one at a time at the men for whom he has been
fighting. Viewed from its streets and in the light of the sun,
Rome no longer seems such a splendid object for his devotion
after all. Campaigning in Rome, Coriolanus confronts the disturbing fact that in serving the city he is at least in part serving the plebeians:

> Your voices? For your voices I have fought;
> Watch'd for your voices; for your voices bear
> Of wounds two dozen odd; battles thrice six
> I have seen and heard of; for your voices have
> Done many things, some less, some more. Your voices?
> Indeed, I would be consul. [II.iii.126–31]

These lines reek of irony, but an irony that could be turned
back upon the ironist. For once, Coriolanus is willing to speak
the lies the Roman regime requires, to claim that he, a patrician, is nothing but the servant of the plebeians. But for a
moment he may begin to suspect that the lies the Roman patricians speak so glibly contain a basic truth, that in reality
all the fighting he has done, all the suffering he has undergone,
have served no other purpose than to protect the plebeians he
despises.[18] If that were true, it would be a bitter pill for the
noble Coriolanus to swallow. In the fable of the belly, Menenius

claims that the patricians want to serve the plebeians, not rule
them. He of course regards the fable as a pretty tale that suits
his immediate purposes, but it may reveal more than he realizes. In some sense the patricians are saddled with the true
burden in Rome, the burden of rule, of protecting the whole
city, and thus principally the plebeians. The mere fact that the
patricians, however much they think they are lying, still feel
compelled to claim to be the servants of the plebeians shows
that the plebeians must have some real power in the city, if
only by virtue of their numbers. A true master does not have
to give an account of himself (I.i.144) to his slaves. Coriolanus sees that as long as a mixed regime prevails in Rome, as
long as one party does not openly rule the other, the city
leaves in doubt for whose sake it really exists, the patricians or
the plebeians. Since a warrior is only as good as the cause he
fights for, the absolute Coriolanus cannot tolerate any ambiguity about the city's purposes in Rome.

Confronted with the duplicity upon which the Roman
mixed regime is based, Coriolanus must wonder whether his
honor is hollow at the core. In his very first speech in the play,
he tells the plebeians that they are no secure foundation for a
man's nobility. To build on them is to build on mud:

> You are no surer, no,
> Than is the coal of fire upon the ice,
> Or hailstone in the sun . . .
> . . . He that depends
> Upon your favors swims with fins of lead,
> And hews down oaks with rushes. Hang ye! Trust ye?
> With every minute you do change a mind,
> And call him noble, that was now your hate;
> Him vild, that was your garland.   [I.i.172–74, 179–84]

Coriolanus likes hard, solid, sharply-defined objects, not soft,
liquid, diffuse objects; to call a woman an "icicle" (V.iii.65)
is his idea of a compliment, but ice that melts earns his scorn.
His choice of imagery reflects on a low level his preference
for the immutable over the changeable, and his consequent

search for something absolutely sure, something on which he can unconditionally depend. What he holds against the plebeians is their fickleness. He thinks he can be sure of his nobility, but the plebeians keep changing their minds as to what is noble. Coriolanus would like his honor to be founded purely on his "own desert" (II.iii.65), but standing for the consulship he is forced to recognize that to be honored in Rome he is in large part dependent on the whims of the plebeians.

A contradiction lies at the heart of Coriolanus' character. He seeks honor but dislikes the requirement of having other men to honor him. Thinking he can stand alone on the basis of his honor, he finds instead that his pursuit of honor binds him more closely to the city. Another aspect Shakespeare has added to the character of Coriolanus is his reluctance to hear himself praised (I.ix.13–15, II.i.168). In part, this is a sign of personal modesty (I.ix.53, 69–70), but it is difficult to think of Coriolanus as genuinely humble, and one might suspect that his antipathy to being honored in public is rooted in his pride. Hearing him praised for his heroism, men might think he acts heroically for the sake of praise (I.i.30–40). The implication that he is in need of praise, and therefore of other men to praise him, would impugn his heroic self-sufficiency.[19] Coriolanus will only accept praise as free acknowledgment of his intrinsic merit, not as payment for services rendered; he wants his honors to come to him, as Cominius tells him, "in sign of what you are, not to reward / What you have done" (I.ix.26–27). Furthermore, Coriolanus wants his deeds to speak for themselves (II.ii.127–28), because only deeds cannot be faked. As long as the world is full of flatterers, anyone can have mere speeches made in his honor. Coriolanus' anger at hearing himself praised in speeches is part of his general disgust at the confusing of appearance and reality in Rome:

> When drums and trumpets shall
> I' th' field prove flatterers, let courts and cities be
> Made all of false-fac'd soothing! . . .

You [shout] me forth
In acclamations hyperbolical,
As if I lov'd my little should be dieted
In praises sauc'd with lies   [I.ix.42–44, 50–53]

In Coriolanus' eyes, Rome, and especially the plebeian class, does not always distinguish sufficiently between real and apparent merit, and thus he scorns its praise.

But Coriolanus' contempt for mercenary praise does not mean that he is wholly indifferent to the opinion other men have of him. On the contrary, he wants to be honored in Rome, but only for what he really is, not for what people say about him. He objects to being confused with the men who have risen to prominence by flattering the people rather than by achieving anything on their own:

his ascent is not by such easy degrees as those who, having been supple and courteous to the people, bonneted, without any further deed to have them at all into their estimation and report.
                                                                    [II.ii.25–28]

Only if Coriolanus can become consul without flattering the people can he feel that being honored does not make him dependent on others. Thus Coriolanus hates the people of Rome precisely because they fail to honor him properly, that is, without any concessions to them on his part. This point is made clear when one of the Senate's officers claims that Coriolanus does not concern himself with what the people think of him:

Faith, there hath been many great men that have flatter'd the people, who ne'er lov'd them; and there be many that they have lov'd they know not wherefore; so that, if they love they know not why, they hate upon no better a ground. Therefore, for Coriolanus neither to care whether they love or hate him manifests the true knowledge he has in their dispositions, and out of his noble carelessness lets them plainly see't.   [II.ii.6–15]

This view is immediately contradicted by another officer:

If he did not care whether he had their love or no, he wav'd indifferently 'twixt doing them neither good nor harm; but he seeks their hate with greater devotion than they can render it him, and leaves nothing undone that may fully discover him their opposite. Now, to seem to affect the malice and displeasure of the people is as bad as that which he dislikes, to flatter them for their love.
[II.ii.16–23][20]

This observation on Coriolanus is borne out by his conduct later in the play. If he did not care whether or not the plebeians honored him, he would not punish them for failing to do so, as Plutarch explicitly observes:

For he that disdaineth to make much of the people and to have their favor should much more scorn to seek to be revenged when he is repulsed. For to take a repulse and denial of honor so inwardly to the heart, cometh of no other cause but that they did too earnestly desire it.[21]

Coriolanus' hatred of the people is based on his secret desire to be worshiped by them, so that his anger against Rome is best understood as that of a god seeking vengeance on the mere mortals who have betrayed their faith in him:

> You speak a' th' people
> As if you were a god to punish; not
> A man of their infirmity.   [III.i.80–82]

Because of the blasphemy of the plebeians against him, Coriolanus turns on Rome and leaves the city:

> Despising,
> For you, the city, thus I turn my back;
> There is a world elsewhere.   [III.iii.134–36]

Ultimately Coriolanus is not satisfied with the honors Rome gives him because they come to him smelling of the plebeians (III.iii.120–23). For him, the Republic's honors are corrupted by their source, but as he leaves Rome, he fails to consider one question: Is there any source of honor for him outside the city?[22]

Coriolanus' hesitation at entering the city's domestic politics reveals that the Roman mixed regime is the patricians' attempt at concealing their own rule. But the tribunes too can hide their power behind the Republican institutions. With both the senators and the tribunes working by indirect means, manipulating men for hidden purposes, no one seems to be willing to stand up in Rome and claim the right to rule the city.[23] Coriolanus' objections to politics in Rome all point in one direction: the city is without a ruler in the fullest sense. Roman peacetime politics is a battleground on which nobody ever claims complete victory, and therefore no one ever has to admit total defeat. As the one man in the city who scorns deceptions and partial victories (I.vi.47–48), Coriolanus appears to be the one man destined to achieve true rule over Rome. But his involvement with Roman politics raises doubts in Coriolanus' mind about the worth of his way of life, particularly because he sees that his goal of living nobly makes him dependent on the plebeians he detests to acknowledge his nobility. Coriolanus comes to despise the city because it demands that he compromise his virtue and prevents him from being self-reliant. His aim therefore becomes to live without a city, even as he forces the city to live without him. Coriolanus and Rome reach a crossroad at the end of Act III, and try to go their separate ways. The city banishes Coriolanus and he banishes the city, for they both think they are self-sufficient (III.iii.135, IV.vi.12–15, 36–37). Their claims are tested in Acts IV and V of the play.

CHAPTER 3

The Man without a City

i

Captivated by the idea of heroic self-sufficiency, Coriolanus sets out from the gates of Rome, hoping to prove not only that he can survive without the city, but also that the city cannot survive without him. Once Rome realizes how much it needs him, it will finally worship him properly, or as he himself says, "I shall be lov'd when I am lack'd" (IV.i.15). Because Coriolanus sees that banishment can provide the one true test of his self-reliance (IV.i.3–11), he insists on departing from Rome alone, "a single man" against the "vast world" (IV.i.42).[1] By banishing him, Rome apparently breaks whatever ties bind him to other men, and thus offers him a kind of freedom. Rejected by his native city, Coriolanus becomes aware of what has always been his deepest wish: "All bond and privilege of nature, break!" (V.iii.25), and he understands that he will have achieved his independence only when he can

> stand
> As if a man were author of himself,
> And knew no other kin. [V.iii.35–37]

At the head of the Volscian army, with his soldiers freely acknowledging his superiority, Coriolanus seems to have reached his goal at last:

> He is their god; he leads them like a thing
> Made by some other deity than Nature,
> That shapes men better. [IV.vi.90–92]

99

Here is what Coriolanus has been striving for all along, the self-sufficiency of a god.

Raised above the level of humanity, the gods are not supposed to be dependent on their worshipers for they are not compelled to make concessions to the city in order to be honored by it. Coriolanus believes the gods look down from their heights and laugh at human fallibility and weakness (I.ix.79, V.iii.183–85). Evidently for him a god should be imperturbable, unmoved by any human spectacle and hence unmoved by any appeal from men. He tries to imitate the gods (V.iii.150) by appearing deaf to all entreaties from Rome (V.ii.88–89, V.iii.5–6, 17–19), showing that he cannot be swayed as ordinary men are: "He's the rock, the oak not to be wind-shaken" (V.ii.110–11). Menenius uses the same metaphor to describe Coriolanus (V.iv.1–6) and goes on to develop a fuller portrait of his divinity:

The tartness of his face sours ripe grapes. When he walks, he moves like an engine, and the ground shrinks before his treading. He is able to pierce a corslet with his eye, talks like a knell, and his hum is a battery. He sits in his state, as a thing made for Alexander. What he bids be done is finish'd with his bidding. He wants nothing of a god but eternity, and a heaven to throne in.
[V.iv.17–24]

If Coriolanus is a god, his divinity is cold and mechanical, the self-sufficiency of a statue or a machine. Menenius' picture accords with earlier descriptions (I.iii.34–37, II.ii.105–13), particularly the repeated associations of Coriolanus with thunder (I.iv.58–61, I.vi.25–27, V.iii.151). His deified status among the Volsces grows out of his original nature:

Sicinius. Is't possible that so short a time can alter the condition of a man?
Menenius. There is a difference between a grub and a butterfly, yet your butterfly was a grub. This Martius is grown from man to dragon: he has wings, he's more than a creeping thing.
[V.iv.9–14]

Here Menenius uses the other principal image for the banished Coriolanus: he is not only a god, but also a dragon (IV.vii.23), a symbol introduced by Coriolanus himself when he leaves Rome as another token of his independence from the rest of mankind:

> I go alone
> Like to a lonely dragon, that his fen
> Makes fear'd and talk'd of more than seen.   [IV.i.29–31]

There is something animal-like about Coriolanus' march on Rome, something of the deliberateness of a predator stalking its helpless prey (IV.vii.34). Although mercy need not be the essential attribute of a god, one might wonder whether Coriolanus' complete lack of it is godlike. Menenius speaks of his imperturbability in animal terms: "There is no more mercy in him than there is milk in a male tiger" (V.iv.27–28). Clearly Coriolanus is trying to cut himself off from humanity in Acts IV and V, but the question remains whether in doing so he will become superhuman or merely inhuman.

In the story of the banished Coriolanus, Shakespeare explores the possibility that a man without a city is either a beast or a god. Several critics have noted the relevance to *Coriolanus* of this idea of Aristotle,[2] which is formulated in the course of his definition of the city in Book I of the *Politics*.[3] Man is a political animal, according to Aristotle—that is, a being whose nature it is to live in the polis—because he can achieve self-sufficiency only in partnership with other men. Once the city has provided for the basic necessities of life (which men are subject to along with other animals), its citizens are able to develop their specifically human potential, to live well, as Aristotle puts it, rather than merely live. Growth into true humanity requires the city because it is contingent upon speech, which can only be developed through human association.[4] Thus a man could have no need of the city only if he were incapable of developing into a full human being, or were raised above the ordinary limitations of humanity to begin with. That is the meaning of saying that someone who by nature, and not just by accident, lives without a city is either lower or higher than a man, or in other words, a beast or a god.[5] If the city is truly the comprehensive human community, then anyone who can do without the city is somehow outside the normal range of humanity.

By facing up to his banishment, Coriolanus is therefore pushing his heroism to new extremes. As he passes through the gates of the city, he passes from one heroic archetype to another. Near the beginning of the play he is compared to Hector (I.iii.41–42, I.viii.11), the hero who piously lived and died for one city, but from the moment Coriolanus sets forth from Rome, he becomes associated with Hercules (IV.i.15–19, IV.vi.99–100),[6] the hero who lived a life of perpetual exile, serving many masters, but knowing himself to be the son of Zeus and thus almost a god in his own right. Coriolanus' initial experience in Antium seems to confirm his quasi-divine status: apparently his greatness is so manifest that he can simply walk into an enemy town and be made commander-in-chief on the spot. He receives the kind of free recognition of his superiority he felt he was denied in Rome, in fact the kind of unconditional recognition only gods merit:

Why, he is so made on here within as if he were son and heir to Mars; set at upper end o' th' table; no question ask'd him by any of the senators but they stand bald before him.   [IV.v.191–94]

In setting himself up as a rival in self-sufficiency to Rome, Coriolanus does in effect rebel against the city gods and try to become a god himself. From the very beginning, the tribunes understand the germ of impiety in his soul: "Being mov'd, he will not spare to gird the gods" (I.i.256). Coriolanus' attempt to live without Rome has a certain titanic grandeur to it, the splendor of a man storming heaven to try to take a place among the gods. Much of the effect of grandeur Coriolanus conveys is due to his being "talk'd of more than seen" (IV.i.31). From Act IV, scene v, line 147, to Act V, scene ii, line 59, he never appears on stage, although he is the main subject of all the intervening dialogue. Coriolanus realizes that to maintain his aura of divinity, he must seem remote to men, and rule with a "speechless hand" (V.i.67). Perhaps he grants audiences only in public because he wants to make as grand an impression as he can, appearing in a cere-monial setting ("he does sit in gold," V.i.63) and speaking with the dignified, rather stilted speech of a monarch (V.ii.82–92).

But the godlike image Coriolanus seeks to project after leaving Rome crumbles in Act V, scene iii. The decisive test of his resolve takes a form that makes his self-reliance look like something other than heroism, namely cruelty, and as we have already seen, Coriolanus is very much concerned about how his actions "show" in public (V.iii.51–52, 191–93). Someone might regard a refusal to listen to the pleas of his mother, wife, and child as a display of superhuman strength, but the more likely reaction would be to treat it as an in-human lack of feeling. In this scene the principle of Corio-lanus' godlike self-sufficiency is reduced to the childish state-ment: "Let it be virtuous to be obstinate" (V.iii.26). Staring at his kneeling family, Coriolanus finds he really does not have the choice of becoming either a beast or a god: his fate is to be a god only by acting like a beast, and his will is broken by a simple reassertion of his humanity:

> I melt, and am not
> Of stronger earth than others.   [V.iii.28–29]

These lines bring about an important reversal of imagery, as Coriolanus, the rock, turns to water. In another complete about-face, for once he drops his scorn of appetite: "But we will drink together" (V.iii.203). Wine will be the pledge of the new-found concord, just as earlier the refusal to "sup

together" was a sign of anger and discord (IV.ii.49–50).
Whatever eros is present in Coriolanus is set free in this scene
(V.iii.44–45), and his hate for Rome begins to dissolve in his
love for his family. Ironically, the city of spiritedness can in
the end be saved only by the power of eros. Rome, the
breeder of warriors, must ultimately rely on the might of
women to win its battles (V.i.70–73, V.iii.206–9, V.iv.52–54).
From being asked to stay at home while the men fight for the
city (I.iii), the women rise to being honored by all of Rome
(V.v).

That the power of eros blocks Coriolanus' access to divinity is by no means accidental, for desire is the sign of man's
incompleteness. Since, as Coriolanus himself says, a love implies a lack (IV.i.15), his yearning for his family proves to
him that he cannot be truly self-sufficient like a god. The
presence of his mother is living testimony that he cannot be
self-generated, especially when he remembers her as "the
honour'd mould / Wherein this trunk was fram'd" (V.iii.22–
23). Volumnia knows she should play upon this fact in trying to convince her son to abandon his campaign against the
city of his birth:

> Thou art my warrior,
> I [holp] to frame thee.   [V.iii.62–63]

> Thou shalt no sooner
> March to assault thy country than to tread
> (Trust to't, thou shall not) on thy mother's womb
> That brought thee to this world.   [V.iii.122–25]

The appearance of his mother, wife, and child confronts
Coriolanus directly with the fact that he cannot stand apart
as a self-sufficient whole. He is himself part of a larger whole,
a family line, linked in one direction with his ancestors and in
the other with his descendants.[7] Even if he is only concerned
about his honor, he is told he still needs his family, to continue his line and help preserve his good name:

Volumnia. This is a poor epitome of yours,
            Which by th' interpretation of full time
            May show like all yourself. [V.iii.68–70]

Virgilia. [I] brought you forth this boy, to keep your name
            Living to time. [V.iii.126–27]

Volumnia extends this point to the whole city, showing Coriolanus that he needs Rome to perpetuate his noble memory,
that in destroying the city he would destroy everything he
ever worked for and earn an eternal curse (V.iii.140–48).
What finally stands in the way of Coriolanus' conquest of
Rome, then, is his concern for what other men will say about
him, particularly what will be said in his "chronicle"
(V.iii.145) or "annals" (V.vi.113).

In worrying about the judgment of history, Coriolanus
shows his basic Romanness, proving once again the durability
of the opinions, or the prejudices, the Republican regime im-
presses upon its citizens. Rome is finally dependent on the
lessons of filial piety it has inculcated in Coriolanus. However
much he rebels against the conventions of the city (II.ii.136),
he still regards the authority of his family as natural (V.iii.31–
33, 58–62, 83–84, 184), with the result that even when Rome
has lost its direct hold over him, it still can influence him
through his mother. Coriolanus begins to believe that his
whole resolve is contrary to nature only when it requires him
to overturn the customary authority of parent over child
(V.iii.29–31, 54–56). As we have seen, Rome tries to subordinate the family to the public good by directing it toward the
goal of producing warriors, to use the family to limit eros as a
source of private interest in the city. In the end, however,
Rome is fortunate that it never succeeds in entirely suppressing the realm of the private: only his special attachment to his
family can sway Coriolanus from his original resolve. Unable
to save itself, the city is forced to turn to a private citizen to
avoid disaster. In that sense Rome is ultimately revealed as
being no more self-sufficient than Coriolanus.

In retrospect one can see that Coriolanus' attempt to live without a city is doomed to failure from the start. He is not the man to achieve self-sufficiency because his special virtue as a warrior and a general requires other men to realize itself. Aufidius understands that a soldier is dependent on the city he fights for:

> I would I were a Roman; for I cannot,
> Being a Volsce, be that I am.   [I.x.4–5]

When Coriolanus is banished from Rome, he makes the triumphant claim: "There is a world elsewhere" (III.iii.135), but the world he goes to is no different from the one he leaves. Turning his back on one city, he can hardly wait, it seems, to find a new one to serve. The first words we hear him speak after leaving Rome are: "A goodly city is this Antium" (IV.iv.1), as if in all his wanderings his mind had never strayed an inch from the subject of the city. He sets forth from Rome on what promises to be a voyage of exploration, but he discovers nothing new on the way, only a mirror image of his native city in Antium. His experience among the Volsces recapitulates in brief his experience among the Romans, as he finds in Antium the same deceptive world of political appearances he tried to leave behind in Rome. Although he is welcomed by the Volsces as a triumphant hero (V.vi.50–51), he soon falls prey to the schemes of his political enemies and is forced to answer once more to the charge of treason (V.vi.84–86). He is killed in Antium just as he would have been killed in Rome, but not before he unconsciously falls back upon his Roman identity. The proximate cause of his death is his attempt to reclaim the name Rome gave him, Coriolanus (V.vi.86–89). In a moment of stress, he cannot resist appealing to his reputation, and his reputation is as a Roman, not a Volsce:

> If you have writ your annals true, 'tis there
> That, like an eagle in a dovecoat, I

[Flutter'd] your Volscians in Corioles.
Alone I did it.   [V.vi.113–15]

Coriolanus here recalls his exploits in Act I, suggesting that
his death has only been postponed from that moment when he
was "himself alone / To answer all the city" (I.iv.51–52), and
a loyal comrade prematurely spoke his eulogy (I.iv.56–61).
He finally dies like a true Roman warrior, slain in the enemy
town.[8]

ii

Coriolanus fails to find the "world elsewhere" he speaks of,
but that does not mean that nothing exists beyond the borders
of the city. Coriolanus carries the city with him wherever he
goes, and stays loyal to his essential Romanness to the end. To
discover what binds Coriolanus to Rome, despite his attempt
to leave it, one can begin with the brief dialogue between
Menenius and the tribunes that opens Act II, scene i:

Menenius. In what enormity is Martius poor in, that you two
have not in abundance?
Brutus. He's poor in no one fault, but stor'd with all.
Sicinius. Especially in pride.
Brutus. And topping all others in boasting.
Menenius. This is strange now. Do you know how you are
censur'd here in the city, I mean of us a' th' right-hand file?
do you?
Both. Why? how are we censur'd? . . .
Menenius. . . . You talk of pride: O that you could turn your
eyes toward the napes of your necks and make but an interior
survey of your good selves! O that you could!
Brutus. What then, sir?
Menenius. Why, then you should discover a brace of unmerit-
ing, proud, violent, testy magistrates (alias fools) as any in
Rome.   [II.i.16–24, 38–45]

Menenius tells the tribunes they lack self-knowledge since
they accuse Coriolanus of being proud without realizing that
they are at least as guilty of pride themselves, condemning

him in terms that could be just as well applied to them
(IV.vi.30–32). Their failure to know themselves is related to
their failure to pay attention to the opinions the patricians
have of them (Sicinius and Brutus must actually ask: "Why,
how are we censur'd?"). Since they cannot turn their eyes in
upon themselves, the only way they could gain self-knowledge
would be to "see themselves as others see them."

The same problem is raised in *Julius Caesar* in almost the
same terms:

Cassius.   Tell me, good Brutus, can you see your face?
Brutus.   No, Cassius; for the eye sees not itself
          But by reflection, by some other thing.
Cassius.   'Tis just.
          And it is very much lamented, Brutus,
          That you have no such mirrors as will turn
          Your hidden worthiness into your eye,
          That you might see your shadow. . . .
          And since you know you cannot see yourself
          So well as by reflection, I, your glass,
          Will modestly discover to yourself
          That of yourself which you yet know not of.[9]

                                      [I.ii.51–58, 67–70]

A man can learn about himself by considering what others
think of him, since observers can be more objective about his
faults and virtues. When men are divided into opposing parties, and their self-conception becomes largely a matter of
party line, their need to consider each other's viewpoints becomes acute. A patrician is likely to be free of the prejudices
of a plebeian if only because he has a different set of prejudices
of his own. This principle works both ways, and the lesson
Menenius teaches Sicinius and Brutus must be turned back on
him as well:

Sicinius.   Menenius, you are known well enough too.
Menenius.   I am known to be a humourous patrician. . . . What
   harm can your beesom conspectuities glean out of this character,
   if I be known well enough too?

Brutus. Come, sir, come, we know you well enough.
Menenius. You know neither me, yourselves, nor anything.
[II.i.46–47, 64–68]

As we have seen, if any members of the opposing parties in
Rome communicate, it is Menenius and the two tribunes, but
here we realize that their communication does not go much
beyond the exchange of demands and commands. Menenius
flatly denies that the tribunes could have anything to teach
him about himself. The ultimate consequence of this refusal
by both parties to consider each other's views is that the citizens of Rome remain trapped in their own self-conceptions.[10]

In Shakespeare's portrayal, the Romans lack inwardness:
they are unable to make an "interior survey" of themselves
because their eyes are always turned outward to a horizon
bounded by the city, a horizon so restricted that Cominius
may be right in his suggestion that Rome has a roof (III.i.204).
The Romans avoid thinking for themselves by taking their
opinions ready-made from the city. In times of crisis, when
they might well be reexamining their assumptions, the Romans
fall back upon what they have always thought to be true, their
conventional beliefs. The wisdom of Rome has a distinctly
proverbial cast, as Coriolanus notes in the case of the plebeians:

> They said they were an-hungry; sigh'd forth proverbs—
> That hunger broke stone walls, that dogs must eat,
> That meat was made for mouths, that the gods sent not
> Corn for the rich men only.   [I.i.205–8]

But the patricians have their proverbs as well, as Coriolanus
reminds his mother:

> You were us'd
> To say extremities was the trier of spirits,
> That common chances common men could bear,
> That when the sea was calm all boats alike
> Show'd mastership in floating; fortune's blows
> When most strook home, being gentle wounded craves

> A noble cunning. You were us'd to load me
> With precepts that could make invincible
> The heart that conn'd them.   [IV.i.3–11]

Shakespeare's Romans are evidently loaded down with precepts, conned in conveniently alliterating form, neatly
phrased so that even children could easily memorize them:
"meat was made for mouths," "common chances common
men could bear." In Rome the tendency is to substitute proverbs and precepts for genuine thought, a fact which goes a
long way toward explaining the peculiar style and poetic
texture of the two Republican Roman plays.[11]

It has frequently been noted that, by comparison with
Shakespeare's other tragedies, *Coriolanus* and *Julius Caesar* are
basically rhetorical in mode, rather than lyrical.[12] In both
plays the verse seems strictly governed by the dramatic context, with the result that neither contains the kind of lyric
poetry that stands out in much of Shakespeare's work, *Antony
and Cleopatra* included. If one were to quote some memorable
lines from either of the Republican Roman plays, they would
almost certainly be from a public speech, say Antony's
"Friends, Romans, countrymen," that is, lines more appropriate to a handbook of oratory than of lyric poetry. There
are no songs in either *Julius Caesar* or *Coriolanus*. The stage
directions of *Julius Caesar* do call for a song (IV.iii.266), but
Shakespeare apparently did not bother to write one for the
play, and in any case Brutus' boy has barely begun singing
when he falls asleep. In *Coriolanus* Volumnia asks her daugh-
ter-in-law for a song (I.iii.1) but, without even pausing for a
reply, assumes none is forthcoming and launches into a long
speech in prose on preferring honor to love. This speech may
explain why Rome is not a city of songs, especially given
Volumnia's final judgment on the subject of sons: "I had
rather had eleven die nobly for their country than one voluptuously surfeit out of action" (I.iii.24–25). Since poets are
exactly the sort of men who are generally thought to "surfeit

voluptuously out of action," they would not be welcome in Republican Rome. After all, the chief subject matter of songs is love, and lyric poetry might threaten Roman austerity, encouraging eros at the expense of spiritedness. What passes for poetry in Rome is apparently the brief ode Volumnia composes on the spot when her son returns from war:

> Death, that dark spirit, in's nervy arm doth lie,
> Which, being advanc'd, declines, and then men die.
>
> [II.i.160–61]

This couplet, "heroic" with a vengeance, is what we get instead of a song in Republican Rome. The only poetry that is not frowned upon in the city is verse in praise of a warrior, since by honoring martial valor it reinforces Rome's dominant or ruling opinions. Like any other private activity, poetry is judged in Rome by a political standard. What matters to the city is not the beauty of a poem, but the effect it will have on its citizens.

The Rome of *Julius Caesar* is actively hostile to poets.[13] Of the two who appear in the play, the first is torn to pieces by a mob that confuses him with a conspirator because it takes names for reality. In an almost surrealistic scene, the dreamer poet, who did not want to go out into the marketplace but was led forth by something he cannot explain (III.iii.1–4), is given a mock trial by the citizens of Rome. Faced with the impossible rhetorical task of answering his accusers "directly," "briefly," "wisely," and "truly" (III.iii.9–12), the poet Cinna finds that even his resources of irony are not enough to save him from execution. As the plebeians carefully check, Cinna does give one answer "directly" (l.23), one answer "briefly" (ll.24–25), and one answer "truly" (ll.26–27), but he never gives an answer "wisely," for in his situation to answer directly, briefly, and truly is not to answer "wisely," in the sense of "prudently."[14] His one attempt to give a wise answer is interpreted by the plebeians as a wisecrack and turns his audience of judges against him:

Cinna.   Wisely I say, I am a bachelor.
2. *Plebeian.*   That's as much as to say, they are fools that marry.
   You'll bear me a bang for that.   [III.iii.16–18]

The questions the plebeians originally fired at Cinna (ll.5–8)
added up to one: Are you with us or against us, are you part
of our city? With his single answer, he apparently declares
himself in the eyes of the plebeians as their enemy, for they
think his claim that it is wise to be a bachelor calls into question the wisdom of all who marry. Cinna's independence is a
challenge to the communal way of life of the city. Later in
the play, Brutus apparently feels a similar challenge to his
authority when a "vilely" rhyming poet breaks in upon a
Roman political conference, claiming the right to advise the
generals on how to make peace (IV.iii.132). Displaying a degree of irascibility unusual for him, Brutus virtually throws
the poet out with the words: "What should the wars do with
these jigging fools?" (IV.iii.137). If poetry has no relevance
to war, if it does not serve the public interest, Brutus does not
want to hear it, and he resents being told what to do by a
merely private man. In general, Rome's hostility to poetry reflects a deeper hostility to any private interest that claims to
be independent of the city, especially independence of mind
or freedom from the city's opinions. Significantly, the poet
Brutus wants expelled is a "cynic" (IV.iii.133), one of those
men who openly despises political life and the honors of the
city.[15]

The absence of any sustained lyrical passages in *Coriolanus* and *Julius Caesar* is in keeping with the focus on political concerns in Republican Rome. With their minds fixed on
public life, the Republican Romans tend to sound as if they
were always speaking at a rostrum, making grandiloquent
oratorical gestures at each other even when they are talking
two at a time (see, for example, *Julius Caesar*, I.iii.89–100). In
both *Julius Caesar* and *Coriolanus*, the measure of a man's

power is his skill as an orator, and most of the turning points
in both plays involve the success or failure of rhetorical attempts at persuading fellow Romans to one course of action or
another.[16] To take only a few examples, *Julius Caesar* opens
with Flavius and Marullus trying to persuade the plebeians to
remember Pompey and abandon Caesar's cause, we then see
Cassius trying to persuade Brutus to join a conspiracy against
Caesar, later Brutus must persuade his fellow conspirators to
do things his way in murdering Caesar, in Act II, scene ii,
Calphurnia tries to persuade Caesar to stay at home, while
Decius Brutus must persuade him to go to the Senate as planned,
and of course the whole play builds up to the great rhetorical
combat between Brutus and Antony for the allegiance of the
citizens of Rome. *Coriolanus* is even more clearly structured
around exercises of eloquence, beginning with Menenius' fable
of the belly and ending with Volumnia's dissuading of her
son, with the central scene of the central act devoted to
Volumnia and Menenius both persuading Coriolanus to court
the people's favor.

As result of the pervasiveness of rhetoric in *Julius Caesar*
and *Coriolanus*, although we are continually witness to characters trying to bring fellow Romans around to their opinions, we rarely get to see how they arrived at those opinions for themselves. The use of rhetoric presupposes that
one thinks one knows the truth: rhetoric is fundamentally an
art of convincing people of truths one thinks one has already
found, not of seeking truth in the first place. The rhetorical
texture of the Republican Roman plays is thus one more indication of the fixity of opinions in Shakespeare's Rome. Everyone in the city thinks that he knows what is right and that the
only problem is winning others over to his own views. This
point is confirmed by looking at the few soliloquies in *Julius
Caesar* and *Coriolanus*, where one might expect to find characters in the process of doubt, self-examination, and the open
search for truth. We will see, however, that the Republican

Romans use rhetoric even when talking to themselves, so dominated are they in their thinking by the city.

In *Julius Caesar* the soliloquy serves mostly as a stage device, a convenient way, for example, for a character to reveal his plans to the audience (I.ii.308–22). Antony's one soliloquy (III.i.252–75) is really a dialogue, an address to the dead Caesar, which has the character of a solemnly pledged oath. The soliloquy is not used to lay bare an actual process of thought, to show a character groping for a decision. Brutus' main soliloquy begins with a conclusion, "It must be by his death" (II.i.10), and then proceeds to justify it, as if Brutus were addressing a crowd. Having already arrived at a decision, he is searching for reasons that would convince the world that what he has decided to do is just; he appeals to "common proof" (l.21), considers how his argument can best be manipulated for rhetorical effect (ll.28–30), and ends with a kind of proverb in the form of a beast fable (ll.32–34). This soliloquy can be viewed as a trial-run for Brutus' oration in Act III, scene ii, which it resembles closely.[17] Certainly Brutus' soliloquy is not in the same category as Macbeth's "If it were done when 'tis done" or Hamlet's "To be or not to be." Since Brutus always sets his sights by what is viewed as noble in Rome, he thinks he has a straightforward principle for resolving the question of his divided loyalties and does not experience the kind of perplexing moral dilemma that grips either Macbeth or Hamlet. Like Volumnia, Brutus automatically places the public interest before his private interest (II.i.10–12), an attitude reflected in the public character of even his most private speech.[18]

Coriolanus' soliloquies are even less like Hamlet's or Macbeth's. In Act II, scene iii, he reaches a turning point in his life, having to decide whether or not to go on deceiving the plebeians. This is how he reflects upon his situation:

> Better it is to die, better to starve,
> Than crave the hire which first we do deserve.

Why in this wolvish [toge] should I stand here
To beg of Hob and Dick, that does appear
Their needless vouches? Custom calls me to't.
What custom wills, in all things should we do't,
The dust on antique time would lie unswept
And mountainous error be too highly heap'd
For truth to o'erpeer. Rather than fool it so,
Let the high office and the honor go
To one that would do thus. I am half through:
The one part suffered, the other will I do.   [II.iii.113–24]

As the only sustained passage of rhymed verse in the entire
play, these lines ought to give a critic pause. The presence of
so much rhyme in a late work of Shakespeare's is in itself
surprising, and that the rhyme should occur in a soliloquy is
doubly surprising. (Nothing comparable occurs in *Antony
and Cleopatra*.) There is not even any attempt to conceal the
rhyme: most of the lines are end-stopped and the verse has an
exceptionally artificial and stilted ring. One might be tempted
to leave the problem at "Shakespeare nods," but the safest assumption is that the playwright deliberately made Coriolanus'
soliloquy sound as wooden as it does. The poetic quality of
the speech would then be a method of characterization:
wooden verse reveals wooden thought. Instead of trying to
reflect, Coriolanus merely spouts sententious maxims in rhyme,
audibly forcing himself to recall lessons he has learned by
rote.[19] He clumsily piles proverb upon proverb in his soliloquy, apparently building to a resolve, but just as he is about to
reach it, his argument tumbles over into an incredibly lame
conclusion, indeed a conclusion completely contrary to the
direction in which his reasoning had been moving. Like his
fellow Romans, in a personal crisis he falls back upon opinions
he already has, instead of seeking to reexamine himself and his
motives, or reevaluate his situation.

To be sure, all Shakespeare's verse soliloquies are in some
sense "artificial," but what distinguishes the most famous ones
is that the poetry is carefully molded to fit the ongoing pro-

cess of the thought. Precisely the reverse occurs in Coriolanus' soliloquy: he fits his thought into the restricting pattern of the rhymed verse.[20] This reflects his attempt to force his mind toward a conclusion, as if he were arguing with someone else. As usual, Coriolanus confuses the public and the private, using rhetoric when talking to himself, even though he fails to use it when talking to others. Hence he remains bound to conventional opinions in soliloquy and does his most original thinking in dialogue. Only in arguing with the plebeians is he able to formulate his penetrating critique of the Roman regime and begin to become independent of Rome. His mistake is to allow everyone to hear his revolutionary ideas about the city, since his frankness brands him as an "enemy to the people" (III.iii.118). Coriolanus is exiled for his free thinking, and that puts an end to his reexamination of Rome. He leaves the city with a string of its proverbs on his lips (IV.i.3–11), and never recovers the insights he achieved in Act III, scene i.

Paradoxically, it is actually Coriolanus' banishment that prevents him from ever becoming free of Rome. His thought had been leading him to see the questionable aspects to devoting himself to the city, but in his exile, the idea of Rome becomes an obsession. Physically removed from Rome, he becomes absorbed in the city in a way that was not possible when he could look around and see Rome before his eyes. In Act IV he cannot bring himself just to walk away from Rome and leave it behind; on the contrary, he wants his exile to become a way of winning the recognition the city always denied him. Coriolanus can never free himself from Rome because in the end he remains bound to its opinions, especially the chief opinion on which Rome is founded, that the city is the fittest object of a man's devotion and the only true judge of his worth. The most one might say for Coriolanus—and even this claim is dubious—is that he becomes indifferent to *which* city he serves; that there might be a way of life independent of the city as such is evidently beyond his comprehension.

Coriolanus has two basic criticisms of Rome. The first fault he sees, that the patricians compromise their virtue, could be corrected in another city, for example, Sparta. But the second fault, that he is dependent in Rome on men he considers beneath him to honor him, cannot be corrected in any city, for the city is by definition a mixture of all types of men, and thus includes the high and the low. If Coriolanus objects to this aspect of Rome, he ought to reconsider whether he wants to be honored by any city at all. Unfortunately for him, such a reconsideration is precisely what he is least suited to do, since he has always tried to avoid thinking on his own. There are several suggestions in the play that Coriolanus' education has been defective (I.iii.55–57), that he has been "ill school'd" (III.i.319) because he was "bred in broils" (III.ii.81).[21] As a soldier, he has been trained to fight, not think, and hence he enjoys thinking only when it presents itelf to him as a kind of fighting. That is why he does his best thinking when arguing: only when confronted with the opposition of contrary opinions is he prodded into mental action and forced to think for himself. Coriolanus' anger normally works against his reason (I.ix.55–58, III.ii.29–31, V.iii.84–86), but if it could be transformed into scorn for false opinion, it might be the means of freeing his mind from bondage to Rome. The only true independence Coriolanus could achieve from Rome would be independence from the city's opinions. That would give him at least one form of self-sufficiency, since a man who is indifferent to the opinions of the city is first and foremost indifferent to whether it honors him or not.

If a man is to remain within the city and yet by virtue of independence of mind not be fully part of it, he must find some way of concealing his independence. As we have already seen in the case of Cinna the poet, the city can become very hostile to a man who questions its assumptions openly, a man, much like Coriolanus (III.iii.28–30), who speaks out his views briefly, directly, and truly, though not wisely.[22] In light of this

problem, we can perhaps interpret the most enigmatic scene
in *Coriolanus*, Act IV, scene iii. In a play so tightly con-
structed, it is something of a shock to find a scene which does
absolutely nothing to advance the plot, which includes none
of the main characters, and which has not the slightest basis in
Plutarch's *Life of Coriolanus*. The scene seems worse than
superfluous: occuring where it does, it obstructs our view of
what we really want to see. The scene stands between Coriolanus' departure from Rome and his arrival in Antium, that
is, at just the point where we might expect to be given a
glimpse of the man without a city. On the road from Rome to
Antium, Coriolanus should for the moment be free of either
city, even if he were only traveling between them, and, in
any case, we would like to witness the journey he has to make
in his mind to get from one to the other.[23] But instead scene
iii gives us a conversation between "a Roman and a Volsce,"
neither of whom we have seen before and neither of whom
we shall ever see again, traveling the same road as Coriolanus,
but for different reasons. Perhaps, the scene must be understood as in some way counterpointing the unseen and unheard
journey of Coriolanus, helping to define by means of contrast
what it is to be without a city, or, more specifically, what it is
to be a traitor to Rome.

Right after watching Rome banish its most loyal defender,
we discover that it has left among its ranks a true traitor, the
spy Nicanor.[24] To develop this paradox further, precisely because Coriolanus is so uncompromisingly devoted to the city,
he seems to be disloyal to it; he arouses his fellow citizens'
suspicion and anger because he cares enough about Rome to
reproach them openly with their failure to live up to his idea
of what it is to be a Roman. Obviously the spy cares about
something other than the city, but to be successful in his pro-
fession he must give the appearance of being loyal to Rome.
The difference between the spy Nicanor and Coriolanus is

that the one is willing to employ appearances, and the other is
not, as shown by their different attitude toward disguises. The
Volsce's remark to Nicanor, "You had more beard when I last
saw you" (IV.iii.8), seems to indicate that the spy has just put
on a new false face, or taken off an old one. In any case,
Nicanor has changed his appearance enough so that an old
friend does not at first recognize him (ll.3–6). In Act IV,
scene v, on the other hand, once Coriolanus has reached
Antium, he can hardly wait to throw off his disguise and reveal himself for what he is (IV.v.54–57), even though he
knows how dangerous being recognized among the Volsces
might be for him (IV.iv.4–6, IV.v.80–82). This conduct is in
keeping with Coriolanus' scorn for appearances, but now we
realize that in addition to learning such scorn, to be free of
the city one must also learn how to use appearances oneself.
Nicanor can stay in Rome and view the city with a critical
eye because he does not parade his disloyalty. He seems characterized by a kind of calm, objective, unimpassioned understanding of humanity, able to speak of the "blaze" and "flame"
of anger in the coolest prose (IV.iii.20–21). Speaking as one
detached from the party conflicts of Rome, he gives the most
nonpartisan account in the play of the "strange insurrections"
in the city (IV.iii.13–26). Presumably he even feels himself
above the conflict of Romans and Volsces, and is in fact the
only Roman in the play, besides Coriolanus, to be seen talking
on friendly terms with a Volsce. Part of Nicanor's disloyalty
is a freedom from ordinary prejudices, which allows him to
know friend and foe alike, to get outside the divisions the city
imposes upon men's thinking. Seizing upon a pun offered by
the text, one might suggest a connection between Nicanor's
espionage and his "intelligence" (l.29). Perhaps Act IV,
scene iii, does give us what we want, after all, though on a
low level: an image of the true man without a city, who precisely because he scorns its opinions becomes all the more
conscious of their nature in order to be free of them.

iii

The story of Coriolanus does lead away from Rome, away
from the city, along a path the hero fails to follow to its end,
but the standard by which Rome is finally found wanting is
not political in any ordinary sense of the term. Rome accom-
plishes its goal of politicizing its citizens, with such success
that it can reveal the limits of the city as such. In the process
of achieving a maximum of loyalty and devotion from its citizens, Rome restricts their access to wisdom, especially to self-
knowledge. With the city's regime itself ultimately founded
upon deception, Rome can hardly afford to let the pursuit of
truth go unhindered. Coriolanus, for example, is ostensibly
banished for wanting to take away the rights of the plebeians,
but the real reason why the patricians accept the banishment is
that, as they see it, he threatens to take away the plebeians'
illusion that they have rights. Coming dangerously close to
exposing the lies involved in the divided rule in Rome, he
could "mar all" (II.iii.58) if permitted to continue in the city.
The city cannot allow men to think on their own, if that independence means they will see through the deceptions politics makes necessary, for these deceptions work better if no
one recognizes them for what they are. The proverbs of
Rome, the quaint little beast fables and high-minded precepts
of nobility, are part of the regime, perhaps the fundamental
part. The Romans in *Coriolanus* are steadfast, or perhaps just
stubborn, in holding to what Rome has taught them, approaching the rock- or statue-like rigidity of Coriolanus in
the unshakeable quality of their opinions. This rigidity is
what critics are referring to when they speak of the lack of
character development in *Coriolanus*;[25] reversals occur in the
play,[26] but no real recognitions.

Just as Coriolanus might have come to realize that as a hero
he cannot live without a city, the Romans might have come
to realize that as a city they cannot live without their hero

(V.ii.38–47). Rome begins with the claim that no man is in-
dispensable, not even the great general:

> Your Coriolanus
> Is not much miss'd, but with his friends;
> The commonwealth doth stand, and so would do,
> Were he more angry at it.   [IV.vi.12–15]

When evidence to the contrary begins arriving, the reaction
of the tribunes would be to have the messenger whipped
(IV.vi.48, 61), as if the best way of dealing with unpleasant
truths were to suppress them. Messengers may be whipped
into silence, but the same technique will not work with Coriolanus, as even the tribunes quickly have to admit, when news
of their old enemy's implacable advance on Rome mounts up.
One would think that the Romans could not fail to draw the
right lesson from the city's brush with disaster: Rome is no
more self-sufficient than is Coriolanus. If the city is at last
saved, its salvation must be attributed not to its own power
(IV.vi.109–14, V.i.18–21), but rather to a kind of miracle
(V.iv.1–8). But Rome acts as if nothing out of the ordinary
has happened at the end of the play, treating what is actually
a defeat as a standard military victory, complete with the
triumphant return of the new conquering heroes, or in this
case, heroines (V.v).

In a curious way, the Republican regime, which Coriolanus wants to shake, is only strengthened by the crisis he
provokes. As we have already seen, the patricians need a way
of keeping the plebeians in their place, and Coriolanus ends up
unwittingly providing it. Only a common enemy, either foreign (the Volsces) or domestic (the Tarquins),[27] can unite the
patricians and the plebeians. With the memory of the Tarquin
tyranny fading, the patricians have to find a new domestic
threat to hold over the plebeians, and as the Coriolanus episode
suggests, the best solution is for the patricians to claim to protect Rome from the more intransigent among their own

numbers. If the people's hatred can be focused on one out-
standing patrician, like Coriolanus (I.i.7–11), it can be di-
verted from the patrician class as a whole.[28] Ironically, Coriolanus does, then, give up his life for his country, going to his
death so that the very regime he despises can go on living. His
march on Rome not only throws fear into the hearts of the
plebeians and makes them aware again of their dependence on
the patricians to protect them (IV.vii.31, V.i.35–38), but it also
discredits the tribunes in their eyes (V.iv.35–36). The whole
Coriolanus episode reenforces the plebeians' conviction that
they are incapable of ruling themselves (IV.vi.140–55), and
thereby reenforces the patricians' hold on them. In short, the
story of Coriolanus serves as a sobering or chastening experience for all Rome, teaching the citizens the moderation necessary to live together in the city, not the daring necessary to
transcend it. From the point of view of Rome, the moral of
the story is spoken by Menenius: "On both sides more respect" (III.i.180). The patricians must learn to deal with the
plebeians more circumspectly, and the plebeians must proceed
with more discretion in asserting their rights. Rome finds it
easy to gloss over those aspects of the story which raise doubts
concerning the city. The story becomes a patriotic parable,
which in Rome means also a lesson in civic piety. The man
who turns traitor to the city and rebel to its gods is destroyed,
while the city that prays together, stays together (V.iv.55,
V.v).

   What one misses most of all at the end of the play is any
recognition on the part of Rome of what it has lost in losing
Coriolanus. We never see anyone in Rome mourning his
death, not even his mother, for, in a fantastic claim that shows
how little the city understands what has happened, Rome
thinks it can repeal his banishment by welcoming home Volumnia (V.v.4–5). The story of Coriolanus highlights in stark
relief the tension between a great man and the community he
tries to serve, but no one in Rome senses any problem at all in

the fact that the very virtues the city encourages can prove unacceptable and unendurable when pursued to an extreme. Certainly Coriolanus does not fit into Rome, and the city is ultimately better off without him, but one must wonder if he fails to fit only because he is too large for Rome, if he really is a kind of Gulliver among Lilliputians, eventually slain in "puny battle" (IV.iv.6) by men far beneath him in stature. What must one say of Rome if it can achieve domestic tranquility only at the expense of expelling the most great-souled man in its midst, the man who is in some sense the fullest embodiment of the city's own ideals?[29] The fact that Rome finds it necessary to banish Coriolanus suggests a fundamental incompatibility between political excellence and human excellence. Or as Aristotle formulated the problem, Coriolanus' banishment raises doubts about the assumption that to be a good citizen and to be a good man are one and the same thing,[30] an assumption that formed the basis of the original bond between Coriolanus and Rome.

To sum up, as Shakespeare portrays the Republic, Rome tries to use Coriolanus, while Coriolanus tries to use Rome. The city needs a hero, just as the hero needs a city, and thus the two do have a common interest. But the city is willing to drop a hero whenever it feels, however mistakenly, it no longer needs him, or whenever he begins to demand too much in return for his services. Instead of being "enroll'd / In Jove's own book" (III.i.290–91), Roman gratitude lasts only as long as the city believes it has something to be grateful for:

Brutus.   When he did love his country
            It honor'd him.
Sicinius.   The service of the foot,
            Being once gangren'd, is not then respected
            For what before it was.   [III.i.303–6]

By the same token, the hero is willing to rebel against the city and go over to its enemies whenever he feels, rightly or wrongly, he no longer needs it, or whenever it begins to de-

mand too much from him in the way of compromise. The fact
that the interests of the city and its hero can and do at times
diverge ought to provoke some serious questions about the
future of Rome. The weaknesses that eventually were to destroy the Republic are already evident in the Rome of *Coriolanus*, and rather glaringly so. Above all, the city is critically
dependent on its military heroes and therefore is open to a
takeover by one of them. But no Roman in *Coriolanus* will
even consider the possibility that the events of the play reveal
any defects in the city's constitution, and hence Rome remains
fundamentally unchanged by those events. In fact, our last
glimpse of Rome in the play (V.iv.49–62) seems to hark back
to our first, as the tribunes are finally ready to heed Menenius'
advice (I.i.73–74), and use their "knees" to the gods, earning
from him in the end praise for the piety he claimed they lack
in the beginning (V.iv.55). In joining together with the
patricians to give thanks to the gods for saving the city, the
tribunes, who originally led the rebellion against patrician
rule, are at last willing to accept Menenius' original claim for
the Roman regime, that the city has divine support. The final
Roman scenes even suggest that the city has cosmic support,
that its existence and safety are rooted in the all-embracing
order of nature. Beginning with the belief that in the party
slogans of the city "nature teaches beasts to know their
friends" (II.i.6), the Romans go on to develop a faith that the
protection of the city from its enemies is "as certain as . . .
the sun is fire" (V.iv.45), forgetting for the moment how
close Rome came to perishing in flames. It is as if Lear were
to come through the scenes on the heath and still think that
storms would peace at his bidding.

PART TWO

Antony and Cleopatra

Eventually . . . a day arrives when conditions become more fortunate and the tremendous tension decreases; perhaps there are no longer any enemies among one's neighbors, and the means of life, even for the enjoyment of life, are superabundant. At one stroke the bond and constraint of the old discipline are torn: it no longer seems necessary, a condition of existence. . . . At these turning points of history we behold beside one another, and often mutually involved and entangled, a splendid, manifold, junglelike growth and upward striving, a kind of *tropical* tempo in the competition to grow, and a tremendous ruin and self-ruination, as the savage egoisms that have turned, almost exploded, against one another wrestle "for sun and light" and can no longer derive any limit, restraint, or consideration from their previous morality. It was this morality itself that dammed up such enormous strength and bent the bow in such a threatening manner; now it is "outlived." The dangerous and uncanny point has been reached where the greater, more manifold, more comprehensive life transcends and *lives beyond* the old morality; the "individual" appears, obliged to give himself laws and to develop his own arts and wiles for self-preservation, self-enhancement, self-redemption. All sorts of new what-fors and wherewithals; no shared formulas any longer; misunderstanding allied with disrespect; decay, corruption, and the highest desires gruesomely entangled; . . . a calamitous simultaneity of spring and fall, full of new charms and veils.

—Nietzsche, *Beyond Good and Evil*, sect. 262[1]

CHAPTER 4

The Politics of Empire

i

In approaching *Antony and Cleopatra* many critics assume the play deals with the opposition of public and private life, that it involves a straightforward confrontation between politics in the abstract and love in the abstract. For this view to be valid as it is commonly formulated, Octavius would have to stand for all politicians, and Antony and Cleopatra for all lovers. But this quasi-allegorization of the story, while perhaps appropriate to a version like Dryden's *All For Love,* is not ture to the complexity of Shakespeare's *Antony and Cleopatra.* Octavius cannot represent politics in general, for he is at most a prototype of the Roman Emperors, and several characters within the play (including Antony) compare him unfavorably with the rulers the Republic produced. A judgment passed on him is by no means a judgment on politics as such, but at most one on Roman Imperial politics. By the same token, Antony and Cleopatra are not typical of lovers in general but claim a special status for their passion. In fact their insistence that they "stand up peerless" (I.i.40) in the eyes of the whole world suggests they have found an imperial form of love to correspond to the imperial form of politics that prevails in their era.

Rather than studying the simple opposition of politics and love in *Antony and Cleopatra,* one might more profitably investigate the interconnection of the two themes, the way in which the political story and the love story are integral to one another. A comparison of *Antony and Cleopatra* with other plays on the subject, such as Dryden's, would show that Shakespeare has taken pains to ground his love story in a very specific political and historical setting, a setting which gives the love its particular character and significance.[1] As Derek Traversi writes, "The passion of Antony and Cleopatra, whatever may be said further of it, shares the weakness, the corruption of the world in which it grows to expression."[2] To give a somewhat more poetic and less moralistic formulation, the early Roman Empire supplies the hothouse conditions necessary for such exotic flowers as the imperial love of Antony and Cleopatra to flourish. Antony, in evaluating the relative merits of politics and love, is confronted with a particular form of politics that encourages a very special brand of love. Clearly the terms of his choice would have been quite different had he lived in the Rome of *Coriolanus*. To dismiss such speculation on the grounds that under such circumstances Antony would never have had the opportunity to meet a Cleopatra is already to draw a distinction between the narrow horizons of the early Roman Republic and the "infinite variety" offered by the cosmopolitan world of the Empire.

To understand why Antony apparently prefers a life of love rather than politics, one must consider how the terms of his choice have changed since the time of the Republic. In the Empire, the rewards of public life begin to look hollow, whereas private life seems to offer new sources of satisfaction. The change from the era of the Republic might be conveniently summed up in the formula: the Imperial regime works to discourage spiritedness and encourage eros, or, more accurately expressed, by removing the premium the Republic places on spiritedness, the Empire sets eros free with a new power. As we have already seen, the rigidity of the Imperial hierarchy limits the access of ambitious men to political life. But though chances for success in Imperial politics might be fewer, if the rewards for success were correspondingly greater, spirited men might still experience the lure of public life with equal force. In terms of range of dominion, length of tenure, perquisites of office, and degree of authority, the Imperial throne does at first seem a far greater goal for an ambitious man's efforts than any political position the Republic has to offer. Yet, though Cleopatra is finally led to proclaim: " 'Tis paltry to be Caesar" (V.ii.2), no one in *Coriolanus* ever asserts " 'Tis paltry to be consul," not even Coriolanus, who surely has grounds for making such a claim but confines himself to questioning his own qualifications for the highest Republican office (II.i.203–4), not its intrinsic value. Since concern for honor is uppermost in the minds of spirited men, the worth of a given political office may be more a function of the quality than the quantity of those ruled. How attractive public life will appear to a man will obviously depend on how he evaluates his public, and in the Empire portrayed in *Antony and Cleopatra* political honors have come to seem empty precisely because of the nature of those who do the honoring. Apparently everyone of importance now shares Coriolanus' contempt for the common people of Rome.[3] Cleopatra, for example, describes them in just the terms Coriolanus likes to use:

> Mechanic slaves
> With greasy aprons, rules, and hammers shall
> Uplift us to the view. In their thick breaths,
> Rank of gross diet, shall we be enclouded,
> And forc'd to drink their vapor.   [V.ii.209–13]

Both Antony and Octavius are convinced of the fickleness of the Romans' opinions (I.ii.185–89, I.iv.44–47), and they must wonder what kind of foundation the "slippery people" can provide for a man's honor.

Above all what the Republic offers and the Empire denies is a sense of being honored by one's equals. The Emperor has no equals and, instead of accepting recognition of his worth freely given by fellow citizens, he can only experience what amounts to the submission of slaves to his will. Coriolanus requires worthy opponents to make his life seem worthwhile (I.i.228–32), and Shakespeare makes a point of depicting the spirit of friendly and generous rivalry that prevails among the patricians under the Republic (I.iv.1–7, I.vi.55–66). Imperial politics, by contrast, requires the elimination of one's rivals, as Octavius well understands in his lament over Antony's death:

> I must perforce
> Have shown to thee such a declining day,
> Or look on thine; we could not stall together
> In the whole world.   [V.i.37–40]

Republican Romans compete with each other against the enemies of the city, and are rewarded with offices in return for foreign conquests. The civil wars thus mark the turning point for Roman politics, as Romans begin contending against each other for dominion of the city itself. The source of Marullus' indignation in *Julius Caesar* is that Caesar was the first to celebrate a triumph for the defeat of fellow Roman citizens:

> Wherefore rejoice? What conquest brings he home?
> What tributaries follow him to Rome,
> To grace in captive bonds his chariot-wheels?
> You blocks, you stones, you worse than senseless things!
>   .   .   .   .   .
> And do you now strew flowers in his way,
> That comes in triumph over Pompey's blood?
>   [I.i.32–35, 50–51]

From the time of Julius Caesar, Roman history becomes the record of the struggle of Roman against Roman, first Brutus and Cassius against the Second Triumvirate, then the members of the Triumvirate against each other. During this internal strife, the possibilities of pursuing a political career with honor rapidly diminish, and the ranks of "honorable men" in Rome are depleted with astonishing speed (*Julius Caesar*, IV.iii.173–80). The lack of true Romans to compete with in the Empire is the wake of Julius Caesar's achievement in surpassing and overcoming all his rivals,[4] an outcome Cassius indignantly foresaw (I.ii.151–57). The feeling pervading the last act of *Julius Caesar* that the race of true Romans is dying out (V.iii.60–64, 98–101, V.v.68) sets an ominous keynote for *Antony and Cleopatra*. It prefigures the loss of the ennobling spirit of contest from Imperial politics, a fact underscored by Antony's vain challenge of Octavius to single combat. The Emperor cannot earn his honors anymore because others do his fighting for him, as Antony points out in Octavius' case:

> He alone
> Dealt on lieutenantry, and no practice had
> In the brave squares of war.   [III.xi.38–40]

> His coins, ships, legions,
> May be a coward's, whose ministers would prevail
> Under the service of a child as soon
> As i' th' command of Caesar.   [III.xiii.22–25]

In short, if being honored means feeling respected by men one respects in turn, the office of the consul in the Republic is a greater honor than the throne in the Empire.

Public service is not only less attractive or satisfying as a career in the Empire, it is also less necessary. The Imperial Romans are freer to give way to their private interests or appetites than the Republican Romans. In thinking over the various means by which the Republic tries to suppress the force of eros, one cannot help being struck by its dependence on being constantly at war: the Republic's austerity is ultimately that of an armed camp. Welcoming the prospect of a new campaign against Rome, Aufidius' servants reveal that war brings out the spiritedness in men, peace the eros:

2. *Serv.* Why then we shall have a stirring world again. This peace is nothing but to rust iron, increase tailors, and breed ballad-makers.

1. *Serv.* Let me have war, say I, it exceeds peace as far as day does night; it's sprightly walking, audible, and full of vent. Peace is a very apoplexy, lethargy, mull'd, deaf, [sleepy],

insensible, a getter of more bastard children than war's a destroyer of men.   [IV.v.218–26]

Peace allows men the luxury of indulging their appetites, notably their sexual desires, but under the pressure of war, they have to suppress their private interests and devote themselves to the public good. Peace, ordinarily associated with love, becomes paradoxically a cause for men to hate each other:

2. Serv.   As wars, in some sort, may be said to be a ravisher, so it cannot be denied but peace is a great maker of cuckolds.
1. Serv.   Ay, and it makes men hate one another.
2. Serv.   Reason: because they then less need one another.
                                                      [IV.v.225–32]

These lines suggest what happens to the Rome of *Antony and Cleopatra.* As long as the city lives under the constant threat of war, the common good is evident, at least in its most rudimentary form: the Romans realize they need each other if only to protect themselves. But once the threat of war is removed, private interests and appetites have the chance to assert themselves, unhindered by the need to unite the community against common enemies. One might in fact trace the absence of any references to the common good of Rome in *Antony and Cleopatra* to the absence of any common enemies for Romans.[5]
     The only statement in all of *Antony and Cleopatra* that even alludes to a common good links it to the notion of political necessity and the prospect of war. Lepidus suggests that Antony and Octavius must suppress their differences in the face of Pompey's threat:

Lepidus.   'Tis not a time
          For private stomaching.
Enobarbus.   Every time
          Serves for the matter that is then born in't.
Lepidus.   But small matters to greater matters must give way.
                                                      [II.ii.8–11]

But Lepidus' statements imply that once the pressure of the

immediate crisis is removed, Antony and Octavius can return
to their private grievances, or as Enobarbus cynically puts it:

> If you borrow one another's love for the instant, you may, when
> you hear no more words of Pompey, return it again. You shall
> have time to wrangle in when you have nothing else to do.
>
> [II.ii.103–6]

This comment evokes a stern rebuke from Antony, perhaps
because it raises an unpleasant truth about the situation of
Rome, a truth even the younger Pompey understands (II.i.42–
49). Once they defeat all their enemies, the Romans will have
"nothing else to do" except indulge their private appetites and
grievances. This line of thought adds new meaning to Act
III, scene i, where Ventidius is shown defeating the last of
Rome's important enemies, the Parthians, and thereby eliminating the last serious external threat that could force the
Romans to unite for the common good. In short, for a country
whose way of life had been closely bound up with the enterprise of war, Octavius' apparently hopeful remark: "The time
of universal peace is near" (IV.vi.4) has an ominous ring.
Rome itself is fast approaching the situation of its Emperor,
with no equals to fight anymore, no more Volsces or Parthians to test and prove its virtue. Perhaps the career of Rome
is prefigured in Valeria's sketch of Coriolanus' son:

> A' my troth, I look'd upon him a' We'n'sday half an hour together;
> h'as such a confirm'd countenance. I saw him run after a gilded
> butterfly, and when he caught it, he let it go again, and after it
> again, and over and over he comes, and up again; catch'd it again;
> or whether his fall enrag'd him, or how 'twas, he did so set his
> teeth and tear it! O, I warrant, how he mammock'd it!
>
> [I.iii.58–65]

As little Martius learns, the game is over once one destroys
one's prey. Rome at first no sooner catches its prey than it lets
it go again, as is evident from the treatment of the Volsces in
Coriolanus,[6] but eventually Rome like little Martius conquers
its "playthings" once and for all, leaving itself alone and with-

out purpose in the world.⁷ By eliminating all its rivals, Rome creates a situation in which it can no longer maintain its martial discipline. In particular, the conquest of the world relieves the Romans of the most elementary, and hence most pressing, of necessities, hunger. In marked contrast to the Rome of *Coriolanus*, the Rome of *Antony and Cleopatra* is never threatened by famine. With conquered territories like Egypt to boast of, Rome seems assured of "foison" rather than "dearth" (II.vii.17–23), and feasts have become the order of the day, of course in Antony's army, but at times in Octavius' as well (IV.i.15–16). The very success of Rome in conquering the world undermines the traditional martial virtues that made that conquest possible. The citizens of an unchallenged empire are freer to indulge themselves in luxuries than are those of a small city struggling for its existence.

For all these reasons, the world of *Antony and Cleopatra* is one in which all kinds of new longings are likely to arise among the Romans, but whether that world can satisfy the desires it awakens remains in doubt. A feeling of dissatisfaction and frustration permeates *Antony and Cleopatra*, to the point where one might choose as a motto for the play Lady Macbeth's bitter lines:

> Nought's had, all's spent,
> Where our desire is got without content.   [III.ii.4–5]

The pattern of a man achieving a long sought-for goal, only to decide it was not worth the effort or to have his accomplishment turn sour in the accomplishing, is repeated again and again in *Antony and Cleopatra*.⁸ In speaking of Antony's final achievement of revenge on Brutus, Enobarbus points out "what willingly he did confound he wail'd" (III.ii.58), and Octavius' reaction to the death of Antony leads Agrippa to comment:

> And strange it is
> That nature must compel us to lament
> Our most persisted deeds.   [V.i.28–30]

Antony sums up the perplexing mutability of values in his world when he hears of his wife Fulvia's death:

> There's a great spirit gone! Thus I did desire it.
> What our contempts doth often hurl from us,
> We wish it ours again. The present pleasure,
> By revolution low'ring, does become
> The opposite of itself. She's good, being gone;
> The hand could pluck her back that shov'd her on.
> [I.ii.122–26]

Obviously it is difficult to hold to any course of action in a world where men are uncertain of their values because goods have a habit of changing into evils, and evils into goods. In this atmosphere, a spiritual malaise infects the characters in *Antony and Cleopatra*, while the strong sense of Roman purpose and indomitable will, so evident in the characters in *Coriolanus*, is disappearing from the scene. Rome as a whole has nothing to do and would welcome anything as a diversion:

> And quietness, grown sick of rest, would purge
> By any desperate change.   [I.iii.53–54]

As Octavius points out, the Roman populace has reached the point of utter stagnation:

> This common body,
> Like to a vagabond flag upon the stream,
> Goes to and back, lacking the varying tide,
> To rot itself with motion.   [I.iv.44–47]

Perhaps this image of rotting best captures the stage Rome has reached by the time of *Antony and Cleopatra*.

The danger of spiritual emptiness—"to be call'd into a huge sphere, and not to be seen to move in't" (II.vii.14–15)—has become widespread in the world of the play, but is acute in Antony's special case. Antony himself realizes that his personal danger is "idleness" (I.ii.129), for as he observes:

> we bring forth weeds
> When our quick winds lie still.   [I.ii.109–10]

Antony's idleness as a soldier could be as much the cause as
the effect of his constant search for new pleasures to relieve
the potential tedium of his life (I.i.46–47). Having missed his
chance to be executed with his master in *Julius Caesar*, a
privilege he requested (III.i.151–63), Antony must search for
another moment when he will be "apt to die," which requires his finding another cause worth dying for. But Antony's tragedy is that he is surrounded by a spiritual vacuum
just when he most needs something to fill the void in his own
soul. To understand more fully why he has trouble finding
an adequate object for his allegiance, one must explore further
what has happened to the ancient city in the world of *Antony
and Cleopatra*.

ii

Merely locating the city of Rome in *Antony and Cleopatra*
has become difficult, for it seems to have been swallowed up
in the vast territory it conquered. Having reached out in its
passion for empire to embrace the entire world, the city,
which in *Coriolanus* "yet distinctly ranges," becomes "as indistinct as water is in water," or as *Rome* is in *Rome*, for by
the time of Antony, the name can refer to either the particular
city or the much vaguer notion of the Empire as a whole. In
Coriolanus one can easily distinguish a separate Rome, a separate Corioli, and a separate Antium because the cities in its
world have walls around them. But there are no sharp boundaries in the fluid world of *Antony and Cleopatra*, and Rome
is not presented as a simple and distinct geographic point. In
Coriolanus and *Julius Caesar*, Shakespeare creates specific
urban environments, making us aware of individual buildings
and monuments, and even of the physical dimensions of the
city. As G. Wilson Knight points out, in the context of *Coriolanus*, the phrase: " 'Tis south the city mills" (I.x.31) sounds
perfectly natural.[9] In *Antony and Cleopatra*, on the other
hand, we do not get a sense of the physical presence of Rome

as a discrete city. Some of the "Roman" scenes undoubtedly occur within the old boundaries of the city, but no reference is made to traditional Roman landmarks like the Forum or the Tarpeian Rock, and other scenes appear to be scattered throughout Italy, for example, at the port city of Mesena or Misenum (II.ii.160, II.iv.5–7). Clearly *Rome* means something less definite and more abstract in *Antony and Cleopatra* than it does in *Coriolanus* and *Julius Caesar*.

Certainly the city is not a character in *Antony and Cleopatra* in the way it is in the Republican Roman plays. There are no crowd scenes to show the Roman populace playing a role in their own destiny.[10] We do hear some talk of the effect the people might yet have on Imperial politics (I.ii.185–92, II.i.8–10), but no one bothers to appeal to them directly and their support for Pompey ultimately does not count for much. Significantly, the patrician and plebeian parties have no role in the action of *Antony and Cleopatra*. In fact, the word *patrician* does not even occur in the play; the word *plebeian* only once (IV.xii.34), and then in a context that suggests the Roman people have become spectators rather than actors. All one can speak of in Imperial Rome are private factions developing around the various contestants for the throne (I.iii.46–47). The absence of the Roman parties, and accompanying offices like the tribunate, means a general lowering of the Romans' participation in politics. One hears nothing of traditional Roman political institutions in the play, even though historically many of them did survive into the era of the Empire. From reading Shakespeare's play, one would never know, for example, that the Senate still existed in Imperial Rome, since Shakespeare omits all of Plutarch's references to it.[11] One can virtually observe the playwright in the act of deleting the Senate from Imperial Rome; at one point where North's Plutarch has "Octavius Caesar reporting all these things unto the Senate and oftentimes accusing [Antony] to the whole people and assembly in Rome,"[12] Shakespeare re-

stricts the action to the much vaguer command: "Let Rome
be thus / Inform'd" (III.vi.19–20). As Shakespeare recasts the
situation, all that remains is the Emperor on one side and the
whole of Rome on the other. All the intermediary bodies such
as the Senate and the people's assembly, which might have
bridged the gap between ruler and ruled, have dropped out of
sight.

One of the chief characteristics of Imperial politics in *Antony and Cleopatra* is thus the remoteness of the ruler from
the ruled. If only because of the geographic extent of the Empire, men have difficulty obtaining clear guidance from the
authorities who govern them. On a distant frontier of the
Empire, Ventidius must try to figure out what his general
really wants him to do, illustrating the problem of obedience
"when him we serve's away" (III.i.15). He apparently was
not given a clear set of instructions, and cannot follow any
simple objective standards, since he "could do more to do
Antonius good, / But 'twoud offend him" (III.i.25–26). Usually a subordinate is given explicit guidance, such as Octavius'
command to Taurus: "Do not exceed / The prescript of this
scroll" (III.viii.4–5), but Ventidius is in the strange situation
of having to guess at his commander's intentions. Menas has
a similar dilemma when he offers to give his commander
Pompey the whole world by murdering the Triumvirs for
him, and receives this most peculiar reply:

> Ah, this thou shouldst have done,
> And not have spoke on't! In me 'tis villainy,
> In thee't had been good service. Thou must know,
> 'Tis not my profit that does lead mine honor;
> Mine honor, it. Repent that e'er thy tongue
> Hath so betray'd thine act. Being done unknown,
> I should have found it afterwards well done,
> But must condemn it now.   [II.vii.73–80]

Menas is trying to do the right thing as a subordinate—to get
direct orders from his commander—but he is told that no such

clear-cut advice is forthcoming for him. He must quite literally be able to read Pompey's mind, and only after the fact will he know if he has done so correctly or not. This is tantamount to having no guidance at all, especially since Pompey strongly implies that Menas will have to act directly contrary to his commander's professed standards (ll.74–75). To have to obey a master's unexpressed commands would be to have a remote commander indeed, even if he were standing right at one's side.

But the most remote commanders in the world of *Antony and Cleopatra* are the gods themselves. Most critics assume the references to the gods in the Roman plays are intended merely to give a certain pagan flavor to the dialogue,[13] but careful analysis will uncover a significant contrast between the religious beliefs of the Republican Romans in *Coriolanus* and those of the Imperial Romans in *Antony and Cleopatra*. This contrast is most clearly revealed in a dialogue between Pompey and the pirate Menecrates:

Pompey.   If the great gods be just, they shall assist
                 The deeds of justest men.
Menecrates.   Know, worthy Pompey,
                 That what they do delay, they not deny.
Pompey.   Whiles we are suitors to their throne, decays
                 The thing we sue for.
Menecrates.   We, ignorant of ourselves,
                 Beg often our own harms, which the wise pow'rs
                 Deny us for our good; so find we profit
                 By losing of our prayers.   [II.i.1–8]

In considering whether any divine support for human justice exists, Pompey places himself in the same position with respect to the gods that he later places Menas in with respect to himself. That is, Pompey does not speak of obeying the gods' expressed commands concerning justice; rather, he talks as if a man should go ahead and do what he thinks is just and then see if the gods support him, a course he doubtless has in mind in challenging the Triumvirs to open war. In other words, an appeal to the gods is an appeal to arms, an approach still in harmony with Republican beliefs:

Cominius.   The Roman gods,
  Lead their successes as we wish our own,
  That both our powers, with smiling fronts encount'ring,
  May give you thankful sacrifice.   [*Coriolanus*, I.vi.6–9]

The Republican consul Cominius, however, expects a straightforward answer from the gods, and expects it almost immediately, for the outcome of the battle will show which side has divine support. But Menecrates makes divine guidance less readily accessible, claiming that the gods may "delay" their judgment and that Pompey cannot tell from their immediate failure to support his cause that they do not really favor him in the long run. Pompey understandably objects that, while he is waiting around for word from heaven, he may lose what he was striving for in the first place.

At this point, Menecrates makes divine guidance even more remote from men, so remote that one has to question whether the gods in his view provide any effective support for human justice at all. He tells Pompey that he cannot go by his own standards of what is good and bad, because divine values may not correspond to human, and, although he may think the gods have injured him and shown their disapproval, they may actually have benefitted him and shown their favor. The Republican attitude toward the gods is simple, if somewhat crude: you go to battle, and if you win, the gods support you; if you lose, they do not. Pompey is at first presented with a slightly more complicated situation: even if you lose a battle, the gods may still show their support at a later date. But as Menecrates finally draws the picture, the lines of divine guidance have been blurred virtually beyond recognition: you go to battle, and if you win, the gods may have prepared a hidden calamity for you (victory itself may be the disaster), and if you lose, the gods may have some secret consolation ready (loss itself may be in some sense to your advantage). For the Republican Romans, the gods in effect confirm human judgments of what is good and bad. In the Empire, as Menecrates portrays the situation, the gods throw these judgments into confusion, as a result of the claim that they know better than men themselves what is in the interest of mankind.

Menecrates is not alone in his way of thinking, for Enobarbus tells Antony that he must give the gods a "thankful sacrifice" for taking away his wife (I.ii.161), and Cleopatra implies that a man must be wary when the gods seem to be favoring him, since they may well turn on him:

> I hear him mock
> The luck of Caesar, which the gods give men
> To excuse their after wrath. [V.ii.285–87]

Having to wonder what divine actions signify is bad enough, but Antony, in the most disturbing view of the gods in the play, claims they make it impossible for a man to judge their intents:

> But when we in our viciousness grow hard
> (O misery on't!) the wise gods seel our eyes,
> In our own filth drop our clear judgments, make us
> Adore our errors, laugh at 's while we strut
> To our confusion. [III.xiii.111–15]

Obviously someone with this view of the gods will have trouble keeping faith in any course of action he chooses for himself. Unlike the gods of *Coriolanus*, who support the Romans' sense of purpose, the gods of *Antony and Cleopatra* undermine it. But perhaps this understanding of things confuses cause and effect. The Republican confidence in the Roman gods expresses the city's faith in itself, epitomized in Menenius' conviction that Rome's acts are "enroll'd / In Jove's own book" (III.i.290–91). By the same token, the Romans in *Antony and Cleopatra* have lost their confidence that they know the will of the gods because they have lost confidence in themselves.

One can study the weakening of the Roman civic religion by tracing the gradual intrusion of the supernatural into Shakespeare's Rome. Critics have seldom made much of the absence of the supernatural from *Coriolanus*,[14] perhaps because they see no reason for Shakespeare to have included supernatural elements. And yet Plutarch's *Life of Coriolanus* contains several supernatural incidents which, on the face of it, seem as worthy of inclusion in a play as are the instances of the supernatural in *Julius Caesar* or *Antony and Cleopatra*. The first battle Coriolanus fights in is marked by a mysterious appearance of Castor and Pollux, but Shakespeare's Cominius makes no mention of this in his otherwise detailed account of the event (II.ii.87–98). After Coriolanus' banishment, "certain sights and wonders in the air" appear in Rome, in Plutarch's account, and a man named Titus Latinus receives instructions from Jupiter to the Senate. Above all, the idea to have Volumnia and Virgilia go to entreat Coriolanus comes to Valeria as an "inspiration" from "some god above."[15] Finally, when the ladies return to Rome, a statue in a temple speaks to them, an incident which prompts Plutarch into a long discussion of the status of supernatural utterances. Since all these instances of the supernatural have analogues in other Shakespearean plays, it seems likely that Shakespeare deliberately excluded the supernatural from *Coriolanus*, probably in an effort to maintain the consistency of his image of Republican Rome. The city would no longer appear self-contained and self-sufficient if in times of crisis it were forced to rely on divine revelations other than official civic religious functions like the auspices. The various supernatural incidents in Plutarch suggest that private individuals have personal access to divine authority, without the mediation of the city, but, as we have seen, Shakespeare presents the gods under the firm political control of the patricians in *Coriolanus*, as part of the city's attempt to form the comprehensive horizons of its citizens. The city must be closed off from supernatural revelation to keep the roof of Rome intact.

But in *Julius Caesar* the roof of Rome begins to crack. To be sure, the play still offers several masterly examples of the old Roman manipulation of religion for political ends.[16] Caesar is able to interpret the news from the augurers to suit his own purposes, turning an obvious ill omen into a confirmation of his will to go to the Senate (II.ii.37–48). The prize for hermeneutic dexterity must, however, go to Decius Brutus, who takes Calphurnia's horrible dream of Caesar's statue spouting blood and calmly expounds its hidden meaning, showing it to be "a vision fair and fortunate" (II.ii.76–91). But terrifying visions (I.iii.3–32, II.ii.14–26) are pressing in upon the Rome of *Julius Caesar* with such force that even the most rational Romans are losing their hold on their religious beliefs. Cassius detects a weakening in Caesar's resolution:

> But it is doubtful yet
> Whether Caesar will come forth to-day or no;
> For he is superstitious grown of late,
> Quite from the main opinion he held once
> Of fantasy, of dreams, and ceremonies.
> It may be these apparent prodigies,
> The unaccustom'd terror of this night,
> And the persuasion of his augurers
> May hold him from the Capitol to-day.   [II.i.193–201]

Though, with the help of Decius Brutus, Caesar does decide to go to the Senate, the way he wavers in his decision suggests that with the change in his religious beliefs he is no longer as sure of himself as he once was. The most striking transformation occurs in Cassius:

> You know that I held Epicurus strong,
> And his opinion; now I change my mind,
> And partly credit things that do presage.

Coming from Sardis, on our former ensign
Two mightly eagles fell, and there they perched,
Gorging and feeding from our soldiers' hands,
Who to Philippi here consorted us.
This morning are they fled away and gone,
And in their stead do ravens, crows, and kites
Fly o'er our heads and downward look on us
As we were sickly prey. Their shadows seem
A canopy most fatal, under which
Our army lies, ready to give up the ghost.   [V.i.76–88]

This theoretical change on Cassius' part soon has important
practical consequences, since his fatalistic conviction that his
luck has turned, together with his superstitious belief that his
birthday should be his death-day (V.iii.23–25), leads him to
give up the fight prematurely and kill himself. When even the
skeptical Cassius becomes subject to mystical promptings, the
supernatural has clearly gained a foothold in the hitherto this-
worldly city of Rome.

If nothing else, the shadowy presence of the soothsayer in
Julius Caesar suggests that a new dimension has entered Roman life, beyond the ordinary political control of the city. By
the time of *Antony and Cleopatra*, soothsayers seem to have
become common household items, and their claim to be able
to interpret "nature's infinite book of secrecy" (I.ii.10) on
their own gives them a new authority over men. Unlike Julius
Caesar, Antony allows himself to be warned away from
Rome by a soothsayer who plays upon his superstitious regard
for his luck (II.iii). No longer is the city the intermediary
between a man and his gods, as in *Coriolanus*. In *Antony and
Cleopatra* the importance of the city gods seems greatly reduced, as the characters turn to new sources of divine authority. For the only time in the Roman plays, personal deities are
mentioned, as the soothsayer tells Antony he must be guided
by his own "daemon" or *daimonion* (II.iii.20–31). And in a
crisis, the Roman Scarus feels he can no longer call upon a
single god of the city, but must appeal to "gods and god-

desses, / All the whole synod of them!" (III.x.4–5). Perhaps one universal deity is needed to correspond to the universal Emperor in the world of *Antony and Cleopatra*. Cleopatra's dream of Antony can be interpreted as an attempt to create the myth of such a universal god:

> His face was as the heav'ns, and therein stuck
> A sun and moon, which kept their course, and lighted
> The little o' th' earth.
> His legs bestrid the ocean, his rear'd arm
> Crested the world.   [V.ii.79–83]

In Cleopatra's eyes, Antony in scope and stature is above not just the city gods but the cosmic gods as well. But if Dolabella is any example, the Romans are not yet ready to believe in such a god (V.ii.94). The most striking supernatural incident in *Antony and Cleopatra* is not the entrance but the exit of a god, suggesting that, whatever will replace it, the traditional Roman religion is coming to its end. The eery scene when "the god Hercules, whom Antony lov'd, / Now leaves him" (IV.iii.16–17) seems to have more than personal significance, faintly suggesting as it does the motif of the flight of the pagan gods, familiar to us from Milton's "Nativity Hymn." In another scene with symbolic resonance, Shakespeare shows the world of classical antiquity drunk and reeling, invoking in song the god of an Eastern mystery religion (II.vii.113–18).[17] Perhaps Shakespeare realized that when Rome turned to foreign gods like Bacchus, it was a sign of the city's decline, and the beginning of a process that eventually dissolved the ancient world.[18]

iii

In a world in which they have lost their old political bearings, the Romans of *Antony and Cleopatra* are figuratively at sea, a metaphor developed by the emphasis in the play on battles at sea as opposed to on land. The most unequivocal call to patriotism is the defense of one's own land, but in the inter-

national imperial wars of *Antony and Cleopatra* the soldiers
are never given a real foothold. A vague expanse of sea cannot call forth the same fighting spirit in Antony's men that a
determinate patch of land could:

> O noble Emperor, do not fight by sea,
> Trust not to rotten planks. Do you misdoubt
> This sword, and these my wounds? Let th' Egyptians
> And the Phoenicians go a-ducking; we
> Have us'd to conquer standing on the earth,
> And fighting foot to foot.   [III.vii.61–66]

The case of Enobarbus shows how the change in the Roman
regime has left soldiers without guidance, undermined their
martial virtue, and introduced a new perplexity into their relation to their superiors. Enobarbus is unquestionably a spirited
man (see, for example, II.ii.4–8), but his circumstances make
it difficult, if not impossible, for him to become public spirited. With his courage and sense of loyalty, he surely would
have found an honored place in the armies of the Republic. In
the world of *Antony and Cleopatra*, however, he cannot at-
tach himself to any cause that is not essentially private in
nature, and Antony cannot hold his devotion in the way the
city could have. Whereas the city could put the blame for its
defeats on individual generals or soldiers, Antony must take
responsibility himself for the fortunes of his cause. In a way,
Antony is too open to the scrutiny of his followers to maintain their unquestioning allegiance. In the battle of Actium,
Enobarbus thinks his master's actions are shameful (III.xiii.10),
and becomes ashamed to follow him. After observing first-
hand Antony's attempts to cope with defeat, Enobarbus decides his master has lost his reason and concludes that serving
him any longer would be irrational (III.xiii.194–200). In
short, although Enobarbus is not afraid of death, he would
only want to die for something he knows to be worthwhile.
He is forced to wonder whether it would be wise or courageous to die for the sake of a fool or a coward, and thus his

doubts concerning Antony eat away at his soldier's resolve. Enobarbus' self-interest gradually comes to the fore as the force he poised against it, his devotion to Antony, gradually weakens. When a soldier is considering risking his life, evidently the public good is a more effective counterweight to his own private good than the mere private good of another man can be.

Yet Enobarbus cannot live with himself after leaving his master. Antony's cause may not have been noble enough to satisfy him, but he cannot find any new and nobler cause that would justify the inherent baseness of his act of desertion. In the Republic, a soldier can be disloyal to his commander and not regard his actions as treachery, if he believes they are in accord with his higher loyalty to Rome. That, after all, is the principle of Brutus' self-defense: "Not that I lov'd Caesar less, but that I lov'd Rome more" (III.ii.21–22). But Enobarbus has no such higher loyalty and can only set his own self-interest against Antony's. He sums up his dilemma in a remarkably penetrating speech:

> Mine honesty and I begin to square.
> The loyalty well held to fools does make
> Our faith mere folly: yet he that can endure
> To follow with allegiance a fall'n lord
> Does conquer him that did his master conquer,
> And earns a place i' th' story.   [III.xiii.41–46]

Enobarbus cannot accept the idea that faith in itself is a value, that one need only be loyal to someone, no matter how undeserving of loyalty he may be. Yet he is living in a world where fidelity to one's master is fast becoming the only virtue recognized. This truth is brought home to him when he goes over to Octavius' camp, only to find himself despised and branded forever a "master-leaver and a fugitive" (IV.vi.10–17, IV.ix.21–22). He dies because he has nothing left to live for, his last moments poisoned by the thought that Antony was more loyal to his servant than he was to his master

(IV.vi.29–38, IV.ix.18–19). The whole scene of Enobarbus' death, illuminated by the moon, the "sovereign mistress of true melancholy" (IV.ix.12), has the atmosphere of a lover dying for the sake of his beloved, even to the point of Enobarbus expiring with the name of Antony on his lips (IV.ix.23).

Enobarbus' story reveals the hold a master is able to exert over a servant under the Imperial regime, a hold that exceeds all rational considerations. However, if servants have a deep need for masters when they have nothing else to give their allegiance to, masters also find they have a deep need for servants. Antony in particular needs a sense that others have faith in him,[19] and many of his actions have the effect of inspiring and maintaining fidelity in his followers. This consideration helps explain the trait in his character that most mystifies his Roman friends, the way he actively courts disaster, or even pursues defeat. If the common good is uppermost in a soldier's mind, victory will be his paramount goal. But if fidelity has become a man's primary value, then situations can arise in which he might prefer defeat to victory. For a subordinate, a defeat might allay any suspicions his commander had formed about his "quick accumulation of renown" (III.i.19). Such thoughts are needed to make sense out of Ventidius' most puzzling statement:

> ambition
> (The soldier's virtue) rather makes choice of loss
> Than gain which darkens him.   [III.i.22–24]

Ventidius begins by merely declining to pursue a victory further, but goes on to raise the possibility of actually seeking out defeat. Nothing could sound more un-Roman, but when speaking of *Roman* here, one is thinking of the Republic, wondering, for example, if Coriolanus could ever be brought to make "choice of loss" in battle. Coriolanus inspires martial spirit in his soldiers through the conviction that he is unbeatable (IV.vi.90–95, V.ii.110–11), and thus his command over men would be endangered by even one defeat or any sign of weakness on his part. In the Empire, however, Ventidius' thoughts of defeat cease to be "un-Roman;" on the contrary, they merit praise (III.i.27–29). They are even given a religious sanction by Menecrates, who introduces the notion that loss might be gain when speaking of the gods with Pompey: "so find we profit / By losing of our prayers" (II.i.7–8).

The idea of a victory that is in some sense a defeat, and a defeat that is in some sense a victory appears already in *Julius Caesar*:

Brutus. I shall have glory by this losing day
More than Octavius and Mark Antony
By this vile conquest shall attain unto.   [V.v.36–38]

This idea of "vile conquest" becomes increasingly important in *Antony and Cleopatra*, as does the idea that one can gain more glory by losing than by winning. This development is linked to the new importance of private bonds in the Empire, for one can win a battle in a way that will make men love one less, and by the same token lose a battle in a way that will make men love one more. For example, Pompey understands that Octavius' triumphs have lessened the personal attachment of men to his cause: "Caesar gets money where / He loses hearts" (II.i.13–14). And Octavius realizes that for some reason the "ebbed man" has an advantage when it comes to winning love from followers (I.iv.41–44). Octavius fails worst as a ruler when he tries to win heartfelt devotion from his followers, as opposed to prudential loyalty, for he consistently neglects the emotional factors involved, and, even when he takes them into account, has a hard time achieving a desired emotional effect because of his cold demeanor.[20] As Pompey implies, Octavius' very success cuts him off from the devotion of his followers. By contrast, Antony, who can give men fewer reasons for following him, is far more capable of inspiring devotion, for he can establish a warm personal bond

with his followers that means more to them than "mere" victories in the conventional sense. Curiously, when Octavius is
invoking Antony's power, he thinks of one of his great defeats, not as we might expect one of his great victories:
"When thou once / Was beaten from Modena" (I.iv.56–57).
But perhaps Octavius knows what he is doing, for Antony's
most remarkable achievement politically is his ability to snatch
victory not *from* but *in* defeat.

   In one way Antony's actions in defeat encourage disloyal
thoughts toward him in Enobarbus. But in another way,
Antony's conduct succeeds in increasing his followers' loyalty.
His readiness to take the blame for his defeats upon himself
disarms criticism, especially when coupled with praise of
those who have remained loyal to him in adversity. The basis
of Antony's power over his followers becomes clear in the
scene of his supper with them just before his last battles with
Octavius:

Antony.   I wish I could be made so many men,
            And all of you clapp'd up together in
            An Antony, that I might do you service
            So good as you have done.
Omnes.   The gods forbid!
Antony.   Well, my good fellows, wait on me to-night.
            Scant not my cups, and make as much of me
            As when mine empire was your fellow too,
            And suffer'd my command.   [IV.ii.16–23]

Mysteriously, Antony's humbling of himself before his men
proves to be the way to make his "dying honor" "live again"
(IV.ii.6–7). Bewildered by his conduct, Cleopatra asks:
"What does he mean?" but Enobarbus sees Antony's purpose
clearly: "To make his followers weep" (ll.23–24).[21] What is
in one way Antony's weakness as a commander, allowing
others to see his limitations as a man, is in another way his
great strength, for it makes even his enemies pity him (I.iv.71,
V.i.26–30, 40–48, V.ii.360–63) and creates in his followers the

deepened bond that comes from their feeling he is in need of them:

> Tend me to-night;
> May be it is the period of your duty;
> Haply you shall not see me more, or if,
> A mangled shadow. Perchance to-morrow
> You'll serve another master. I look on you
> As one that takes his leave. Mine honest friends,
> I turn you not away, but like a master
> Married to your good service, stay till death.
> Tend me to-night two hours, I ask no more,
> And the gods yield you for't!   [IV.ii.24–33]

This is strange talk from a commander on the eve of a battle; it is, to say the least, defeatist in tone, and Enobarbus actually cautions Antony against unmanning his soldiers (ll.33–36). Contrary to all military considerations, Antony indulges himself in morbid thoughts. What can console him is his belief that the fidelity of his followers will survive even his defeat and death. He considers the possibility that they may betray their allegiance to him, but after a speech such as this he can be certain that they will not do so with peace of mind (as the fate of Enobarbus soon demonstrates).

By the end of Act IV, scene ii, Antony has seen to it that he cannot be judged by the standards usually applied to military commanders. His soldiers cannot blame him if he is defeated; on the contrary, they will feel guilty if they fail to stand by him in defeat. Somehow Antony has placed himself above the ordinary standards of human virtue (I.iv.10–15), so that no deed of his, no matter how base, can totally destroy the impression of nobility he has made on his followers, and the mere memory of his past greatness is enough to maintain their faith in him. His ability to endure moral censure is based in the changed ethical situation in the Empire. As the relationship of master and servant replaces the relationship of city and citizen, the Imperial regime puts a new emphasis on fidelity as a virtue, thus creating a need for new standards for judging men. With the premium now on faith, knowledge of what is in men's hearts becomes necessary. The Republic judges a man directly by his deeds, by what he does for the city. Coriolanus, for example, is willing to stand or fall with his deeds (I.ix.15–19, II.ii.127–28), feeling it beneath him to call upon excuses or extenuating circumstances to justify himself. Antony, on the other hand, asks to be judged by his intentions, rather than his deeds, and insists that his intentions are not always evident from his deeds. This new standard, which allows Antony to preserve his honor in circumstances that would disgrace another man, can be seen at work in Act II, scene ii, where Antony quarrels with Octavius. Octavius charges Antony with failing to live up to the terms of their agreements, and cites several actions to support his accusations, such as the wars Antony's wife and brother made against him, the disdain Antony showed for his messenger, and Antony's refusal to supply him with "arms and aid" when he requested them (II.ii.42–44, 72–74, 88–89). Antony does not dispute Octavius' facts—apparently he sees no need to deny any of his actions—but instead claims that Octavius has simply misinterpreted them (ll.45–56). In order to excuse himself from Octavius' charge of violating their agreements, Antony is willing to accuse himself of various faults that one is surprised to hear a political leader freely admitting to, such as inability to control himself (ll.75–77) as well as his supporters (ll.50, 67–71), even ignorance of what his supporters were doing (l.96) and evidently of what he himself was doing (ll.89–91). The only charge Antony will not stand by and hear himself accused of is that of breaking faith:

Caesar.   You have broken
          The article of your oath, which you shall never
          Have tongue to charge me with.
Lepidus.   Soft, Caesar!

Antony.   No, Lepidus; let him speak.
The honor is sacred which he talks on now,
Supposing that I lack'd it.   [II.ii.81–86]

Evidently Antony will let men think anything of him rather than allow them to suppose he has been unfaithful to his oath. His conviction of the sacredness of the honor of his oath, together with his willingness to "play the penitent" to uphold it (II.ii.92), shows how important the value of fidelity has become in the world of *Antony and Cleopatra*. And as long as Antony can claim his honor is separable from his deeds, he can maintain his reputation on the basis of his ability to convince men of the nobility of his thoughts alone.[22]

The care with which Antony and Octavius spar with each other in Act II, scene ii, the cautious way they probe for each other's responses, each trying to catch at the intent of the other (ll.40–42), suggests the delicacy required in Imperial diplomacy. The absence of the city as a focal point for the loyalty of these two leaders has introduced a new element of uncertainty and insecurity into their political calculations. Without a common object of allegiance, they are forced to rely on their direct loyalty to each other which, as their quarrel reveals, does not have a very secure foundation. Antony tells Octavius that he cannot be known by his deeds; how then, Octavius might well ask, can his partner be sure of his loyalty? Antony's wish to be judged by his intents rather than his deeds thus ends up as a wish to be judged merely by a different kind of deed, what we would call an act of good faith. Agrippa proposes to create a personal bond between the two leaders by having Antony marry Octavia (II.ii.124–27). This offer literally becomes a test of faith between Antony and Octavius, a kind of love test. In describing how the marriage would put an end to the doubts that infect the relationship of Antony and Octavius, Agrippa in fact talks of them as if they were

insecure lovers, as if they were getting married to each other
so that an "unslipping knot" would end their suspicions:

> By this marriage,
> All little jealousies, which now seem great,
> And all great fears, which now import their dangers,
> Would then be nothing. Truths would be tales,
> Where now half tales be truths. Her love to both
> Would each to other and all loves to both
> Draw after her.   [II.ii.130–36]

At this point consideration of political problems in *Antony
and Cleopatra* unites with consideration of problems in private life. For Agrippa's talk of "little jealousies" and "great
fears," of "half tales" taken for "truth," characterizes the love
relationship of Antony and Cleopatra at least as well as it does
the political relation of Antony and Octavius. The problem
of fidelity, central in the politics of Empire, is also the central
problem in the love story of *Antony and Cleopatra* and provides the closest point of contact between public and private
life in the play. Antony and Cleopatra are as much in need of
tests of each other's faith, of love tests, as any of the figures
related in political terms.[23] The need for tests of love in a
world in which old forms of loyalty have given way to new
is the keynote of *Antony and Cleopatra*, sounded by Cleopatra herself in her very first line in the play: "If it be love
indeed, tell me how much" (I.i.14).

CHAPTER 5

The Liberation of Eros

i

We have seen that Antony's tragedy is rooted in his specific political and historical circumstances. He is not simply a man who has been seduced away from a standard Roman career of military conquest by the enchantments of an Egyptian witch. The view that, but for Cleopatra, Antony would have been a Roman warrior of the old stamp, voiced by Philo in the opening lines of the play, can be held only by someone who assumes that the Imperial Roman way of life is so obviously choiceworthy that any deviation from it must be explained by reference to occult powers. But Antony has no such blind attachment to the Roman cause, and sees more clearly than most of his contemporaries the questionable aspects of public life in the Empire. If, as we have seen, conquests have become "vile," if military victories can no longer establish a man's honor but may on the contrary cost him the devotion of his followers, if, in short, success no longer has the value it once had in Rome, then Antony's half-hearted conduct as a soldier has a certain logic to it, a peculiar logic perhaps, but one that may be more appropriate to his world than the concentration on victory of a Coriolanus. From what we know of Antony, we might speculate that even if he had never met Cleopatra he would have found it difficult to pursue singlemindedly a military and political career in Rome. Perhaps Antony's failure to find satisfaction in Imperial politics is what makes him so sus-

ceptible to Cleopatra's charms. In any event, searching for a
fit object of his allegiance, Antony finally chooses Cleopatra
as the noblest cause he can fight for. Paradoxically, Antony's
love for Cleopatra is really in harmony with his deepest political purposes, if one understands that he regards the abiding
loyalty of his followers as more important than the temporary
triumph of military conquest. His love for Cleopatra provides
him with a noble justification for the losses that bind his men
to his cause, while Cleopatra herself, as the most faithful of
his retainers, provides a model of devotion for his men to follow (IV.iv.14–15).

Similarly, the love story of Antony and Cleopatra cannot
be understood apart from its political dimension.[1] In talking
about them as lovers, one cannot ignore the fact that they are
emperor and queen, because their political positions lend stature to their love. Moreover, one can detect a strategy in their
love, a policy they pursue which is remarkably similar to the
plan of "choice of loss" outlined by Ventidius as the appropriate course in Imperial politics. In defeat Antony is able to
bind his followers more closely to him than ever before, and
similarly adversity proves to strengthen the bond between him
and Cleopatra. The ultimate test of love in *Antony and Cleopatra* is how much one is willing to sacrifice for one's beloved,
so that Antony's military losses become a pledge of his faith to
Cleopatra, and her willingness to stand by him in his downfall
becomes in turn her token of allegiance. Once again we see
that the problem of fidelity is the bridge that connects the
political story and the love story in *Antony and Cleopatra*.

The love of Antony and Cleopatra is a curious mixture of
deep passion and profound insecurity, and seems all too ready
to pass over into its opposite, a deeply felt hate, or at least a
bitter mistrust of each other's fidelity. Their love follows a
pattern of doubt succeeded by reassurance, the new proof of
love apparently lasting only until the next occasion for doubt
arises. At first sight, the lack of faith in each other that An-

tony and Cleopatra display might seem to belie the depth of
their passion, but a consideration of the special nature and circumstances of their love will uncover the close connection
between their passion and their insecurity. The distinctive
qualities of the relationship of Antony and Cleopatra are best
seen by contrast with the thoroughly different relationship of
Antony and Octavia.

Antony and Octavia celebrate what ought to be a standard
Roman marriage, familiar to us from the world of *Coriolanus.*
Octavia should make the perfect partner for a Roman general,
since Enobarbus describes her in terms that recall Virgilia:
"Octavia is of a holy, cold, and still conversation" (II.vi.122–
23). Antony can be certain that the chaste Octavia will be
faithful to him, and she has reasons to believe that he will remain faithful to her. After all, a great deal depends on this
marriage: it is entered into for weighty reasons of state, and
if Antony breaks faith with Octavia, he will have to face
serious consequences (III.ii.24–33). The marriage, in short,
has everything in favor of it, including the full support of the
highest political authority. Unfortunately, the marriage proves
to have too much in its favor. The fact that it is politically
motivated means that the love of the partners is at best a sec-
ondary element, as Menas observes: "I think the policy of that
purpose made more in the marriage than the love of the
parties" (II.vi.118–19). Thus the political support which ought
to give Octavia security in her marriage actually works to
undermine it. Precisely because Antony has good cause for
giving the impression of loving her, she can never know if he
really does love her, that is to say, love her for herself and
not out of prudential considerations. The marriage of Antony
and Octavia is a fully conventional relationship, made along
conventional lines, supported by the conventional authorities,
and restricted to the most conventional expressions of love
(II.iii.1–8, III.ii.43–44, 47–50). Even if Antony really did love
Octavia, to convince her of his sincerity he would face the

difficult task of breaking through the wall of conventions that in one sense holds them together, but in a deeper sense keeps them apart.

The loveless marriage of Antony and Octavia is another token of the hollowness of traditional Roman institutions in the Empire, especially when contrasted with the marriageless love of Antony and Cleopatra. Antony and Cleopatra cannot derive any external support for their love because it occurs outside all authority except their own. The various trans-Mediterranean invocations in the play, Octavius' of Antony (I.iv.55ff), Cleopatra's of Antony (I.v.18ff), and Pompey's of Cleopatra (II.i.20ff), stress the physical distance that can separate the lovers, but they have an even wider gulf to overcome. One can get a sense of the nature of this gulf by recalling that they do not worship the same gods, that Antony understands his love for Cleopatra as a kind of impiety to his gods (III.xi.58–61). Since Antony and Cleopatra do not recognize any higher authority in common, their love can find support only in their own wills, and the closest they come to a marriage ceremony is a rite that they must perform on their own, in which they themselves act as the presiding deities (III.vi.1–19). No law can bind them together, for they are a law unto themselves.

The love of Antony and Cleopatra is a thoroughly unconventional relationship, and its cosmopolitan or transpolitical character is the source of both their insecurity and their passion. The fact that no civic authority supports their love means that they have cause to doubt each other's fidelity. No one will step in to enforce their love vows when no one encouraged them in the first place. Antony and Cleopatra have no "reasons" for loving each other, no prudential considerations that recommend their match. On the contrary, everything seems to be working against their love. At different times their closest advisers counsel them against their mutual involvement, and events repeatedly conspire to make it in the interest of one to betray the other. These considerations can-

not help but arouse in them doubts of each other's fa
ness: hence their insecurity. But at the same time, th
carious character of their love offers them continuir
dence of its genuineness. Since nothing forces them to love
each other—no marriage contract, no family pressures, no
political necessities—they know that if they are loyal to each
other it is only out of love, and not at all out of prudence.
Ultimately they derive the strength of their love from the
feeling that they stand together against the rest of the world.
As Cleopatra understands (I.iii.1–10), a love that runs
smoothly loses its force, and the opposition she and Antony
encounter works to keep their passion alive, providing the
relish in the "cloyless sauce" (II.i.25) of their love.[2]

To sum up the problem raised by the disjunction of marriage and love in *Antony and Cleopatra* (I.i.41), a conventional relationship offers a security of a kind, but the emotions
involved may go dead; an unconventional relationship can
maintain and even increase the original force of its passion,
but only at the price of radical insecurity. For this reason, a
love that runs counter to conventions is potentially tragic,
whereas a love that is ultimately in harmony with conventions
is comic. The relation of conventions and love is a pervasive
theme in Shakespeare's plays, and one would have to go well
beyond *Antony and Cleopatra* to give an adequate treatment
of it. The basic difficulty is that while conventions provide
form and structure for emotions, they threaten to kill them in
the very act of giving them stability. Shakespeare's romantic
comedies explore the ways in which social masks and poses
can interfere with genuine expressions of emotion, and the
comic antics in these plays, especially the mistaken identities,
serve to break the hold outworn habits of thought and feeling
have on men's minds, thereby revitalizing the life of society.
In *Much Ado About Nothing*, for example, the plot to deceive Claudio and the plot to deceive Beatrice and Benedick
both have the result of founding or refounding a true love.

Claudio must be brought to drop his pose as the idealizing young Petrarchan lover and accept the fact that he is to marry a flesh-and-blood woman, while Beatrice and Benedick must be tricked into dropping the opposite, and equally sterile, pose of cynical doubters of love, a stance which is in part a matter of pride and in part just a matter of habit.

The language of love is one of the conventions that Shakespeare often shows interfering with love. Language is after all socially acquired, and the fact that lovers must resort to language reveals their problematic relation to the society in which they live. On the one hand, language facilitates communication and understanding between lovers, but, on the other, if it becomes too conventional, in the sense of hackneyed, it actually prevents communication. Since love language tends to be poetic, and lovers do not usually invent their own metaphors, they are especially dependent upon the language of the great poets of love. But the metaphors of poetry may lose their meaning through overuse, as Shakespeare's Troilus understands when he speaks of "truth tir'd with iteration" (III.ii.176). Thus speeches of love may be insincere in the sense of being trite (not to mention the possibility of their being simply false, since, as the saying goes, "talk is cheap"). Lovers are therefore forced to go beyond speeches of love to deeds of love in order to guarantee the genuineness of their emotion. In *Romeo and Juliet*, for example, Romeo begins as the conventional idealizing lover in his devotion to the fair Rosaline, and his language is appropriately poetic, as Mercutio indicates: "Now is he for the numbers that Petrarch flow'd in" (II.iv.38–39). But in the course of his love for Juliet, the stock language of love, Petrarchan figures of speech like "brawling love" or "loving hate" (I.i.176), which have become stale from overuse, acquire a new meaning as the oxymorons spring to life in the actual situation of the young lovers (III.ii.73–79), culminating in a frightening realization of the most tired of love's clichés, the living death.[3]

The affinity of *Romeo and Juliet* with the world of Shakespeare's romantic comedies has often been noted.[4] If, for example, the metaphors of tragic love become hopelessly trite, and their translation into action remains unconvincing because of faulty dramatic illusion, one has the play-within-the-play of *A Midsummer Night's Dream*, the "most lamentable comedy" of Pyramus and Thisby. Even the tragic love story of Antony and Cleopatra seems at times to border on comedy, for example in Act II, scene v, in which Cleopatra receives the news of Antony's marriage to Octavia. As she herself admits (II.v.82–83), Cleopatra is at her most petty in this scene, and the comedy stems from the incongruity of a queen's acting like a common jealous housewife.[5] Our amusement at this scene is a good reminder that sexual jealousy is usually a theme of comedy rather than tragedy; in particular, the problem of fidelity in love was always a subject for comic treatment in classical literature, never for tragic.[6] The fact that one cannot simply laugh at the jealousy of Antony and Cleopatra, not even in Act II, scene v, is one more proof of the new importance fidelity has acquired in their world. Because their love means so much to them, Antony and Cleopatra react to suspicions of infidelity with a depth and authenticity of passion that would be completely out of place in a comedy. In the middle of her antics with the messenger, Cleopatra's despair breaks out with such force that her jealousy ceases to be laughable (II.v.78–79).

The magnitude of the stakes involved in the love of Antony and Cleopatra is ultimately what lifts their suspicions above the level of the jealousy of lovers in domestic comedy. That is one reason why their public status is integral to their special kind of relationship: they must act out their passions on a grand scale. Their political power allows them to create a hyperbole of deeds to correspond to their hyperbole of speeches.[7] Anyone can mimic Antony in his sweeping rhetorical gesture to express his love:

> Let Rome in Tiber melt, and the wide arch
> Of the rang'd empire fall!   [I.i.33–34]

But only a Roman Triumvir can work to bring this result
about, in other words, to translate the speech of love into a
deed of love. Antony's strategy is to prove his love in his actions; more specifically, the test of his love is how much he is
willing to sacrifice for his beloved. Antony has his main
chance to prove his love for Cleopatra at the battle of Actium,
where he gives up victory to follow his queen's ship. He at
first regards his flight as a disgrace to his honor, but when
confronted with Cleopatra's contrition, he finally treats his
loss as just one more gambit in their continuing love game:

> Fall not a tear, I say, one of them rates
> All that is won and lost. Give me a kiss.
> Even this repays me.   [III.xi.69–71]

Cleopatra's love is more important to Antony than any victory, but the magnitude of his loss is necessary as a true
measure of the depth of his passion.

Cleopatra undergoes a love test shortly after Antony's at
Actium. She has the opportunity of betraying him in order to
win the favor of Octavius (III.xiii), and her politic handling
of the situation calls forth from Antony a jealous rage that
exactly parallels hers in Act II, scene v, even to the point of
his basely mistreating a guiltless messenger. One can see in
this scene that the trouble with deeds is that they are ambiguous: since deeds cannot speak for themselves and must be
interpreted, they are open to being misinterpreted. The source
of the quarrels of Antony and Cleopatra is invariably misunderstanding, an uncertainty about reading each other's minds
from ambiguous deeds that leads them to answer questions
with further questions:

Cleopatra.   Not know me yet?
Antony.   Cold-hearted towards me?   [III.xiii.157–58]

In this scene, Cleopatra is able to silence Antony's doubts with a hyperbolic declaration of her love, a curse upon herself, her issue, and her land if she has been unfaithful (III.xiii.158–67). When, two battles later, Antony is again convinced that she has betrayed him (IV.xii.9–15, 24–29), Cleopatra, realizing that speeches will no longer serve to calm her lover, sends Antony word of a deed to restore his belief in her fidelity. She knows that the final proof of her love for him would be her willingness to die for him, and therefore dispatches a messenger to tell Antony she has killed herself. This sincere deception has the effect of a self-fulfilling prophecy (IV.xiv.120–21), for it sets in motion a train of events that finally does bring about Cleopatra's suicide. The plot works to show each lover's reaction to the other's death, so that we feel each dies for the sake of the other, a dramatic construction Shakespeare had used earlier in *Romeo and Juliet* (something similar happens with Cassius and Brutus in the last act of *Julius Caesar*). Suicide promises to be the ultimate test of love, involving as it does the irrevocable sacrifice of everything for the sake of the beloved. Antony and Cleopatra each find no value in a world that does not contain the other (IV.xiv.45–49, IV.xv.60–68), and their deaths bring to life another cliché of love: they prove they cannot live without each other. Their loyalty in defeat must finally extend to loyalty in death, and suicide seems to offer the one unambiguous—and hence final—deed of love.

ii

The connection between love and death in the story of Antony and Cleopatra merits further exploration. Anyone familiar with the legend of Tristan and Isolde should be prepared to find that the deaths of Shakespeare's lovers are not accidental to their story but in some sense its proper fulfillment.[8] They actively seek out their tragedy to avoid becom-

ing trapped in a world they find dull and stale. Conventional
happiness is beneath them and is even, as they see it, a barrier
to their higher aspirations. Theirs is a kind of infinite yearning, a search for a satisfaction that is not to be found in this
world. The love of Antony and Cleopatra carries them to the
borders of ordinary life and, at least in their eyes, beyond this
world into the realm of death. If all this sounds like Romantic
ranting, it is only a paraphrase of the opening words Antony
and Cleopatra speak to each other:

Cleopatra.   If it be love indeed, tell me how much.
Antony.   There's beggary in the love that can be reckon'd.
Cleopatra.   I'll set a bourn how far to be belov'd.
Antony.   Then must thou needs find out new heaven, new
               earth.   [I.i.14–17]

The self-proclaimed boundlessness of their desire for each
other is what drives Antony and Cleopatra beyond any given
moment of satisfaction, for the only image of an infinite love
in the finite human world is a love that seems to grow without
limit. The notion that love for Cleopatra is an insatiable desire, ever on the increase, is of course the point of the most
celebrated description of her:

    Age cannot wither her, nor custom stale
    Her infinite variety. Other women cloy
    The appetites they feed, but she makes hungry
    Where most she satisfies.   [II.ii.234–37]

In the end, however, Antony and Cleopatra must face the fact
that no earthly act is adequate to express their limitless love,
for all acts in this life are finite by nature. As Troilus tells
Cressida:

This [is] the monstruosity in love, lady, that the will is infinite
and the execution confin'd, that the desire is boundless and the
act a slave to limit.   [III.ii.81–83]

Antony and Cleopatra certainly learn to measure their love

on the grandest scale, in terms of whole kingdoms (I.iv.18, I.v.43–47, III.x.7–8), but finally not even this extravagance is enough. Since a kingdom is after all a patch of land with definite boundaries, it represents a finite value. The limitless expanse of the sea provides a fitter image of the passion of Antony and Cleopatra, but ultimately they cannot weigh their boundless love against anything in this world, but only against the world itself.

Paradoxically though, at the moment Antony and Cleopatra are ready to use the whole world as a measure of the value of their love, the world has come to seem worthless to them, and thus their ultimate sacrifice is reduced to a form of self-indulgence. An infinite yearning not only fails of satisfaction in this world, it also tends to make this world pale by comparison. Remove the infinite value of the beloved from the world, and the world becomes completely valueless as a result. Consider Antony's reaction when he hears of what he believes to be Cleopatra's death:

> I will o'ertake thee, Cleopatra, and
> Weep for my pardon. So it must be, for now
> All length is torture; since the torch is out,
> Lie down and stray no further. Now all labor
> Mars what it does; yea, very force entangles
> Itself with strength. Seal then, and all is done.
>
> [IV.xiv.44–49]

Cleopatra's reaction to the death of Antony is even more extreme:

> Noblest of men, woo't die?
> Hast thou no care of me? Shall I abide
> In this dull world, which in thy absence is
> No better than a sty? O, see, my women:
> The crown o' th' earth doth melt. My lord!
> O, wither'd is the garland of the war,
> The soldier's pole is fall'n! Young boys and girls
> Are level now with men; the odds is gone,

> And there is nothing left remarkable
> Beneath the visiting moon. . . .
>   . . . It were for me
> To throw my sceptre at the injurious gods,
> To tell them that this world did equal theirs
> Till they had stol'n our jewel. All's but naught.
>   [IV.xv.59–68, 75–78]

The bedrock of nihilism underlying the mountainous passion of Antony and Cleopatra is here finally exposed, or, to vary the metaphor, the oasis of their love is at last revealed to be surrounded by a spiritual desert. We have already seen in Antony's case that it is his loss of faith in all his old values that makes his love for Cleopatra assume such a vast importance for him. Thus the world-weariness which his love for Cleopatra held in check returns in full force once he thinks she is dead. And Cleopatra, too, finally betrays a contempt for the world as the basis of her worshiping Antony with such devotion. The consequences of her longing for a heaven on earth (ll.77–78) are clear from her speech: the fading of the Roman dream of earthly glory (ll.64–65), a general leveling of orders of rank (ll.65–68), and finally an abdication of worldly power (ll.70–75), perhaps even a transfer of the Imperial "sceptre" to the gods (ll.75–76). No wonder Cleopatra at first seems to follow Antony immediately into death (ll.67–68).

If life is worthless and death desirable, then suicide for the first time in the Roman world threatens to become a sin because it is now a selfish act:

> Patience is sottish, and impatience does
> Become a dog that's mad. Then is it sin
> To rush into the secret house of death
> Ere death dare come to us?   [IV.xv.79–82]

Suddenly we find the pagan attitude toward suicide transformed, and by implication the pagan attitude toward death. To be sure, the suicides of Antony and Cleopatra are in part "after the high Roman fashion" (IV.xv.87), familiar to us from the examples of Brutus and Cassius in *Julius Caesar*.[9] By killing himself, a Roman prevents his enemies from disposing of his life; death is the alternative to slavery (*Julius Caesar*, I.iii.89–100). The Roman who commits suicide judges that living without liberty is not worthwhile, and hence Roman suicide is actually based on the conviction of the value of life, albeit a certain kind of life, and not life simply. These motives do appear in the suicide of Antony (IV.xiv.62–68, IV.xv.14–15, 55–58), and even that of Cleopatra (IV.xiv.60–62, V.ii.51–52, 208–26). Nevertheless, motives of honor are not sufficient to explain why the lovers approach suicide with eagerness, not resignation:

> But I will be
> A bridegroom in my death, and run into't
> As to a lover's bed.   [IV.xiv.99–101]

For Cleopatra, too, death has ceased to be a fearful, or even a painful thing, as she observes in the case of Iras:

> If thou and nature can so gently part,
> The stroke of death is as a lover's pinch,
> Which hurts, and is desir'd.   [V.ii.294–96]

The joy with which Antony and Cleopatra greet their deaths indicates that they no longer understand suicide purely in the traditional Roman manner. Roman suicide is based on the premise that death is simply the end of life and as such the end of all human pains (*Julius Caesar*, II.ii.32–37). But Antony and Cleopatra view death as the prelude to new pleasures, for their last speeches are unintelligible unless they are expecting to meet again in another world (IV.xiv.50–54, V.ii.228–29, 301–3). Their infinite love has driven them to thoughts of an afterlife; it has awakened "immortal longings" in them (V.ii.281). They are the only characters in all three Roman plays to think of their personal survival after death, as opposed to the immortality of their names through fame.

Given the changed estimates of life and death in *Antony and Cleopatra*, the paradoxical situation arises in which the loved one is in some way worth more dead than alive. Once dead, Antony exists only in Cleopatra's imagination, thus setting her free to idealize him as never before.[10] At times the living Antony had disappointed her expectations and failed to live up to her image of him. But in his absence, Cleopatra becomes free to indulge herself in fantasies about her godlike lover:

> O Charmian,
> Where think'st thou he is now? Stands he, or sits he?
> Or does he walk? Or is he on his horse?
> O happy horse, to bear the weight of Antony!
> Do bravely, horse, for wot'st thou whom thou mov'st?
> The demi-Atlas of this earth, the arm
> And burgonet of men. He's speaking now,
> Or murmuring, "Where's my serpent of old Nile?"
> (For so he calls me). Now I feed myself
> With most delicious poison.   [I.v.18–27]

In her imagination, Cleopatra is able to reconcile the contradictions in Antony's character; what can be exasperating in fact, the variation in his moods, becomes exhilarating in fancy:

> O well-divided disposition! Note him,
> Note him, good Charmian, 'tis the man; but note him.
> He was not sad, for he would shine on those
> That make their looks by his; he was not merry,
> Which seem'd to tell them his remembrance lay
> In Egypt with his joy; but between both.
> O heavenly mingle! Be'st thou sad or merry,
> The violence of either thee becomes,
> So does it no man's else.   [I.v.53–61]

This vision of Antony is his absence prepares the way for Cleopatra's dream of him in his death,[11] in which he appears as a lord of contraries:

> his voice was propertied
> As all the tuned spheres, and that to friends;

> But when he meant to quail and shake the orb,
> He was as rattling thunder.   [V.ii.83–86]

Only in Cleopatra's dreams is Antony able to reach perfection, and that in effect means only in death.

The idea that a person can gain new status by dying is prevalent in *Antony and Cleopatra*, summed up somewhat callously by Antony when he hears of Fulvia's death: "she's good, being gone" (I.ii.126). Cleopatra understands death as a way of escaping the imperfections of life, more specifically of putting an end to the doubts that have infected her love for Antony:

> And it is great
> To do that thing that ends all other deeds,
> Which shackles accidents and bolts up change.   [V.ii.4–6]

Having lived all her life as a goddess of mutability, resisting any efforts to predict her actions (I.i.48–51, I.iii.1–10), Cleopatra is seeking a form of stability in death. To achieve stability, she thinks she must experience the freeing of her spirit from her body:

> I am fire and air; my other elements
> I give to baser life.   [V.ii.289–90]

In death Cleopatra must abandon what had always been the source of eros for her—her body—but she thinks that eros will be purified when separated from bodily appetite. If from one point of view her suicide appears as self-indulgence, from another it is an act of asceticism. But this is only an apparent contradiction: by repudiating bodily pleasure, Cleopatra hopes to achieve a more secure satisfaction, as symbolized by the fact that she regards her death as the marriage she never achieved in life (V.ii.287–88).

One curious fact remains to be observed about this marriage-in-death of Antony and Cleopatra: like any lawful ceremony it seems to require the presence of at least two witnesses. Cleopatra assumes as a matter of course that her servant Iras will accompany her wherever she goes:

> If she first meet the curled Antony,
> He'll make demand of her, and spend that kiss
> Which is my heaven to have.   [V.ii.301–3]

Whether Antony expects Eros to follow him in another world is unclear, but in any case Antony's vision of an after-life has room for a whole army of followers:

> Where souls do couch on flowers, we'll hand in hand,
> And with our sprightly port make the ghosts gaze.
> Dido and Aeneas shall want troops,
> And all the haunt be ours.   [IV.xiv.51–54]

Death at first appears to be the final way for Antony and Cleo-patra to escape from "the world's great snare" (IV.viii.18), but when Antony comes to imagine a paradise, he does not insist, as Andrew Marvell does, that "the grave's a fine and private place." The other world is to provide Antony with a whole new audience, even the opportunity of winning fol-lowers away from famous rivals. Perhaps death will only mean a new type of command for Antony, with a more satis-factory loyalty from his new troops. Shakespeare has intro-duced the notion of an afterlife into Antony's story,[12] and the way Antony pictures the fulfillment of his love may be an important clue to its nature. When Wagner's Tristan and Isolde come to die, they give no further thought to Kurwenal and Brangäne. Nor do they imagine themselves ascending to a resurrected Valhalla to steal away the following of Siegfried and Brünnhilde. Antony and Cleopatra more closely resemble the lover in Donne's "The Canonization," who, beginning with an impatient desire to be left alone—"For Godsake hold your tongue, and let me love"—proceeds by means of a mys-terious love-death to become canonized as a saint of love, claiming the right to be worshiped by the whole world. Ap-parently even after exploring the connection between love and death in the story of Antony and Cleopatra, one must still account for the distinctive form of love-death they picture for themselves.

iii

As we shall see in the next chapter, Antony's imaging of the afterlife is in part a matter of pride, a very Roman desire to have competition, though on the new battlefield of love. But he and Cleopatra have a more basic reason for wanting followers in an afterlife. In the end they feel they need some sort of objective recognition of their subjective experience. Cleopatra's dream of Antony reveals the problem raised for the lovers by the intensely private character of their love. Cleopatra's grief breaks the hold the world has on her, and a dream of her beloved overpowers her sense of reality. Antony seems to her more real than anything in the world, as if the very thought of him were enough to assure her of his existence, as if in Antony's case, and in his case alone, there were no gap between appearance and reality:[13]

> But if there be, nor ever were one such,
> It's past the size of dreaming. Nature wants stuff
> To vie strange forms with fancy; yet t'imagine
> An Antony were nature's piece 'gainst fancy,
> Condemning shadows quite. [V.ii.96–100]

Cleopatra's dream fulfills all her desires, but the question remains, Does it do so in deed or only in speech? Despite her conviction of the truth of the dream, Cleopatra must be in some way uncertain of its reality. Otherwise she would keep the dream to herself, in all the assurance of subjective certainty, and not profane it by attempting to share the experience with Dolabella. She knows that practical men make fun of lovers' dreams:

> You laugh when boys or women tell their dreams;
> Is't not your trick? [V.ii.74–75]

Yet she goes ahead and narrates the dream anyway, despite all
signs that Dolabella does not understand what she is talking
about. She wants to convert him to her belief, for if he could
accept the vision too it would no longer be merely a dream:

Cleopatra.   Think you there was or might be such a man
                    As this I dreamt of?
Dolabella.   Gentle madam, no.
Cleopatra.   You lie, up to the hearing of the gods!   [V.ii.93–95]

Cleopatra's oath reveals how much it would mean to her for
Dolabella to relieve the burdensome loneliness of her vision.
Shakespeare often portrays the dreamlike quality of an intense
experience of love, most fully of course in *A Midsummer
Night's Dream*, but also in its tragic companion piece, *Romeo
and Juliet*. The beloved so fully absorbs the lover's attention
that he loses sight of all the rest of reality, until it becomes
difficult to distinguish dream from reality (*Romeo and Juliet*,
V.iii.79). At one point, Romeo's experience of love is so powerful that he begins to doubt its truth:

> O blessed, blessed night! I am afeard,
> Being in night, all this is but a dream,
> Too flattering-sweet to be substantial.   [II.ii.139–41]

Precisely because Romeo's experience is so in accord with
what he wishes, he has to wonder if it really happened to him.
Perhaps Cleopatra has such doubts about her perfect vision of
Antony when she seeks confirmation of it from Dolabella.
She too must worry that "wishers were ever fools" (IV.xv.37).

Antony and Cleopatra, as well as Romeo and Juliet, have
some objective evidence of the existence of their love, even if
subjective experience has a certain dreamlike quality. But in
the unreal world of comedy, where everything is possible,
Shakespeare shows that the most perfect experience of love
would necessarily be indistinguishable from a dream, and
hence imperfect. The most unusual and therefore the most
absurd and in a sense the most archetypical love match in all

of Shakespeare is the romance of Bottom and Titania in *A Midsummer Night's Dream*. Bottom is the only character in Shakespeare's plays to be granted the love of an authentic goddess. But the price he pays for the vision he is vouchsafed in the woods outside Athens is that he will go on wondering for the rest of his life if he ever truly experienced it at all:

I have had a most rare vision. I have had a dream, past the wit of man to say what dream it was. Man is but an ass, if he go about [t'] expound this dream. Methought I was—there is no man can tell what. Methought I was, and methought I had—but man is but [a patch'd] fool, if he will offer to say what methought I had. The eye of man hath not heard, the ear of man hath not seen, man's hand is not able to taste, his tongue to conceive, nor his heart to report, what my dream was.   [IV.i.204–14][14]

In the words of Cleopatra, Bottom has truly had a dream "past the size of dreaming." Yet he can never have any evidence of its truth, for he must always keep it to himself. He would like to share the experience with his friends, but he knows that they would only laugh at him and in any case never believe his story. One can sense his bewilderment when he returns to the city, the conflict between his eagerness and reluctance to talk of his vision:

Bottom. Masters, I am to discourse wonders; but ask me not what; for if I tell you, I am not true Athenian. I will tell you everything, right as it fell out.
Quince. Let us hear, sweet Bottom.
Bottom. Not a word of me. All that I will tell you is, that the Duke hath din'd.   [IV.ii.29–35]

Bottom's vision is perfect as pure vision but, like a dream, it is private and incommunicable, and in that sense imperfect.

The comic episode of Bottom's dream reveals that the lover achieves gains in love only by retreating into a subjective world where he is open to a new form of uncertainty. Antony and Cleopatra are free to idealize each other without limit in the moment of their deaths, for once they exist only in each other's eyes, they become in effect the free creations of each other's imaginations.[15] But if their vision ever were to become fully private, they would no longer have any guarantee of its truth. And even on the verge of death their love has not entirely transcended the need for confirmation. Antony must die, after all, with a new instance of Cleopatra's duplicity fresh in mind, and she must hear him returning to the theme of his Roman honor with his last words (IV.xv.51–58), instead of paying her a final tribute. Moreover, just before his death Antony apparently tests Cleopatra once more with the temptation of betraying his memory with Octavius (IV.xv.45–46), and Cleopatra, just before her death, seems to be having jealous thoughts about Antony's behavior in the other world (V.ii.301–3). And the fact is they make their greatest speeches of mutual devotion out of earshot of each other, so that they themselves do not have the evidence we possess for evaluating the meaning of their suicides. One could easily make too much of these slight hints of insecurity surrounding the deaths of the lovers. Certainly the keynote of their last speeches is their final assurance of their mutual faith. But this conviction is, when all is said and done, only a personal and subjective feeling, the power of which may well suspend judgment. Objectively considered, the relationship of Antony and Cleopatra at the end of the play is no less shrouded in ambiguities than it was at the beginning. If anything, untangling the complex web of motivation in their last actions might be more difficult than ever. In considering suicide, Antony talks as much about the shame of being taken alive by Octavius as he does about the shame of outliving Cleopatra (IV.xiv.72–77), and she, in turn, does not actually kill herself until she is certain that Octavius intends to lead her in triumph through the streets of Rome (V.ii.198–226). Again, the point of such seemingly cynical observations is not to question the sincerity of Antony and Cleopatra, but only to show that even at the moment of their deaths the facts in their case have not altered, only their view of the facts. In the end, as in the beginning, they have only each other's words as a pledge of their faith, magnificently eloquent words to be sure, but words nonetheless.

The marriage-in-death that was to put their fidelity beyond question turns out to be the greatest leap of faith Antony and Cleopatra have to face. For that reason, they want their love story not to end with death, but to continue in an afterlife, and Antony craves followers wherever he goes. Again like the lover in Donne's "The Canonization," Antony and Cleopatra ignore the world's criticism of their love, but welcome its approval. Precisely when they decide to stand alone, they long for a crowd to applaud the nobility of their decision. Their love affair is by no means clandestine, but is emphatically carried out in the public eye.[16] No doubt the faith of others in their love strengthens their own faith in each other. When Antony is told "the worship of the whole world" "lies" in his "noble countenance" (IV.xiv.85–86) and Cleopatra learns that Dolabella "makes" a "religion" out of his "love" for her (V.ii.199), they both have some sense that they are not alone in their high estimation of themselves and their love. Antony's notion of paradise reveals that he really covets praise, provided he receives it on his own terms. He is not averse to being honored, only to having to adapt his conduct to someone else's standard of honor. It would unquestionably relieve some of the burden of uncertainty he has been forced to live with to know that he will be remembered as a faithful and noble lover (V.ii.358–60). To the end he is genuinely moved by the thought of the loyalty of his followers (IV.xiv.135–40).

The need Antony and Cleopatra feel to verify their experience of love is made more acute by the unsettling effect of their gradual entrance into a private and subjective world as the play progresses. The Roman world portrayed in *Coriolanus* is one of hard, solid objects, palpable to the touch and thus unquestionably real. In *Antony and Cleopatra* this tangi-

ble world begins to dissolve into a realm of shadows that
seems to hide the true reality. Images of melting or "discandy-
ing" are among the most frequent in the play, especially toward its close.[17] Antony finally feels he is losing his hold on
physical reality, even on his own body, to the point where he
must actually check with his servant to see if he still exists:

Antony.   Eros, thou yet behold'st me?
Eros.   Ay, noble lord.
Antony.   Sometime we see a cloud that's dragonish,
            A vapor sometime like a bear or lion,
            A [tower'd] citadel, a pendant rock,
            A forked mountain, or blue promontory
            With trees upon't that nod unto the world,
            And mock our eyes with air. Thou hast seen these signs.
            They are black vesper's pageants.
Eros.   Ay, my lord.
Antony.   That which is now a horse, even with a thought
            The rack dislimns, and makes it indistinct
            As water is in water.
Eros.   It does my lord.
Antony.   My good knave Eros, now thy captain is
            Even such a body. Here I am Antony,
            Yet cannot hold this visible shape, my knave.
                                                    [IV.xiv.1–14]

In a sense this is the moment Antony has been waiting for—
Rome, and everything else, melts as he once desired (I.i.33)—
but characteristically once his wish is granted the result ap-
pals him. He feels his body dissolving, but finally free of its
limitations he now fears the loss of his identity. Sensing himself being absorbed into the shapeless world of the clouds, he
feels he will no longer have anything definite to depend on,
anything just to tell him he exists. His only recourse is to
reach out for the nearest human being and try to get a firm
grip on common reality. At least his servant can assure him he
is still visible to other men.

    Antony's vision of the clouds at last reveals fully the paradoxical basis of his love for Cleopatra. He rejects the thought of melting, even though dissolution is the ultimate aim of his erotic longing. Eros seeks union with its object, and in the fullest case requires the overcoming of the separateness of lovers, and hence the annihilation of their distinct personalities until they are able to lose themselves in each other precisely "as water is in water." The pervasive imagery of melting in *Antony and Cleopatra*, particularly of one thing dissolving into another (I.ii.192–94) and finally in Antony's cloud speech of all things losing their distinct shapes and blending together into a formless whole, is closely related to the prevalence in the play of erotic vision, which seeks to overcome the articulation of the world into separate parts. Only in music was Wagner able to give a kind of form to the formlessness infinite desire seeks out, but even these bare lines from the libretto of *Tristan und Isolde* give some indication of the one possible resolution for a boundless eros:

Isolde.	Du Isolde.
Tristan.	Tristan du.
Isolde.	Tristan ich,
Tristan.	ich Isolde,
Isolde.	nicht mehr Isolde!
Tristan.	nicht mehr Tristan!
Tristan & Isolde.	Ohne Nennen, ohne Trennen
	Ewig!
	Neu Erkennen, neu Entbrennen,
	Endlos!

Tristan and Isolde struggle to express their ineffable yearning, first by claiming to exchange identities, then by denying their identities entirely. To be without names would mean to be without the possibility of separation, eternally and endlessly. But unlike Tristan and Isolde, or for that matter Romeo and Juliet (II.ii.33–51), Antony and Cleopatra are unwilling to renounce their names, holding on to their separate identities tenaciously when challenged (III.xiii.92–93, 185–86).

This difference remains in force to the end of their story, giving their love-death its distinctive character. Unlike the Romantic Tristan and Isolde, who sink unconsciously and blissfully into a form-obliterating night-world of love and death, Antony and Cleopatra regard death as a way of reasserting their identities, of reliving former "victories" and perhaps achieving new ones:

> I am again for Cydnus
> To meet Mark Antony.   [V.ii.228–29]

The way Antony and Cleopatra pull back at the last moment from the logical fulfillment of their erotic longing perhaps explains the striking reversal of imagery that occurs at the end of the play. Cleopatra, normally associated with soft and melting things, finally pictures herself as something hard and unyielding:

> My resolution's plac'd, and I have nothing
> Of woman in me; now from head to foot
> I am marble-constant; now the fleeting moon
> No planet is of mine.   [V.ii.238–41]

The same reversal occurs in *Coriolanus* when the hero, normally pictured as a solid rock, claims to melt. Similarly, Coriolanus, who consistently rejects food and drink, at last is brought to call for wine, while Cleopatra, the epicure, finally refuses to eat or drink anymore:

> Sir, I will eat no meat, I'll not drink, sir;
>
> . . . . .
>   . . . Now no more
> The juice of Egypt's grape shall moist this lip.
>   [V.ii.49, 281–82]

The fact that Cleopatra, the virtual high priestess of eros, ultimately displays this spirited contempt for appetite suggests the impossibility of developing one side of human nature to the total exclusion of another. When Coriolanus tries to push his spiritedness to an extreme, he finds he is still subject to the

promptings of eros; when Cleopatra tries to live a life of pure
eros, she finds she is still too spirited to allow her identity to
be submerged completely in her beloved or in death. The reversals of imagery in *Coriolanus* and *Antony and Cleopatra*
suggest that man cannot become simply a part of a larger
whole with no separate identity (like a bee in a hive), nor
simply a whole unto himself (like a god). Coriolanus' spiritedness demands that he try to be self-sufficient and stand alone,
but he learns that ultimately he is in need of others and is part
of a larger whole, his family and his city. Antony and Cleopatra, on the other hand, feel radically deficient without each
other and want to merge into a greater whole, but hesitate
when they realize their separate identities will become lost in
that whole.[18] Obviously the seeds of tragedy lie dormant in
this conflict of desires. We have already seen Coriolanus tragically torn between his will to be independent of Rome and
his need for a city to serve. Now we see a similar tragic contradiction at the heart of the love story of Antony and Cleopatra.

The mutually contradictory desires Antony and Cleopatra
experience are what drive them quite literally in and out of
each other's arms, and help explain why they create obstacles
for themselves—tragic obstacles—at just the moment they seem
on the verge of achieving erotic fulfillment. Since in one sense
their desire is driving them toward mutual annihilation and
loss of self, they must work to prevent its total satisfaction
just to prolong their enjoyment. Their love thus swings back
and forth between moments of union and separation, and, to
adapt Volumnia's words (*Coriolanus*, I.iii.3–5), they in some
respects "freelier rejoice" in each other's "absence" than in
the "embracements" of their "bed where" they "would show
most love." Antony formulates their paradox explicitly:[19]

> Our separation so abides and flies,
> That thou residing here, goes yet with me;
> And I hence fleeting, here remain with thee.   [I.iii.102–4]

Once one understands that being apart can somehow bring
Antony and Cleopatra closer together, one can see why death
tempts them as the fitting culmination, though in their eyes
not the end, to their story. In talking of their suicides, they
stress how death will eventually reunite them, but they also
dwell on how for the moment it has opened up a gap between
them (IV.xiv.44, 50, V.ii.286). Death somehow seems to allow them to be forever near each other and yet forever remote from each other. Or to put it differently, once dead they
can in a sense never be united again, but in another sense they
can no longer be separated. Death cannot resolve the paradoxes of their love, but it can fix them in a final form for all
time.[20]

iv

The paradoxical nature of the love of Antony and Cleopatra is emphasized by the aura of uncertainty and even mystery surrounding their deaths. The key to the complication of
our response at the end of the play is Cleopatra's strange conversation with the rustic who brings her the means to her
suicide, the "pretty worm of Nilus." This brief interlude goes
well beyond injecting a moment of comic relief into the high
tragedy being acted out. With the naiveté of a rustic or the
license of a clown, the "rural fellow" goes ahead to cast doubt
on the grand proceedings that are about to take place. Beginning ominously by confusing mortality and immortality
(V.ii.246–47), he leaves the matter of the effect of the worm's
bite in multiple uncertainty: "those that do die of it do seldom
or never recover" (ll.247–48). Here is a man who by virtue
of his trade should have knowledge of death, if any man does,
but his speech is full of riddles (many of them sexual puns)
that conceal whatever wisdom he has won from long ac-
quaintance with the dying (ll.249–50). He talks in paradoxes
(ll.251–52), yet his puzzling speech does revolve around a
serious question: How can the living ever hope to have knowl-

edge of death, if one must die to find out what it is like? The
rustic can only go by a "report o' th' worm," and perhaps he
realizes that what people say about suicide may be quite different from the act itself: "he that will believe all that they
say, shall never be sav'd by half that they do" (ll.255–57). All
that is certain in suicide is the deed itself ("how she died of
the biting of" the worm); any report of the subjective experience of suicide ("what pain she felt") must be taken on
faith (ll.253–54).

The rustic's riddling speech resembles closely the words of
the Jailer in *Cymbeline*, who in a similar situation (talking to
Posthumus on the day he is to be hanged) raises the same
doubts about knowledge of life after death:

Jailer. Look you, sir, you know not which way you shall go.
Posthumus. Yes indeed do I, fellow.
Jailer. Your death has eyes in's head then; I have not seen him
  so pictur'd. You must either be directed by some that take
  upon them to know, or to take upon yourself that which I am
  sure you do not know, or jump the after-inquiry on your own
  peril; and how you shall speed in your journey's end, I think
  you'll never return to tell one.   [V.iv.174–84]

The Jailer perhaps gives a fuller and clearer account of what
the rustic in *Antony and Cleopatra* is trying to say. In any
case, the gentle undercurrent of skepticism the rustic introduces moderates any exultation at Cleopatra's death.[21] She
thinks the worm is sending her to meet Antony, but all its
keeper can pronounce with certainty is that "the worm's an
odd worm" (ll.257–58), and his attempts at expanding this
enigmatic statement only add sinister overtones to it ("there
is no goodness in the worm," "it is not worth the feeding"),
until finally it sounds as if the worm will do the devil's work
(ll.266–67, 269–70, 272–76). In the end the rustic seems to
offer Cleopatra a sort of fifty-fifty chance (ll.255–56, 276–
77). The worm cannot itself provide knowledge of death, for
one must already possess wisdom in order to make use of it:

"Look you, the worm is not to be trusted but in the keeping of wise people" (ll.265–66). The rustic's knowledge never really goes beyond a thoroughly ambiguous and hence empty tautology: "You must think this, look you, that the worm will do his kind" (ll.262–63), that is to say, the worm will do what it will do.

The rustic's wisdom, which seems about as clear "as water is in water," reminds one of the knowledge of Egyptian mysteries Antony parades before the drunken Lepidus:[22]

Lepidus. What manner o' thing is your crocodile?
Antony. It is shap'd, sir, like itself, and it is as broad as it hath breadth. It is just so high as it is, and moves with its own organs. It lives by that which nourisheth it, and the elements once out of it, it transmigrates.
Lepidus. What color is it of?
Antony. Of its own color too.
Lepidus. 'Tis a strange serpent.
Antony. 'Tis so, and the tears of it are wet.   [II.vii.41–49]

Antony shows how easy it is to disguise ignorance as wisdom, especially with men curious about exotic subjects who are willing to take words for facts. As long as the rustic sounds as if he is saying something profound, Cleopatra, like Lepidus, is tempted to assume she is being initiated into a mystery, in her case the mystery of death. But what from one point of view seems infallible, by a simple and perhaps innocent slip of the tongue, is seen to be from another point of view "most falliable" indeed (V.ii.257). The cloud cover that obstructs the prospect of the skies promises to dissolve and lift at the end of *Antony and Cleopatra* (V.ii.299), offering new vistas to the eyes of man, but what lies beyond "black vesper's pageants" remains unclear. The mood of uncertainty with which the play closes is expressed in a different context by Macbeth:

> function
> Is smother'd in surmise, and nothing is
> But what is not.   [I.iii.140–42]

With its unusually complex texture—its puzzling blend of dreams and visions, riddles and paradoxes—the ending of *Antony and Cleopatra* underscores the subjectivity of the lovers' experience. To the moment of their deaths, particularly at the moment of their deaths, their vision remains their own, never fully shared by those around them. Nevertheless, they speak as if they wanted to share their experience with others. If their love cannot be accepted by the world they live in, Antony would like to find or found a new world in which their status as lovers would be recognized by all. In their last moments, their vision has a certain hallucinatory quality, and no doubt Eros is as puzzled by Antony's attempt to explain his experience of the clouds as Dolabella is by Cleopatra's narration of her dream. Cleopatra's last moment is one of pure hallucination, but she tries to make Charmian verify it for her, to confirm her private vision:

> Dost thou not see my baby at my breast,
> That sucks the nurse asleep?   [V.ii.309–10]

To the extent that Antony and Cleopatra take their private vision with them to the grave, their story remains a tragedy. But to the extent that they do leave behind them believers in the legend of their love, their story becomes a comedy. Moreover, although from one point of view their story, like a tragedy, ends in death, from another, like a comedy, it ends in marriage (IV.xiv.100, V.ii.287). That it why, of all Shakespeare's tragedies, *Antony and Cleopatra* has the least painful ending. The hero and heroine suffer defeat, but if one can accept their subjective view of events, they achieve a form of triumph. Although they cannot be married in the Roman world, at least as they see it, "there is a world elsewhere." In the end, however, one is forced to add: for their story to be a comedy, it would have to be a kind of divine comedy.

CHAPTER 6

Love and Tyranny

i

The love of Antony and Cleopatra, as we have seen, cannot
be regarded simply as a form of private as opposed to public
life. Though their passion leads them away from conventional
forms of "publicity" for love, such as a marriage contract, when
their experience becomes oppressively subjective, when they
seem to be left with nothing but dreams and visions to rely on,
they make a partial return to the realm of the public, seeking
out at least a small following of believers in their love. But
Antony and Cleopatra are not indifferent to public life even
in the ordinary sense of the term. Before assuming that they
sacrifice politics for love, one ought to consider the straightforward question: "Why don't Antony and Cleopatra ever
consider abdicating in order to be free to love each other as
they choose, if their political positions really mean nothing to
them at all?" To point to Antony's request to live "a private
man in Athens" (III.xii.15) is not a sufficient answer, for Antony's suit is joined with a request that Cleopatra retain her
crown (III.xii.16–19), and he may be looking to create a new
romantic situation of "Queen loves commoner." In any case,
the only point of his request would be to avoid becoming a
fugitive, to reserve his right to appear in public. Otherwise he
would have no reason to ask Octavius to grant him the *right*
to live in Athens. Presumably if Antony and Cleopatra were
willing to give up public life entirely, they could steal away

184

at any time and lose themselves in the mass of humanity the Empire encompasses. We know how easily they blend into the populace of Alexandria (I.iv.18–21).

But one would hate to think of a Mr. and Mrs. Mark Antony living somewhere under an assumed name, hiding from Caesar's legions. Once having renounced the public world, they would no longer be the Antony and Cleopatra we know, and one can imagine to what bitter recriminations the decision to abdicate would lead. To be out of the reach of the arm of the law, they would have to be out of the sight of the public eye, and if out of sight is out of mind, they might soon be forgotten by even their most devoted followers. Certainly the glamour of their romance would be gone, and they would have to confront the day-to-day necessities of making a living. The only thing that would be left for them if they truly gave up politics for love would be to settle down into the comfortable but dull relationship that they have been trying to avoid all along. The fact that one cannot conceive of Antony and Cleopatra restricted to private life and still retaining their identities suggests that there is something essentially public about the life of love they desire for themselves.

To prove Antony's indifference to public life, critics usually cite his first speech:

> Let Rome in Tiber melt, and the wide arch
> Of the rang'd empire fall! Here is my space,
> Kingdoms are clay; our dungy earth alike
> Feeds beast as man; the nobleness of life
> Is to do thus—when such a mutual pair
> And such a twain can do't, in which I bind,
> [On] pain of punishment, the world to weet
> We stand up peerless.   [I.i.33–40]

Only by ignoring the second half of this passage can one maintain the customary interpretation of it. In the very speech in which Antony is usually taken to be rejecting his public role, he feels compelled to invoke his political authority, to "bind" the world on *"pain of punishment"* to acknowledge the uniqueness of his love. To be sure, Antony voices disenchantment with his ordinary political role, but that does not mean he intends to renounce public life. On the contrary, the love he seeks out is itself a form of public life, and is perhaps a substitute for conventional political office, which has lost its attractiveness in the new Roman Empire.[1] Antony does not want to be burdened by the responsibilities of politics, but he does covet the advantages that come with high public office, especially the feeling that all eyes are turned on him. Despite his doubts about the worth of Roman politics, Antony will not accept a humble or obscure position in life. Since he cannot do without a sense of being noble, he must revalue nobility, making it a matter of excellence in love, not politics.[2]

Antony's "nobleness of life" speech shows that in addition to confirmation of their love, he and Cleopatra seek recognition of it from the world, an acknowledgment that they are the greatest of lovers. Antony and Cleopatra want to excel in love just as the Republican Romans want to excel in war, which explains why, like Coriolanus, they desire the competition of worthy rivals (in their case not Aufidius but Dido and Aeneas). To distinguish themselves from the common run of lovers, Antony and Cleopatra conceive the notion of a noble love, which can take place only between two persons raised above the ordinary necessities of life, hence free from mercenary motives and capable of bounteously expressing their emotions. Antony and Cleopatra want their love to be "liberal" in the classical meaning of the word, the love of free men and women as opposed to that of "mechanic slaves" (V.ii.209). When Antony defines "the nobleness of life" as love, he makes it clear that not just any love at all will do. He immediately adds the qualifier "when such a mutual pair / And such a twain can do't,"[3] excluding ordinary mortals from the ranks of noble lovers. If he gestures to the surrounding court with these words, alluding to the lavish scale on which he and

Cleopatra conduct their affair, Antony indicates why such a love is beyond the means of all but a privileged few. For Antony and Cleopatra, love is no more governed by economic considerations than war is for the patricians in *Coriolanus*, and thus it requires the conventional privilege of wealth. Only a woman born to wealth could bring herself to spend quite as much as Cleopatra does in preparing to receive Antony at Cydnus. For anyone else the temptation to economize on perfume, or at least to hold the line on Cupids and Nereids, would be just too great. In trying to understand fully the love of Antony and Cleopatra, one must not forget that Antony conceives of the opposite of his liberal love as "beggary" (I.i.15), and that he intends by his love to "stand up peerless" (I.i.40).[4]

The love of Antony and Cleopatra is not unmixed with pride, and the two are not as free of ambition as many critics suppose. At times the love of Antony and Cleopatra seems to be not an alternative to the Roman quest for public eminence, but rather an alternative path to a new kind of public eminence itself. As soon as one realizes that in addition to pure eros, pride is at work in the love of Antony and Cleopatra, one begins to see how extraordinarily complex their relationship is. As we saw in analyzing Republican Rome, pride and eros are ordinarily two separate forces, working against each other and thus moderating each other. But for Antony and Cleopatra pride and eros have become united: since they take pride in their love, their pride only serves to increase the force of eros in their lives. Once Antony and Cleopatra derive their sense of achievement from their status as lovers, they begin to demand a great deal more from love than most men and women do, and they also allow love to assume an importance for them that goes well beyond its usual role. Love of course is the central concern in Cleopatra's life: she has truly made a career of it, with as many glorious victories to her credit as any Roman legion:

> Broad-fronted Caesar,
> When thou wast here above the ground, I was
> A morsel for a monarch; and great Pompey
> Would stand and make his eyes grow in my brow.
> [I.v.29–32]

Cleopatra's achievement in having "a hand that kings / Have lipp'd, and trembled kissing" (II.v.29–30) is perhaps her way of showing that she is somehow above politics, that politicians must bow to her, not she to them. In this sense, far from being nonpolitical, her ambitions are in effect transpolitical: she wants to be able to rule the rulers of Rome.[5]

Antony has not devoted himself as singlemindedly to a career in love, and does have some conventional military triumphs to his credit. Nevertheless, as the play progresses it becomes clear that Antony has staked his whole sense of his worth as a man on the fact that Cleopatra loves him, for ultimately he chooses her as the only competent judge of his deeds. At times Antony seems to fight for no other reason than to win Cleopatra's praise, occasionally showing off or bragging in front of her like a schoolboy:

> O love,
> That thou couldst see my wars to-day, and knew'st
> The royal occupation, thou shouldst see
> A workman in't.   [IV.iv.15–18][6]

Antony's boast conceals a serious doubt, that as he grows older he is losing his capacity for both love and war, a suspicion that can approach the surface only in his moments of greatest self-confidence:

> Mine nightingale,
> We have beat them to their beds. What, girl, though grey
> Do something mingle with our younger brown, yet ha' we
> A brain that nourishes our nerves, and can
> Get goal for goal of youth.   [IV.viii.18–22]

Antony's consciousness of his age may affect his relationship with Cleopatra deeply. Despite his claim: "Things that are past are done with me" (I.ii.97), he and Cleopatra are all too aware that they approach each other with long and somewhat tarnished histories in love, their record spotted by specific instances of betrayal and surrounded by general suspicions of infidelity.[7] The notion of a life of unending infidelity in love is introduced in the play by the barely comic prophecies of a queen who widows one great husband after another (I.ii.26–28) and of a man with a limitless succession of wives, who are apparently unable to satisfy him but somehow manage to cuckold him over and over again nonetheless (I.ii.63–67). With a little imagination, these visions transpose into a "parody" or "nightmare version" of the careers of Cleopatra and Antony in love.[8] Perhaps their desperate need to believe they are loyal to each other, evidenced in the readiness with which Antony accepts Cleopatra's denials of her infidelity,[9] is to be traced to their conviction that this love is their last chance to redeem their reputation as lovers, to earn a name for faithfulness, not faithlessness, in love. Antony, for one, does not want his "remembrance" to "suffer ill report" (II.ii.156).

The need of the lovers for each other is in many ways clearer in Antony's case than Cleopatra's, for his despair at the thought of her infidelity breaks out with greater force. Antony's whole world, together with his sense of personal identity, seems to melt away when he thinks Cleopatra has betrayed him (IV.xii.20–29, IV.xiv.1–20). Antony has staked his entire self-conception, his sense of manhood, on his love with Cleopatra, hence on her love for him. In warfare Antony always likes to keep his options open, to leave himself something to fall back upon (III.vii.52–53). As a result, he and his soldiers do not fight with all the fury of men feeling their backs against the wall until it is too late (III.xiii.177–82). But in his love with Cleopatra, Antony has no place to retreat to if he suffers a defeat. Ordinarily a man faced with a setback in love can at least try to make up for it by turning to satisfaction in other areas of his life. But Cleopatra has become involved in all aspects of Antony's life, and he certainly cannot look to military victories to console him for amatory defeats when his wars have been in the service of his love. Only in love does Antony at last come face to face with real necessity, only in love does he finally experience the true need that calls upon the deepest resources of his soul. Only in love can Antony finally learn what it is to feel "the very heart of loss" (IV.xii.29).

In their effort to achieve independence and preeminence as lovers, Antony and Cleopatra become overwhelmingly dependent on love itself. Love gradually extends its dominion in their lives until it becomes the sole value for them, and hence an unconditional value. According to them, no other value can even be compared to love, and nothing could possibly compensate for its loss. This situation could not occur in the Rome of *Coriolanus,* with its compartmentalization of life: love is love and war is war, and the one activity is not allowed to run over into the other. The city keeps the activities of its citizens distinct and within their proper bounds, so that no single activity can become the whole of life and absorb the full attention of a citizen, for the city itself claims to be the only true whole. Virgilia does not attempt to become involved in her husband's life as a warrior but is, as we have seen, content to stay at home while Coriolanus does his fighting. If Virgilia's respect for the Roman "threshold" (I.iii.75) means she cannot be at the battlefield to give aid and comfort to her husband, it also means that she does not add to his worries when he most needs to have his mind free.

By the time of *Julius Caesar,* love has evidently begun to increase its role in Roman life. Portia claims the right to share her husband's state secrets, involving herself in his public affairs to an extent that Virgilia would think presumptuous (*Julius Caesar,* II.i.280–82, 291–302). Though Brutus may

find comfort in unburdening himself of his secrets to his wife
(II.i.302–8), he thereby endangers his great enterprise, for
Portia almost betrays the conspiracy against Caesar by her
suspicious conduct in Act II, scene iv. Refusing to be seques-
tered within a corner of Brutus' life, Portia chafes under the
limits the Republican regime sets to love:

> Am I yourself
> But, as it were, in sort or limitation.
> To keep with you at meals, comfort your bed,
> And talk to you sometimes? Dwell I but in the suburbs
> Of your good pleasure? If it be no more,
> Portia is Brutus' harlot, not his wife.   [II.i.282–87]

Portia hits the point precisely: love is in the "suburbs" of
Brutus' life, for Rome is at the center. Portia's moderate wish
to be something more than a domestic companion to her husband is a faint prefiguration of Cleopatra's immoderate urge
to take part in every phase of Antony's existence, above all, to
accompany him right into battle. Cleopatra's presence might
conceivably add something to Antony's fighting spirit, but it
also distracts him from the real business at hand, as Enobarbus
warns the Queen:

> Your presence needs must puzzle Antony,
> Take from his heart, take from his brain, from's time,
> What should not then be spared.   [III.vii.10–12]

But Cleopatra disregards Enobarbus' warning, for she cannot allow Antony any activity that is not in some way bound
up with his love for her. To admit that he had any legitimate
interests outside their love would be to acknowledge objects
as worthy of Antony's devotion as she herself. That is why
she must transform the battle of Actium into a test of love: it
is her way of proving that she is all that really matters to Antony (III.xi.69–71). By contrast, Virgilia is content to share
Coriolanus with the city, and would not dream of demanding
from him a kind of unconditional surrender to his love for

her. Even when she and Volumnia try to talk Coriolanus out
of his march on Rome, although at first they couch their appeal in personal terms, it gradually becomes apparent that they
are speaking in the name of the city (V.i.73, V.iii.44, 186).
One could imagine their argument going no further than this:
"You're right not to care about Rome, Caius Martius, but you
ought to care about us, your loved ones. For our sake, and our
sake alone, don't destroy the city. If you really love us, you
won't do this terrible thing." As such, their appeal would have
been a straightforward test of Coriolanus' love, much like the
suit of Menenius that failed so miserably. But Volumnia em-
phasizes that she and Virgilia are not asking Coriolanus to
sacrifice his honor in the name of his love for them; they are
there to show him the path to his true honor (V.iii.131–55),
to convince him that he needs his native city to preserve his
good name intact. They do not want to prove the power they
presumably hold over Coriolanus, but rather the power the
city of Rome holds, in part of course through them as his
Roman family. The notion of an unconditional love is wholly
alien to them. Volumnia loves her son only on the condition
that he remain the valiant Roman she raised him to be, for she
cannot love him as a Volsce (V.iii.178–80). Cleopatra, on the
other hand, cannot love Antony as long as he feels any remaining allegiance to the cause of Rome (I.ii.82–83). By making an unconditional demand upon Antony's devotion at the
battle of Actium, she is able to win from him an admission that
her command over him is absolute:

> Egypt, thou knew'st too well
> My heart was to thy rudder tied by th' strings,
> And thou should'st [tow] me after. O'er my spirit
> [Thy] full supremacy thou knew'st, and that
> Thy beck might from the bidding of the gods
> Command me. [III.xi.56–61]

Cleopatra experiences a feeling of power in love. Using her
own metaphor, one might say she is fishing for Antony's soul

(II.v.10–15), and thinks she can reel him in anytime she wants.[10] By playing upon Antony's infinite need for her, she is able to exert a form of rule over him that, in view of her absolute demands upon him, one might call an absolute rule, or, to put it differently, a tyranny. The metaphor of desire as a tyrant is common enough, and Shakespeare often suggests in passing a connection between love and tyranny in his plays.[11] But in *Antony and Cleopatra* the idea that love can become a kind of tyranny is basic. Once the value of love becomes infinite or absolute, refusing its demands becomes impossible, and one might answer Antony: if there's beggary in the love that can be reckoned, there's slavery in the love that cannot. A boundless desire plays the same role in a man's soul that a tyrant plays in the city, overpowering all other desires and making them follow its lead just the way the tyrant crushes all opposition in order to have his own way.[12] Cleopatra certainly exerts as strong a hold over Antony as the city of Rome does over any of its citizens, as witness the fact that Antony finds it at least as difficult to leave Cleopatra as Coriolanus does to leave Rome. Even when Antony becomes aware of his bondage to Cleopatra (I.ii.116–17, 128) and wants to "break off" from her, his will falters or his motives are suddenly transformed, and he presents his leaving Egypt as a sign that Cleopatra's hold over him is increasing, rather than decreasing.[13] Antony's departure only serves as "an honorable trial" to prove his love (I.iii.74–75), for his wars are in Cleopatra's service and will be governed by her will (I.iii.43–44, 68–71). In the absence of the security provided by the city and its conventions, Antony and Cleopatra are forced to cling to each other with a new and deepened passion. Although their exploration of the subjective world seems like the conquest of a whole new kingdom, it also requires a surrender of self-control to certain forces within their own souls which the ancient city had held in check. Hence their freedom from the city turns into a freedom to become enslaved to each other, under a "benevolent" despotism to be sure, but a despotism nonetheless.

ii

In exploring the relation of love and tyranny in *Antony and Cleopatra*, one finally realizes how inextricably intertwined the realms of public and private life have become in the world of the play. For if the lovers' conduct toward each other can be understood as tyrannical in a metaphorical sense, their conduct toward their subjects can be viewed, as we shall see, as tyrannical in the literal sense of the word. Thus one can say that they are governed in their public and private lives by the same principles. Their inability to keep their public and private roles clearly separate is in fact almost a defining characteristic of Antony and Cleopatra. We have already seen that they never make any attempt to keep their love affair strictly private but are instead proud to flaunt it in the public eye. Examination of their conduct as rulers shows that they also make no attempt to prevent private motives from obtruding upon their handling of public affairs. Above all, they allow their private demands and needs to warp their political judgment. Since so much is at stake in their love, it would be remarkable if they could keep their political judgment unclouded by despair when they feel unloved. Moreover, for these monarchs of love, every domestic quarrel takes on the scope of an international incident, since any slight they feel as lovers is magnified into an affront to their dignity as rulers. This difficulty is compounded by the fact that their political authority is not entirely independent of their love, but threatens to crumble away along with it. In Cleopatra's case, whatever real political power remains to her depends upon her hold over Antony. She is so shaken by the news of Antony's marriage to Octavia that she wants to have Herod beheaded, but he suddenly realizes that if she has lost Antony's love, she has at the same time lost the power she needs to vent her anger:

> That Herod's head
> I'll have; but how, when Antony is gone
> Through whom I might command it?   [III.iii.4–6]

Believing herself unloved is doubly frustrating for Cleopatra because she loses her feeling of power over both Antony and her subjects. Antony's political authority is not as derivative as Cleopatra's, for he has battalions of his own. Nevertheless, since his cause has become bound up with the fact that Cleopatra loves him, any signs of infidelity on her part weaken the hold he has over his followers, as Enobarbus observes:

> Sir, sir thou art so leaky
> That we must leave thee to thy sinking, for
> Thy dearest quits thee.   [III.xiii.63–65]

The reverse side of the exhilarating sense of power Antony and Cleopatra feel in love is a frustrating sense of impotence when their love seems threatened.[14]

If the deepest desire of Antony and Cleopatra were simply to give up politics for love, one would expect them to welcome any loss of power, since that would truly free them from all public obligations. But both Antony and Cleopatra are deeply shaken by the prospect of losing their authority because they derive their sense of dignity from their public eminence. Cleopatra's self-regard is threatened by the lack of regard others show her in defeat:

> What, no more ceremony? See, my women,
> Against the blown rose may they stop their nose
> That kneel'd unto the buds.   [III.xiii.38–40]

However much Antony may boast of his indifference to political power, when he finds he has lost command, he bitterly regrets that men are no longer at his beck and call:

> Authority melts from me. Of late, when I cried "Ho!"
> Like boys unto a muss, kings would start forth
> And cry, "Your will?"   [III.xiii.90–92]

Antony has particular reason to fear the loss of his political position, given his knowledge of Cleopatra's special taste for public figures in love.[15] Once he no longer seems a worthy successor to Pompey the Great and Julius Caesar, perhaps Cleopatra will abandon him; that at least seems to be Antony's suspicion in Act III, scene xiii, where he begins to wonder whether the change in their fortunes has now made Octavius the more attractive of the two to Cleopatra. Earlier, Antony even worries that his loss of personal preeminence might affect his relationship with Octavia:

> If I lose mine honor,
> I lose myself; better I were not yours
> Than [yours] so branchless.   [III.iv.22–24]

The inability of Antony and Cleopatra to separate their public and private roles makes one complication lead to another in their lives. A threat to their love gives them cause to doubt their political authority (this is particularly true in Cleopatra's case). By the same token, a threat to their political authority gives them cause to doubt their love (this is particularly true in Antony's case). For them, insecurity in one area of life quickly spreads to another, an inescapable consequence of their attempt to make their love into the whole of their lives, a whole that turns out to have the shape of a vicious circle. In Act II, scene v, and Act III, scene xiii, where we see first Cleopatra and then Antony experiencing a sense of frustration in both love and politics, we realize how truly vicious this circle can become.

In Act II, scene v, Cleopatra responds to the messenger's gradual revelation of Antony's marriage to Octavia with a frantic alternation of moods of benevolence and cruelty:

I'll set thee in a shower of gold, and hail
Rich pearls upon thee.

Thou shalt be whipt with wire, and stew'd in brine,
Smarting in ling'ring pickle.   [II.v.45–46, 65–66]

What the messenger receives for his errand will bear no relation to his own merits or demerits, but will be strictly in pro-
portion to Cleopatra's momentary moods, which vary between
exultation and despair. Cleopatra will richly reward news to
her liking (ll.28–30, 68–69), and horribly punish news to her
distaste (ll.33–35, 73), thereby working to corrupt the basically honest messenger by making it extremely tempting for
him to lie and highly imprudent for him to tell the truth.
Hence the basic injustice of Cleopatra's conduct: she sets the
messenger an impossible task, to fulfill the contradictory demands of telling her the truth and telling her what she wants
to hear, and then punishes him for failing to do what was
clearly beyond his capacity (ll.100–1). In her wrath, Cleopatra completely ignores the principles of ordinary justice,
dismissing all thoughts of the difference between guilt and
innocence: "Some innocents scape not the thunderbolt" (l.77).
Unspeakable tortures leap to Cleopatra's lips with frightening
ease. When Antony seems to fail her, she begins to feel insecure and must reestablish her self-image as a powerful woman
by forcing the poor messenger to grovel before her. His
cowardly submission is to make up for what appears to her as
Antony's manly defiance.

The connection between insecurity and the will to lord it
over others is even clearer in Antony's parallel conduct toward Octavius' ambassador in Act III, scene xiii. Antony tries
to shore up the tottering realm of his pride with the prop of
Thidias' humiliation. Antony's frustration as a lover and as a
ruler reaches its peak in this scene, and quickly transforms his
usual generosity toward men into an extraordinary cruelty.

The more he has cause to doubt his power as a ruler the more he needs assurance of Cleopatra's love for him, but he finds that the very incident that made him feel his authority was melting away also creates doubts about Cleopatra's fidelity:

> To let a fellow that will take rewards
> And say "God quit you!" be familiar with
> My playfellow, your hand, this kingly seal
> And plighter of high hearts!   [III.xiii.123–26]

Obsessed by the thought of his former strength and current weakness (ll.140–47), Antony apparently must prove to himself he still has power over others in the basest way, by having Thidias savagely whipped. Antony wants to see him whimper:

> Whip him, fellows,
> Till like a boy you see him cringe his face,
> And whine aloud for mercy.   [III.xiii.99–101]

In his fury, Antony becomes completely indifferent to the welfare of his old subject Hipparchus, whom Octavius now has in his camp:

> If he mislike
> My speech and what is done, tell him he has
> Hipparchus, my enfranched bondman, whom
> He may at pleasure whip, or hang, or torture,
> As he shall like, to quit me. Urge it thou.   [III.xiii.147–51]

Antony has evidently become blind to any normal standards of human accountability: he punishes Thidias for what is Octavius' responsibility, while Hipparchus is to be punished for what Antony himself has done.

The way Cleopatra treats the messenger in Act II, scene v, is almost a parody of what one expects from a tyrant, indeed a caricature of an Oriental despot; Antony's treatment of Thidias is not at all amusing, but it is equally tyrannical. Antony and Cleopatra are as moody in rule as they are in love. As a lover, Cleopatra will not allow herself to be governed by Antony's moods but wants instead to make him accommodate himself to hers (I.iii.3–10). She realizes that this is the way to exert a form of mastery over Antony, and the principle by which she rules in love is the same by which she—and Antony —rule in politics. They are both constantly trying to make their subjects' moods correspond to their own, as is evident if one compares Act IV, scene ii, with Act IV, scene viii. Since Antony's soldiers "make their looks by his" (I.v.56), they become infected with the frantic alternation of his moods:

> Antony
> Is valiant, and dejected, and by starts
> His fretted fortunes give him hope and fear
> Of what he has, and has not.   [IV.xii.6–9]

In particular, when Antony and Cleopatra feel miserable as lovers they are not averse to using their political power to spread the misery around among their subordinates. At times they seem to care about the happiness of their subjects only when it is required for their own, to bolster up their faltering spirits (III.xiii.182–90), and occasionally they talk as if they did not care at all what happened to their subjects.[16] They would never call out in public for the destruction of Rome and Egypt if they were at all concerned about accommodating themselves to ordinary notions of how rulers should behave.

In this respect, their conduct is in sharp contrast to that of Octavius, who seems acutely sensitive to the problem of laying an adequate foundation for his rule in a world in which old forms of political legitimacy have lost their force. Octavius is always careful to give a good account of himself, to offer reasons for his political decisions and to justify publicly his course of action, especially the wars he conducts against Antony:[17]

> Go with me to my tent, where you shall see
> How hardly I was drawn into this war,
> How calm and gentle I proceeded still
> In all my writings. Go with me, and see
> What I can show in this.   [V.i.73–77]

One might object that Octavius' regard for public opinion is all "show" or sham, that he merely wants to "let the world see / His nobleness well acted" (V.ii.44–45) and does not care at all for justice in itself. But Octavius' concern for public justification is not immaterial, since it causes him to act moderately and prudently as a ruler, and therefore, in a limited but significant sense, justly.

By contrast, Antony proceeds as if he had no need to justify himself to anyone, except perhaps Cleopatra, and thus he is tempted into acting immoderately and imprudently as a ruler, and, in a basic sense, unjustly. The most important decision he makes as a commander is to fight the battle of Actium at sea. When asked to explain why he is doing exactly what Octavius wants him to do, he replies curtly: "For that he dares us to't" (III.vii.29). Antony will not explain why fighting Octavius is necessary or why doing so at sea is a rational course of action. He feels he has said enough if he can show that his personal honor has been challenged. Because he is unwilling to consider the objections raised by his followers, Antony dangerously overestimates his capabilities (III.vii.49–53). Canidius and Enobarbus advance weighty reasons against the decision Antony has made (ll.30–48), and one of his "worthy" soldiers points out that in fighting at sea Antony is going against his own tradition (ll.61–66). But in politics, as in love, Antony scorns both prudential reasons and custom. He refuses to give an account of himself, simply keeps on repeating his original decision, and finally puts an end to all further discussion. The sum total of his arguments against his counselors amounts to no more than this:

> By sea, by sea.
>
> . . . . .
> I'll fight at sea.
>
> . . . . .
> Well, well, away!   [III.vii.40, 48, 66]

Antony's arbitrariness as a commander serves as a love-test of sorts for his soldiers, who must obey his commands no matter how surprising or even absurd they seem in the circumstances. Antony assures that whatever loyalty his men have for him will be the result not of habit or prudence, but of pure faith in him as a leader. But if his rule is as unconditional as his love, it is also as insecure, for his arbitrariness works to drive even his most loyal followers to desert him (III.xiii.194–200).[18]

What unites in principle the love and rule of Antony and Cleopatra is a certain lack of moderation or prudence, based on a contempt for whatever seems reasonable or traditional to ordinary men. More specifically, the element common to their love and rule is an attempt to do without law. We have already seen that their personal relationship can be understood as at best a marriage outside the law, and the clearest definition of tyranny is "rule without law," first in the sense of rule established illegally, but more importantly in the sense of arbitrary rule, that is, rule according to the sovereign's personal will and not according to publicly promulgated statutes.[19] It is characteristic of Antony and Cleopatra as rulers that, unlike even the revolutionary tribunes in *Coriolanus*, they never appeal to law or custom in making or announcing their decisions.[20] Laws would circumscribe their authority, and one may see in their lawlessness as rulers the same drive to go beyond all limits that manifests itself in their love. Their rule is, so to speak, as unconventional as their love, as uniquely their own and as free of external constraints. In public as in private life Antony and Cleopatra never do the expected thing, as if they were as unwilling to issue a hackneyed command as they are to give a trite pledge of love. Recalling that the highest claim that can be made for Cleopatra is that "custom" cannot "stale her infinite variety," one might say that the guiding principle of Antony and Cleopatra in both public and private life is open hostility to stale custom.

Once we see the rule of Antony and Cleopatra as the mirror image of their love, we can understand why judgments concerning their characters diverge so widely. For what appears quite positive from the perspective of private life is not so attractive when viewed from the perspective of public. The same absoluteness that makes Antony and Cleopatra look glorious as lovers makes them appear despotic as rulers, even though they pursue the same goal in rule that they do in love, namely, to bring reality into accord with their own desires, to have their world exactly the way they want it, without compromise. The tyrant lives in a private universe just as the lover does, for the tyrant is as likely to substitute illusions for reality when he is surrounded by sycophants and flatterers. As is clear from the scenes of Cleopatra with her messenger, tyrannical behavior shields her from unwelcome truths and leaves her in a world built up by her own hopes and wishes. After the beating the messenger receives in Act II, scene v, he returns in Act III, scene iii, apparently having learned how to adapt his speech to the queen's vanity. He simply lets her construct in her mind's eye as unflattering a portrait as she likes of Octavia, his "good judgment" (III.iii.25) affording a spurious confirmation of Cleopatra's fantasies. Cleopatra is clearly living in a dream world in this scene, indulging herself in thoughts of her supremacy as a woman, but because the messenger and Charmian spring forward to second her every observation, she remains unaware of the subjectivity of her vision.

Although we might be tempted to allow Cleopatra to enjoy her pleasant (and essentially valid) thoughts of her power as a woman, we react differently when she overestimates her power as a monarch: "I have sixty sails, Caesar none better" (III.vii.49). The same sort of vanity is at work here, but it has dangerous consequences, tempting Cleopatra (and through her, Antony) into a foolhardy battle. Somehow the fantasies of a ruler seem less innocent than those of a lover, and An-

tony and Cleopatra cannot lay claim to the self-defense of
Donne's lover in "The Canonization":

> Alas, alas, who's injured by my love?
> What merchants ships have my sighs drown'd?

Unlike purely private lovers, Antony and Cleopatra do not
live in a self-contained world of harmless metaphor. On the
contrary, they try to use the real world as a metaphor for
their love, and Antony ends up with a "drown'd ship" or two
on his conscience. In short, a trait that seems acceptable in a
lover—faithfulness to his desires—is unacceptable in a ruler,
where the same trait appears as selfishness, arbitrariness, and
willful blindness to reality. Whether one allows one's evalua-
tion of the rule of Antony and Cleopatra to color one's view
of their love depends on whether one chooses to interpret
their love story in light of their tendency as rulers to live in a
world of flattering illusions.

iii

We have seen that, rather than sacrificing public for private
life, Antony and Cleopatra give up security for the excitement
and novelty of going their own way, a description that fits
their conduct both as rulers and as lovers. Hence Enobarbus'
criticism of Antony's military strategy at Actium expresses
the principle of his strategy in love as well:

> [you] quite forgo
> The way which promises assurance, and
> Give up yourself merely to chance and hazard
> From firm security.   [III.vii.45–48]

This decision to live dangerously, to sail into uncharted seas,
is what is fundamentally heroic about Antony and Cleopatra,
for it represents a forthright response to the fundamental fact
of their world, the dissolution of the ancient city and the
resulting hollowness of old conventions and traditional values.
In this sense, to understand the special case of Antony and

Cleopatra is to take a major step toward understanding life in general under the Imperial regime. For the insecurity the lovers encounter in their attempt to live without the support of convention, the difficulty of validating subjective modes of thought and feeling, is the characteristic problem of life in the Empire. It is, for example, precisely the dilemma facing Enobarbus, who, with the city gone, is left entirely on his own to answer the difficult question: What is loyalty and what is treason? He clearly cannot appeal to any authority when his whole problem is deciding what authority he should accept. How the characters in *Antony and Cleopatra* react to this feeling of being at sea, of suddenly being without guidance in a morally perplexing world of divided allegiances, seems to be the only true test of heroic fortitude remaining to them.

Enobarbus for one allows himself to be destroyed by his inability to find anything he can believe in. Other characters, foremost among them Octavius, seem content with the changed terms of life in the Empire, lowering their sights and following a prudent course of moderation. Satisfied with being "the universal landlord" (III.xiii.72), the unheroic administrator of an imperial bureaucracy that could just as well operate without him (III.i.16–17, III.xi.38–40, III.xiii.22–25), Octavius is apparently willing to forgo the old Roman sense of personal preeminence, in particular the heroism of being willing to fight to the death for mastery (III.xiii.29–31, IV.i.3–6, IV.ii.1–4). Only Antony and Cleopatra struggle against the leveling effects of the Imperial regime (IV.xv.65–68), fighting to remain above the common run of men, whose aspirations do not exceed "sleep and feeding" (II.i.26, V.ii.187). Since Antony and Cleopatra are unable to find values in traditional sources, they are forced to create values for themselves.[21] With the Empire no longer able to supply its citizens with the sense of wholeness the Republic provided, Antony and Cleopatra try, as we have seen, to make their love into the whole of their lives, to use their own passion as a narrower but more intense focus for the meaning of their existence. Hence of all the characters in the play they are the only ones who can be said to respond heroically to the challenge presented by the dissolution of the Republican regime. No longer provided with a definition of nobility, they do not give up the pursuit of nobility out of bewilderment or complacency, but try to find a new path to nobility, beyond the city's borders, however dangerous that search proves to be.

Viewed in this light, the story of Antony and Cleopatra reveals its inner unity with that of Coriolanus. In taking the uncharted sea as their element and seeking out "new heaven, new earth," Antony and Cleopatra resemble Coriolanus setting out alone from the gates of Rome in hopes of finding "a world elsewhere." In trying to live without the city, all three exhibit the same pride and daring, the same urge to transcend the conventional limits of humanity. Hence Antony and Cleopatra are characterized by the same pattern of god-beast imagery we observed in *Coriolanus*. On the divine level, Antony plays the roles of Mars and Jove, while Cleopatra appears as Venus and Isis. On the bestial level, Antony is generally associated with horses, and Cleopatra most frequently with serpents, although occasionally the two turn up in more curious metaphoric garb, Cleopatra, for example, compared to "a cow in June"[22] and Antony to a "doting mallard" (III.x.14, 19). Cleopatra neatly sums up the double perspective in the imagery when she says of Antony: "Though he be painted one way like a Gorgon, / The other way's a Mars" (II.v.116–17).

The god-beast imagery in *Antony and Cleopatra* has the same significance it does in *Coriolanus*: it reflects the new possibilities that have opened up in the world of the play to rise above or sink below the ordinary human level, possibilities facing all men, however, and not just someone like Coriolanus, banished from his native city. For the world of *Antony and Cleopatra* is essentially cityless from the beginning, and exile has become the basic human condition, as the characters find themselves displaced and disoriented in a new order. "Ill-rooted" in shifting soil and "quicksands," they sometimes feel as if "the least wind i' th' world will blow them down" (II.vii.2–3, 59). In a moment of defeat, Antony gives voice to the feelings of confusion that are never far from the surface in the play:

> I am so lated in the world, that I
> Have lost my way for ever.   [III.xi.3–4]

Antony's bewilderment, here and elsewhere, reminds us that the absence of boundaries implies the absence of guideposts. The freedom from the restrictive world of the ancient city the Romans experience when the Republic dissolves is thoroughly problematic: boundlessness is also rootlessness, and if the liberation of eros creates new opportunities, it also closes off certain old ones and brings new difficulties in its wake. Somehow the independence that makes for an intoxicating spectacle in the case of Antony and Cleopatra provides a sobering sight in that of Enobarbus. Finding a new source of nobility is difficult enough for Antony and Cleopatra; for those who lack the imaginative resources necessary to forge a private world in accord with their own desires, the public world of the Empire becomes desolate indeed. If the dissolution of the Republic cannot be said to be an unequivocal gain, then one understands why the situation of Shakespeare's Romans is fundamentally tragic. While the Republican regime exists, it works to check their aspirations, but once it dissolves, they are no longer sure what to aspire to. To put it another way, the Romans, at least the greatest of them, chafe under the regime's restraints or even rebel against them, but if successful in breaking out of the city's control, they find they have difficulties living without its guidance. In that sense, Coriolanus' story reveals most clearly the dilemma of Shakespeare's Romans: Coriolanus finds he cannot live within the city, but he finds he cannot live without it either.[23]

It is to achieve this perspective on the Roman plays that one must read *Coriolanus* and *Antony and Cleopatra* as companion pieces. If one read *Coriolanus* alone, one might wonder what could be positive about the restrictive nature of the ancient city. By the same token, if one read *Antony and Cleopatra* alone, one might accept as a given the hollowness of political life in the play, and not consider whether alternative regimes might be possible, in which politics would nourish the public spiritedness of men. The two plays are therefore complementary, since the one helps to define what is lacking in the world of the other. The Rome of *Coriolanus* curbs its citizens in their aspirations, but at least it provides them a home, giving their lives meaning in the context of the city. The Rome of *Antony and Cleopatra* permits its characters their "immortal longings," but by their very nature these longings can no longer be satisfied within this world, and force the characters to seek out a world beyond. Either Rome, Republic or Empire, is potentially tragic in the disparity between human aspirations and the reality they encounter. Ultimately the source of tragedy in Rome can be traced to the fact that the Republic seems to offer men nobility only at the price of wisdom and self-knowledge, while the Empire offers freedom in private life only at the price of a lasting and meaningful public context for nobility. Reading *Coriolanus* and *Antony and Cleopatra* in light of each other, one comes away from Shakespeare's Rome with the impression of a city great because of the kinds of human greatness it fosters, and yet tragically at odds with the full and independent development of that greatness.

In the end, however much one may gain from treating *Coriolanus* and *Antony and Cleopatra* as companion pieces, one cannot escape the fact that the plays make entirely different impressions on almost all readers. One rarely finds a critic who even attributes to the two the same level of artistic achievement.[24] At the moment, *Coriolanus* is generally discussed in the shadow of *Antony and Cleopatra,* like a well-formed but plain child who must be kept from pushing his way into the spotlight with a more famous and handsome brother. One quality that apparently elevates *Antony and Cleopatra* above *Coriolanus* in the minds of most critics is that the issues in the play seem broader in scope and less partisan in nature, reaching far beyond the rather mundane disputes of patricians and plebeians. However, instead of regarding *Antony and Cleopatra* as one of Shakespeare's wide-ranging works, in opposition to the "narrowly conceived" *Coriolanus,* we can view the universal character of the former as the complement to the parochial character of the latter. It is above all the cosmopolitan setting of *Antony and Cleopatra* that is responsible for the impression of universality the play makes, and this expansiveness is but the reverse side of *Coriolanus'* restriction to the narrow horizons of a single polis. Both plays revolve around the same issue, namely, what is meant by being bounded by the city and what is meant by being free of it, or, alternatively phrased, what is meant by being rooted in the city and what is meant by being uprooted from it. Though *Coriolanus* seems to focus on man confined within the city, the play does open up in the direction of universality with the hero's attempt to leave Rome. Similarly, though *Antony and Cleopatra* ranges all over the Mediterranean world, it gradually narrows its scope to the confines of a single tomb, as the lovers seek a stable refuge within their rootless cosmopolitan life.[25] The plays thus approach from different angles the one problem of the relationship of the city and man. And in revealing the potentially tragic nature of this relationship, the tension between the heroic character and the political community, the two Roman plays provide a profound clue to the nature of Shakespearean tragedy in general.

Notes

Notes to Preface

1. Goethe is the most famous spokesman for this view, although he merely alludes to it in passing. See Johann Peter Eckermann, *Conversations with Goethe*, January 31, 1827.

2. Samuel Johnson, *Works* (New Haven: Yale University Press, 1968), VII, 65–66.

3. See, for example, John Palmer, *Political Characters of Shakespeare* (London: Macmillan, 1945), pp. 308–9.

4. See M. W. MacCallum, *Shakespeare's Roman Plays and Their Background* (London: Macmillan, 1910), p. 513, for the claim that the departures from Plutarch in *Coriolanus* "may have arisen quite naturally and unconsciously from Shakespeare's indifference to questions of constitutional theory and his inability to understand the ideals of an antique self-governing commonwealth controlled by all its free members as a body."

5. See James Phillips, Jr., *The State in Shakespeare's Greek and Roman Plays* (New York: Columbia University Press, 1940), p. 206: "In *Coriolanus* democracy is tried and found wanting." Norman Rabkin, *Shakespeare and the Common Understanding* (New York: The Free Press, 1967), p. 135, speaks of Coriolanus "searching for a way to accept public office in a democracy."

6. See, for example, Phillips, p. 104.

7. On this general subject, see Kurt von Fritz, *The Theory of the Mixed Constitution in Antiquity* (New York: Columbia University Press, 1954). The idea of the mixed regime originated with Aristotle, was applied to Rome by the Greek historian Polybius, and later in a different form became the basis of Machiavelli's analysis of the Republic. See in particular Aristotle, *Politics*, 1293b–1294b, Polybius, *Histories*, VI.10–18, and Machiavelli, *Discourses on the First Ten*

Books of Livy, I.ii. On the relevance of the idea of the mixed regime to the Roman plays, see Clifford Chalmers Huffman, *Coriolanus in Context* (Lewisburg: Bucknell University Press, 1971), pp. 30–34. Huffman's book is an impressively documented study of how important and how widespread the idea of the mixed regime was in Renaissance political thought, even among English writers. For evidence that English Renaissance poets were aware of the mixed regime, see Fulke Greville's *A Treatise of Monarchy*, stanzas 618–19, in *The Remains* (London: Oxford University Press, 1965), p. 190.

8. See Machiavelli, *Discourses*, III.xxiv, and Charles de Secondat, Baron de La Brède et de Montesquieu, *Considerations on the Causes of the Greatness of the Romans and Their Decline*, tr. by David Lowenthal (Ithaca: Cornell University Press, 1965), p. 91.

9. Montesquieu, pp. 92–93.

10. For a summary of the latest evidence for dating *Coriolanus* and *Antony and Cleopatra*, see the *Riverside Shakespeare*, ed. by G. Blakemore Evans (Boston: Houghton Mifflin, 1974), pp. 55, 1343, 1392. The consensus is that the two plays were written sometime during the years 1606–1608. Virtually no basis exists for deciding which of the two was written first, although most editors place *Coriolanus* after *Antony and Cleopatra*. In the absence of any evidence to the contrary, it is quite possible that the two plays were conceived and executed more or less simultaneously.

11. At almost the same time that Shakespeare was working on *Coriolanus*, a French playwright, Alexandre Hardy, wrote a tragedy called *Coriolan*. See Geoffrey Bullough, *Narrative and Dramatic Sources of Shakespeare* (London: Routledge & Kegan Paul, 1964), V, 474–76. Later dramatizations of the Coriolanus story, such as James Thomson's or Bertolt Brecht's, appear to be direct responses to Shakespeare's version. The same must be said of Beethoven's *Coriolan Overture* and T. S. Eliot's poem "Coriolan." Whether any major artist would have touched the Coriolanus theme without Shakespeare's example is doubtful.

12. See Huffman, pp. 29–30, Jan Kott, *Shakespeare Our Contemporary* (London: Methuen, 1965), p. 146, and T. J. B. Spencer, "Shakespeare and the Elizabethan Romans," *Shakespeare Survey* No. 10 (1957), p. 31.

13. Harold Goddard, *The Meaning of Shakespeare* (Chicago: University of Chicago Press, 1951), p. 595.

14. See Bullough, p. 454.

15. Machiavelli's discussion of the Roman Republic virtually begins

with the tribunate and its distinctive role in Roman political life (*Discourses on Livy*, I.iii). See also José Ortega y Gasset, *Concord and Liberty* (New York: Norton, 1946), pp. 41–47.

16. *Plutarch's Lives of the Noble Grecians and Romans*, tr. by Sir Thomas North (New York: The Limited Editions Club, 1941), II, 302–3.

17. Bullough advances the intriguing theory that Shakespeare came upon the life of Coriolanus through the medium of the life of Alcibiades (V, 455). In Bullough's hypothetical reconstruction, Shakespeare, starting with Plutarch's life of Antony, became interested in the story of Timon, which Plutarch tells in the course of narrating Antony's life. To find material for a play about Timon, Shakespeare turned to Plutarch's Life of Alcibiades, which in turn led him to the parallel life of Coriolanus. As speculative as Bullough's account may be, it has a certain plausibility. See also T. J. B. Spencer, *William Shakespeare: The Roman Plays* (London: Longmans, Green, 1963), p. 38.

18. Cf. Bullough's formulation of the contrast, V, 454–55: "Antony and Coriolanus 'were at once like and unlike,' both victims of passion, but of very different passions. . . . They exemplified the two complementary aspects of human nature defined by many ethical writers since Aristotle; for if Antony was a slave to the 'concupiscible' forces, Coriolanus was at the mercy of the 'irascible' elements in his personality. They are indeed parallel portraits."

19. Though *Titus Andronicus* should in some sense be classified as one of Shakespeare's Roman plays, I have left it out of consideration entirely, because it is obviously an immature work and does not display the understanding of Rome Shakespeare developed in his later Roman tragedies.

20. See especially Allan Bloom's essay, "*Julius Caesar*: The Morality of the Pagan Hero," *Shakespeare's Politics* (New York: Basic Books, 1964), a discussion which suggested many of the basic ideas of this book.

21. Goddard, pp. 593–94: "*Antony and Cleopatra* may be taken not only by itself, but as the final part of Shakespeare's Roman trilogy—*Coriolanus, Julius Caesar, Antony and Cleopatra*—last not in order of composition but in historical sequence. Coriolanus, Brutus, Antony; Volumnia-Virgilia, Portia, Cleopatra: the men, and even more the women, give us a spiritual history of Rome from its austere early days, through the fall of the republic, to the triumph of the empire."

22. For all quotations from Shakespeare, I have used the new

Riverside edition. References to line numbers follow the lineation of this edition. Fortunately for a study relying heavily on textual evidence, the texts of both *Coriolanus* and *Antony and Cleopatra* (and *Julius Caesar* as well) are in comparatively good condition. The sole authority for all three plays is the First Folio, and there are relatively few disputed readings in the texts, and almost none of any real significance. I have, however, checked all the standard emendations against the Folio original, and in a few cases restored the Folio reading where it seemed to make sufficient sense as it stood not to warrant emendation. I have followed Evans in his practice of bracketing all emendations of the original text, so that readers may be aware of editorial intervention.

Notes to Introduction

1. For a list of similar images, see Maurice Charney, *Shakespeare's Roman Plays* (Cambridge: Harvard University Press, 1961), pp. 103–5.

2. Charney, p. 93.

3. Charney, pp. 102–3.

4. Charney cites them both, pp. 105–6.

5. Cf. Janet Adelman, *The Common Liar* (New Haven: Yale University Press, 1973), p. 132.

6. See Charney, pp. 109–12, and Adelman, pp. 153–54. However, Rome sometimes seems as liable to idleness as Egypt (I.iv.76). Ultimately the difference between Egypt and Rome in *Antony and Cleopatra* reduces to the difference between a country which has long had an imperial regime and way of life and one which is just developing them. That is why Rome has so much to learn from Egypt.

7. II.i.16–20, 28–30, III.vi.64–66, III.vii.20–23, 56–57, 74–75.

8. Charney, pp. 106–7.

9. Charney, p. 95.

10. Charney, pp. 142–57.

11. Cf. J. Leeds Barroll, "The Characterization of Octavius," *Shakespeare Studies*, VI(1970), 248.

12. Barroll, pp. 238–41.

13. See Adelman, p. 131: "Although Octavius is the spokesman for measure, he is by no means the spokesman for the idea of Rome itself: our sense of ancient Roman virtue comes not from Octavius but from the descriptions of Antony as he used to be."

14. See Charney, p. 143, on the connection between "images of temperance and austerity" and "an heroic aristocratic ideal."

15. Austerity makes strange bedfellows in Goddard, p. 612: "Digestive comfort . . . would have made as little difference to Coriolanus as to Saint Francis himself." This statement is correct as it stands, but it might be somewhat misleading.

16. See Goddard, p. 612.

17. This word should be thought of as a translation of the Greek word *thumos*, which, unlike *eros*, has not found its way into English usage. A reading of Plato's discussion in the *Republic* of *eros* and *thumos*, the two irrational parts of the soul, is very helpful for understanding the relationship between *Antony and Cleopatra* and *Coriolanus*. See especially 369b–376c and 439a–441c, and above all 440c–d, a passage which associates *thumos* with anger, austerity, and a concern for justice.

18. Brutus points out that "he is given / To sports, to wildness, and much company" (II.i.188–89). See also II.ii.116.

19. See MacCallum, p. 513.

20. On the link between these scenes, see Derek Traversi, *Shakespeare: The Roman Plays* (London: Hollis & Carter, 1963), p. 218.

21. On the availability in England of Machiavelli's writings, including the *Discourses*, see Huffman, pp. 110–12, 119–20.

22. A. C. Bradley points out that Shakespeare goes beyond Plutarch in attributing this fate to Sossius. See "Antony and Cleopatra," *Oxford Lectures on Poetry* (London: Macmillan, 1909), p. 306.

23. See MacCallum, p. 461.

24. Cf. Traversi, p. 208.

25. Cf. Adelman, pp. 132–34.

Note to Part One

1. Quoted in the translation of Walter Kaufmann (New York: Vintage Books, 1966), p. 210.

Notes to Chapter 1

1. For a definition of the polis, see Aristotle, *Politics*, 1253a–b. For a fuller discussion of the difference between the modern state and the ancient city, see Harry Jaffa, "Aristotle," in *History of Political Philosophy*, ed. by Leo Strauss and Joseph Cropsey (Chicago: Rand McNally, 1963), pp. 65–67.

2. Aristotle, *Politics*, 1276b, 1–12.

3. See Aristotle, *Politics*, 1252b, 30–31.

4. On the style of this speech, see Reuben Brower, *Hero and Saint: Shakespeare and the Graeco-Roman Heroic Tradition* (Oxford: Oxford University Press, 1971), pp. 354–60.

5. *Shakespeare's Plutarch*, ed. by T. J. B. Spencer (Baltimore: Penguin Books, 1964), p. 305.

6. In *Julius Caesar* (I.i), "the tribunes are even put in the position of defending the traditional role of the senatorial class, so that the constitution can remain intact!" (Bloom, p. 82).

7. For the sake of parallelism, it is tempting to use the word *erotic* to characterize those in whom the force of eros predominates, but this word has such strong connotations in English that its use might be misleading. The most prudent course seems to be to use the adjective *appetitive* for describing people like Menenius and the majority of the plebeians, in whom eros generally takes the form of appetite.

8. Cf. Rabkin, p. 138.

9. See Rabkin, p. 122, Traversi, pp. 208–12, Judah Stampfer, *The Tragic Engagement: A Study of Shakespeare's Classical Tragedies* (New York: Funk & Wagnalls, 1968), p. 295, and Roy Battenhouse, *Shakespearean Tragedy* (Bloomington: Indiana University Press, 1969), pp. 341–47.

10. See *Shakespeare's Plutarch*, pp. 300–1.

11. See Bloom, pp. 79–80.

12. One of the many critics who apparently see nothing problematic about the fable of the belly inadvertently confirms this point. Phillips (p. 155) views Menenius as a straightforward spokesman for Shakespeare, but when he tries to state the moral of the patrician's tale, he cannot help speaking of the "head" where Menenius spoke of the "belly": "The chief implication of Menenius' fable, and of his reference to one citizen as the 'great toe of this assembly,' is that as the feet cannot supplant the head in the government of the natural body, no more can the commoners supplant the aristocrats in the government of the political body."

13. Cf. Goddard, pp. 616–17.

14. See Bloom, p. 81.

15. See *Coriolanus*, II.ii.144–45.

16. On "the corruption of the people" as "the key to the mastery of Rome," see Bloom, pp. 80–83.

17. The disparity between nature and convention is perhaps hinted at during the weird moment in *Julius Caesar* (II.i.101–11) when the

conspirators try to determine where the sun rises, only to decide the precise point keeps changing throughout the year and does not correspond with due east, where Rome has built its Capitol. The city tries to remain fixed, while nature varies. On the importance of this scene, see Goddard, pp. 316–17.

Notes to Chapter 2

1. For a psychoanalytic view of Coriolanus, see Otto Rank, *Das Inzest-Motiv in Dichtung und Sage* (Vienna: Franz Deuticke, 1926), pp. 214–17. Positing an Oedipus complex in Coriolanus, Rank claims that from a "hater of his father," he becomes a "hater of his fatherland" (p. 216). On Coriolanus' relation to his mother, see R. Browning, "Coriolanus, Boy of Tears," *Essays in Criticism*, IV (1954), 18–31, Michael McCanles, "The Dialectic of Transcendence in Shakespeare's *Coriolanus*," *PMLA*, LXXXII (1967), 51–3, Katherine Stockholder, "The Other Coriolanus," *PMLA*, LXXXV (1970), 232–3, and Lawrence Danson, *Tragic Alphabet: Shakespeare's Drama of Language* (New Haven: Yale University Press, 1974), pp. 152–55.

2. See J. L. Simmons, *Shakespeare's Pagan World: The Roman Tragedies* (Charlottesville: The University Press of Virginia, 1973), pp. 51–52.

3. On the importance of the definition of a citizen, see Aristotle, *Politics*, 1274b–1275b.

4. In the Folio, these lines are ascribed to Menenius. However, in view of the obviously incorrect ascription of the preceding line to Coriolanus, it is reasonable to assign this speech to Coriolanus, especially since Volumnia attributes precisely these sentiments to him earlier in the play (I.iii.30–32). All editors follow this practice.

5. Consider I.i.171–72, I.iv.34–36, II.i.246–53, III.i.137–39. Cf. Aristotle's discussion of natural slavery, *Politics*, 1254b.

6. See Polybius, *Histories*, VI.48–50, and Machiavelli, *Discourses*, I.ii, v–vi. Sparta was the other principal example of the mixed regime in antiquity. See Huffman, p. 34. Battenhouse, p. 365, points out that Coriolanus has "a Spartan view of society."

7. Polybius, *Histories*, VI.45.3–5.

8. See Huffman, p. 70.

9. See Polybius, *Histories*, VI.10.13–14, and Machiavelli, *Discourses*, I.ii. Polybius discusses Lycurgus in *Histories*, VI.10, but does not bother to mention the legendary founder of Rome, Romulus, in his discussion of the Roman regime. Machiavelli (*Discourses*, I.ii) does

mention Romulus after discussing Lycurgus, but points out that the laws Romulus gave his people were suitable to a monarchy and could not provide the basis for a republic.

10. Several characters within the play understand that Rome is dependent upon the good fortune of its citizens. See I.iv.44, I.v.20–22, V.iii.119–20, V.vi.117.

11. Plutarch makes this point at the beginning of his comparison of Coriolanus with Alcibiades. See *Lives*, II, 299. See also Livy, *Histories*, II.38, and Machiavelli, *Discourses*, III.xiii.

12. Consider I.i.199–200, I.iv.28–29, 38–40, III.i.223–224, 241–42.

13. Brower, p. 377.

14 Plutarch's Coriolanus has no hesitations about showing his wounds. See *Shakespeare's Plutarch*, p. 319.

15. Traversi, pp. 249–51.

16. What is suggested to Coriolanus in III.ii is in effect Aristotle's idea that natural right is part of political right. See *Nicomachean Ethics*, 1135b.

17. Shakespeare's departures from Plutarch in this minor incident show how carefully he rethought the character of Coriolanus. In Plutarch's account, the Volsce is simply an "old friend," who was once "host" to Coriolanus, and, far from being poor, was an "honest wealthy man" (*Shakespeare's Plutarch*, p. 312). No mention is made of any services he performed for Coriolanus, and Coriolanus does not forget his name. All the changes Shakespeare made have the effect of bringing out Coriolanus' reluctance to be dependent on another man, especially one beneath him in dignity. Shakespeare might have derived the idea for this incident directly or indirectly from Aristotle's description of magnanimous men in the *Nicomachean Ethics*, 1124b: "They seem also to remember any service they have done, but not those they have received (for he who receives a service is inferior to him who has done it, but the magnanimous man wishes to be superior)" (quoted in the translation of W. D. Ross). A reading of the entire section on *megalopsychia*, or "greatness of soul," in the *Nicomachean Ethics* is very helpful in studying *Coriolanus*, since at many points Aristotle could be describing Shakespeare's hero. (For example: "He is free of speech because he is contemptuous, and he is given to telling the truth, except when he speaks in irony to the vulgar," 1124b.) See also Rodney Poison, "Coriolanus as Aristotle's Magnanimous Man," *Pacific Coast Studies in Shakespeare* (Eugene: University of Oregon, 1966), pp. 210–24, and Battenhouse, pp. 365–69.

18. See McCanles, p. 46, and Simmons, pp. 45–46.

19. McCanles, p. 47, and Stockholder, pp. 231–32.

20. This passage is directly based on the comparison of Coriolanus with Alcibiades in Plutarch's *Lives*, II, 299–300: "He is less to be blamed that seeketh to please and gratify his common people than he that despiseth and disdaineth them, and therefore offereth them wrong and injury because he would not seem to flatter them to win more authority. For as it is an evil thing to flatter the common people to win credit, even so is it besides dishonesty—and injustice also—to attain to credit and authority, for one to make himself terrible to the people by offering them wrong and violence."

21. *Lives*, II, 305. Plutarch's remark might be traced to Aristotle's discussion of greatness of soul, *Nicomachean Ethics*, 1124a.

22. See Bloom, pp. 83–85.

23. On the importance of hidden or indirect government in Republican Rome, see Harvey C. Mansfield, Jr., "Machiavelli's New Regime," *Italian Quarterly*, XIII (1970), 63–95.

Notes to Chapter 3

1. In Plutarch, Coriolanus "went on his way with three or four of his friends" (*Shakespeare's Plutarch*, p. 334).

2. See, for example, Bloom, pp. 85–86, Charney, p. 187, and F. N. Lees, "*Coriolanus*, Aristotle, and Bacon," *Review of English Studies*, I (1950), 114–25.

3. *Politics*, 1252b28–1253a5.

4. *Politics*, 1253a8–18.

5. *Politics*, 1253a25–29.

6. On the significance of Hercules in *Coriolanus*, see Eugene M. Waith, *The Herculean Hero* (New York: Columbia University Press, 1962), pp. 121–43.

7. See Danson, pp. 154–55.

8. On Coriolanus' death, see Danson, pp. 159–62. On Coriolanus' failure to transcend Rome, see McCanles, pp. 50–51.

9. Cf. *Troilus and Cressida*, III.iii.103–11. See also Plato, *Alcibiades I*, 132d–133d, and Simmons, pp. 95–98.

10. See D. J. Enright, *The Apothecary's Shop* (London: Secker & Warburg, 1957), who sees in the play (p. 51) "the dangers that are often implied in the word 'political'—the dangers of a situation in which each opposing side understands the other (in the way that Coriolanus is right about the plebeians, and the plebeians are right about Coriolanus), but neither side understands itself." See also

Traversi, pp. 227–28, and L. C. Knights, *Public Voices* (London: Chatto & Windus, 1971), pp. 42–43.

11. On the connection between style and meaning in the Roman plays, see Charney, chapter 2.

12. See Harry Levin, "Introduction to *Coriolanus*," *The Complete Pelican Shakespeare* (Baltimore: Penguin Books, 1969), p. 1213, and Brower, pp. 217–18.

13. See Charney, pp. 65–66, and Danson, pp. 62–63.

14. A comparison of Brutus' speech with Antony's in the preceding scene will confirm the point that in addressing the people, to speak directly, briefly, and truly is not to speak wisely.

15. In North's Plutarch, the character who breaks in upon Brutus and Cassius "cared for never a Senator of them all." See *Shakespeare's Plutarch*, p. 146, and Bloom, p. 101, p. 110.

16. See Levin, p. 1213.

17. See Brower, pp. 224–26.

18. See Bloom, p. 95.

19. Hence W. I. Carr's apt characterization of Coriolanus as "a bundle of assertions in a suit of armour" in " 'Gracious Silence'—A Selective Reading of *Coriolanus*," *English Studies*, XLVI (1965), 234.

20. Coriolanus' second soliloquy (IV.iv.12–26), though not in rhyme, is almost as artificially composed as the first and just as platitudinous, starting from the trite exclamation: "O world, thy slippery turns!" See Sailendra Kuman Sen, "What Happens in *Coriolanus*," *Shakespeare Quarterly*, IX (1958), 338.

21. Coriolanus' "lack of education" is the first point Plutarch makes about the Roman in his biography (*Shakespeare's Plutarch*, p. 297). In the corresponding point in Plutarch's parallel life of Alcibiades, we learn how readily the Greek took to education. Moreover, he had no less a teacher than Socrates.

22. Plutarch describes the Cynic who broke in upon Brutus and Cassius as a man who "took upon himself to counterfeit a philosopher not with wisdom and discretion but with a certain bedlam and frantic motion," "a hasty man and sudden in all his doing," who had a "bold manner of speech." See *Shakespeare's Plutarch*, p. 146.

23. On the importance of this "missing scene," see Stockholder, p. 231.

24. Where Shakespeare found the name *Nicanor*, or why he used it here, is difficult to discover, but Plutarch in his *Life of Phocion* does mention a Nicanor who would be an excellent namesake for both a spy and a foil to Coriolanus. See T. J. B. Spencer, *William Shake-*

speare: The Roman Plays, p. 40. Plutarch's Nicanor achieves command over the city of Athens by deceit, uses "secret means" and bribes to keep himself in power, and can be persuaded to court the favor of the Athenians, and even to "give the people the pastime of common plays" (see *Lives*, VI, 41, 39). The unpunished treachery of Plutarch's Nicanor contrasts with the punished loyalty of Plutarch's Phocion in much the same way that the unpunished treachery of Shakespeare's Nicanor contrasts with the punished loyalty of Shakespeare's Coriolanus. The story of Phocion parallels that of Coriolanus in its broad outlines, a fact to which the mention of Nicanor in IV.iii may be intended to call our attention, thereby extending to Coriolanus the parallel Plutarch draws at the end of his biography between Phocion and another Athenian unjustly sentenced to death by the city (*Lives*, VI, 48). See also Jean Bodin, *The Six Bookes of a Commonweale*, tr. by Richard Knolles (London: 1606), 532g, 704i.

25. See, for example, Rabkin, p. 143.

26. See Kenneth Burke, "*Coriolanus* and the Delights of Faction," *Hudson Review*, XIX (1966), 191–92.

27. For the importance of the exiled Tarquin kings, see Machiavelli, *Discourses*, I.iii. For the association of Coriolanus with the Tarquins, see V.iv.42–43.

28. According to both Livy and Machiavelli, the Roman Senate's policy was to make one man bear the brunt of popular anger and then sacrifice him to appease the plebeians. See Livy, *Histories*, II.xxxv.3–4 and Machiavelli, *Discourses*, I.iii, viii, xxxiv–v. See also Mansfield, pp. 76–77.

29. See Carr, p. 223, and Simmons, pp. 7, 16–17.

30. See *Politics*, 1276b–1277b, 1294a–b.

Note to Part Two

1. Quoted in the translation of Walter Kaufmann, pp. 211–12. See also Nietzsche, *The Gay Science*, sect. 23.

Notes to Chapter 4

1. See Lord David Cecil, *Poets and Story-Tellers* (New York: Macmillan, 1949), pp. 8–9: in *Antony and Cleopatra* "the private life is, as it were, a consequence of the public life."

2. Traversi, p. 101.

3. See A. P. Riemer, *A Reading of Shakespeare's Antony and Cleo-*

patra (Sidney: Sidney University Press, 1968), p. 34, MacCallum, p. 344, and Simmons, p. 43.

4. See Bloom, p. 90.

5. The one appeal to political principle in the play, however insincere it may be, is to the principle of the Republic (II.vi.10–19), and has an archaic ring. The absence of the common good threatens to obliterate the distinction between a soldier and a pirate. Menas claims they differ no more than a thief "by land" and a "thief by sea" (II.vi.83–96). Cf. Bradley's judgment on the Triumvirs: "They are no champions of their country like Henry V. . . . Their aims . . . are as personal as if they were captains of banditti; and they are followed merely from self-interest or private attachment" ("Antony and Cleopatra," p. 291). See also MacCallum, p. 345.

6. In *Coriolanus*, Rome appears intent on preserving the Volsces as enemies, perhaps as part of a patrician policy of using foreign wars to divert attention from domestic strife. Notice how certain the Volsces are that their town will be "deliver'd back on good condition" (I.x.2).

7. On the parallel between war and "boys pursuing summer butterflies," see *Coriolanus*, IV.vi.94.

8. See Maynard Mack, "Introduction to *Antony and Cleopatra*," *The Complete Pelican Shakespeare*, p. 1170, and Ann Slater, *Notes on Antony and Cleopatra* (London: Ginn, 1971), pp. 22–23.

9. G. Wilson Knight, *The Imperial Theme* (London: Oxford University Press, 1931), p. 156.

10. See MacCallum, p. 344.

11. See, for example, *Shakespeare's Plutarch*, p. 247. The word "senators" appears only once in the play (II.vi.9), and even then is misapplied.

12. *Shakespeare's Plutarch*, p. 243, and Barroll, "Octavius," p. 264.

13. See, for example, Charney, p. 214.

14. But see A. C. Bradley, "Coriolanus" (British Academy Shakespeare Lecture, 1912), reprinted in *Studies in Shakespeare*, ed. by Peter Alexander (London: Oxford University Press, 1964), pp. 220–21, Battenhouse, pp. 330–31, and Jay Halio, "*Coriolanus:* 'Shakespeare's Drama of Reconciliation,'" *Shakespeare Studies*, VI (1970), 299.

15. *Shakespeare's Plutarch*, pp. 299, 339, 351.

16. On this subject, see Machiavelli, *Discourses*, I.xiv.

17. On the identity of the song, see Peter J. Seng, "Shakespeare's Hymn-Parody?" *Renaissance News*, XVIII (1965), 4–6.

18. Perhaps in this context one might interpret the otherwise puz-

zling Biblical allusions in *Antony and Cleopatra*. The most striking of
these are what seem to be several quotations from the Book of Revelation, concentrated at the point of Antony's suicide (compare
IV.xiv.106–8 with Rev., viii:10, x:6, viii:13, and ix:6; these parallels,
and several others, were first pointed out by Ethel Seaton using the
Geneva Bible in *"Antony and Cleopatra* and the Book of Revelation," *Review of English Studies*, XXII [1946], 219–24. See also Battenhouse, pp. 176–81). Also suggestive is the number of times Herod
of Jewry is mentioned in the play (I.ii.28–29, III.iii.3–4, III.vi.73,
IV.vi.12), perhaps an attempt to bring Roman events into line with
the Biblical chronology, especially since Herod's name comes up in
conjunction with talk of "three kings" and a miraculous birth
(I.ii.26–30). See Battenhouse, p. 173, and William Blisset, "Dramatic
Irony in *Antony and Cleopatra*," *Shakespeare Quarterly*, XVIII
(1967), 164–65. Finally, by referring to the Biblical "hill of Basan"
(III.xiii.127), Antony in effect compares himself to the roaring bulls
of Psalm 22, whose opening line does convey something of the emotion Antony is feeling in this particular scene. See J. A. Bryant, Jr.,
Hippolyta's View (University of Kentucky Press, 1961), pp. 179–80.
One could go on uncovering Biblical allusions in *Antony and Cleopatra*, but these are enough to make the point that Shakespeare may
be trying to remind us of what was happening almost contempora-
neously with the Roman drama he unfolds, a drama on another plane
that was soon to eclipse in importance the history of Rome, or at
least turn it in a new direction. On this general subject, see Simmons,
especially pp. 7–14.

19. See J. Leeds Barroll, "Shakespeare and the Art of Character: A
Study of Anthony," *Shakespeare Studies*, V (1969), 196–97.

20. This defect in Octavius' rule is evident in his treatment of
Pompey, but betrays itself most clearly in his ineffective dealings
with Cleopatra, who easily sees through his plans and defeats his
purposes, in part because of Dolabella's disloyalty to Octavius. See
Barroll, "Octavius," pp. 273–83.

21. Antony's ability to summon up tears and call on men's pity is
already evident in *Julius Caesar* (III.ii.169–70, 193–96). See also
Shakespeare's Plutarch, p. 193, pp. 230–32. On the interpretation of
IV.ii, see Battenhouse, p. 173, and Arnold Stein, "The Image of
Antony: Lyric and Tragic Imagination," *Kenyon Review*, XXI
(1959), 594.

22. The principle of Antony's defense of himself to Octavius is
enunciated in a different context by Cleopatra: "And when good will

is show'd, though't come too short, / The actor may plead pardon" (II.v.8–9). (When Coriolanus speaks in favor of "good will," he still insists that it be "effected," [I.ix.18–19].) The idea of the contrast between deeds and intentions is appropriately introduced by the eunuch Mardian at I.v.15–18.

23. Antony tests the loyalty of his troops in the same way he tests Cleopatra's—by smoothing the way to betrayal and making the prospect of a deal with Octavius seem attractive. Compare III.xiii.17–19 with III.xi.4–6.

Notes to Chapter 5

1. See Cecil, p. 10: the love of Antony and Cleopatra "would be essentially altered were it to be transferred to a private setting. If Antony and Cleopatra had been private persons, their story simply could not have happened." See also C. E. Nolan, "*Antony and Cleopatra* and the Triumph of Rome," *University Review*, XXXII (1966), 200.

2. Cf. Stampfer, pp. 241–43.

3. See Rabkin, pp. 179–84.

4. See, for example, Henry Alonzo Myers, *Tragedy: A View of Life* (Ithaca: Cornell University Press, 1956), pp. 110–28.

5. Note, for example, the similarity between Cleopatra's comparing herself with Octavia in III.iii and Hermia's comparing herself with Helena in III.ii of *A Midsummer Night's Dream*.

6. See Bloom, p. 53.

7. For a more detailed discussion of hyperbole in the play, particularly its role in lifting the lovers above the comic plane, see Adelman, pp. 110–21.

8. For the link between love and death in the Tristan legend, see Denis De Rougemont, *Love in the Western World* (New York: Pantheon Books, 1956).

9. For a discussion of suicide in Shakespeare's Roman plays, see Charney, pp. 209–14.

10. See Riemer, p. 113.

11. See David Daiches, "Imagery and Meaning in *Antony and Cleopatra*," *English Studies*, XLIII (1962), 351.

12. Only the barest hints of an afterlife can be found in Plutarch's *Life of Antony:* when Antony hears of Cleopatra's death, he tells her "I will not be long from thee" and when she is offering a funeral

sacrifice to him, she speaks of "the gods where thou art now" (*Shakespeare's Plutarch*, pp. 277, 290).

13. See Stein, pp. 595–97, and Traversi, p. 103.

14. Cf. 1 Corinthians, ii:9.

15. See Traversi, pp. 183–86.

16. See III.vi.1–19, III.xiii.182–85, IV.viii.29–39, and Julian Markels, *The Pillar of the World: Antony and Cleopatra in Shakespeare's Development* (Columbus: Ohio State University Press, 1968), p. 45.

17. See I.i.33–34, III.xiii.90, 162, IV.xii.20–23, IV.xv.63, V.ii.298–99. See also Adelman, pp. 147–48.

18. Cf. Adelman, p. 149. The tragedy of Rome itself has its origins in similar tensions. Like Coriolanus, Rome cannot stand alone against the whole world, and like Antony and Cleopatra, it cannot make itself into the whole world either without losing its separate identity as a city. From the point of view of the individual citizen the city may appear to be the only true whole, but as the limits of Rome indicate, the city's "wholeness" is in its own way partial, especially in relation to the cosmic whole (see above, Chapter 1, note 17). For a suggestive discussion of the polis in terms of the classical problem of the whole and the part, see Hans Jonas, *The Gnostic Religion* (Boston: Beacon Press, 1963), pp. 247–50, 330–31.

19. Cf. 11.25–48 of Shakespeare's "The Phoenix and Turtle," a poem which explores the same paradoxes of love and death that *Antony and Cleopatra* does. See Adelman, p. 112.

20. Cf. Adelman, p. 160.

21. Cf. Battenhouse, p. 168.

22. See Elias Schwartz, "The Shackling of Accidents: *Antony and Cleopatra*," *College English*, XXIII (1962), 557.

Notes to Chapter 6

1. One might at first assume that politics and public life are identical, but it is possible to be a public figure without being strictly speaking political. Our world offers numerous examples of people who use fame in a nonpolitical field (entertainment, athletics, education, etc.) as an entrance into politics; by contrast, Antony and Cleopatra seem to regard politics as the springboard, into some new but as yet undefined form of celebrity.

2. *Noble* must mean something different in *Antony and Cleopatra* from what it does in *Coriolanus* if Octavius is able to speak of "noble

weakness" (V.ii.344). Most of the paradoxes or oxymorons in *Antony and Cleopatra* are a result of the revaluation of Roman values that takes place as the play progresses, with defeat becoming victory, and the high and the low as traditionally understood in Rome exchanging places. See I.v.33–34, II.ii.226, 237–39, III.iv.29–30, IV.xiv.78, 108, 136–38, IV.xv.84, V.ii.1–8, 236–37, 316.

3. On "the force of this restrictive clause," see Ernest Schanzer, *The Problem Plays of Shakespeare* (New York: Schocken Books, 1963), p. 155.

4. See Cecil, pp. 11–12, John Holloway, *The Story of the Night* (London: Routledge & Kegan Paul, 1961), pp. 101–5, and Louis Auchincloss, *Motiveless Malignity* (Boston: Houghton Mifflin, 1969), pp. 56–57.

5. See Matthew Proser, *The Heroic Image in Five Shakespearean Tragedies* (Princeton: Princeton University Press, 1965), p. 194. Charmian's request of the soothsayer (I.ii.26–30) reveals the full extent of transpolitical ambitions.

6. See also III.xiii.172–82, 191–94, IV.iv.29–33, IV.viii.19–22.

7. See I.i.41, I.iii.27–29, 62–65, II.v.107–8, II.vi.64–70, III.xiii.105, 116–22.

8. John Danby, *Poets on Fortune's Hill* (London: Faber & Faber, 1952), p. 136.

9. See III.xi.69–70, III.xiii.167, IV.xiv.34–36.

10. See Stephen Shapiro, "The Varying Shore of the World: Ambivalence in *Antony and Cleopatra*," *Modern Language Quarterly*, XXVII (1966), 25.

11. See, for example, *A Midsummer Night's Dream*, I.ii.22, *Troilus and Cressida*, III.ii.119, *Romeo and Juliet*, I.i.21–23, 169–70, and *Twelfth Night*, III.i.120.

12. In the correlation of forms of regimes with forms of souls in Books VIII and IX of the *Republic*, tyranny in the city corresponds to boundless desire in the soul. See 573b, 575a.

13. See Danby, p. 135, p. 139.

14. See Simmons, p. 126, p. 148.

15. See Simmons, pp. 120–21, 136.

16. See I.i.33, I.v.77–78, II.v.78, 93–95, III.xiii.164. See Paul Lawrence Rose, "The Politics of *Antony and Cleopatra*," *Shakespeare Quarterly*, XX (1969), 382–83.

17. See also I.iv.1–3, II.ii.30–35, III.vi.1–38, V.i.35–49, 65–66. Even Antony understands that Octavius is particularly concerned about the "public ear" (III.iv.5). See Barroll, "Octavius," pp. 265, 272.

18. Octavius' soldiers do not desert him when he suffers a setback, but take the turn in their fortunes rather calmly (IV.vii.1–3, IV.ix.4–5), whereas the followers of Antony seem peculiarly given to desertion. In fact we never learn how many men Antony has lost *in* a battle, but only how many he has lost *after* a battle (III.x.25–34, IV.vi.10–17).

19. See Aristotle, *Politics*, 1295a, Xenophon, *Memorabilia*, IV.vi.12, and *Cyropaideia*, I.iii.18.

20. The word *law* appears only once in *Antony and Cleopatra* (III.xii.32–33), and then is used by Octavius, and only in a rather extralegal context: Thidias is told to "make his own edict." The closest Antony ever comes to laying down a law for his subjects is at I.i.38–40, but this is hardly a conventional statute, even if Thidias is eventually convicted and punished under it.

21. The creativity of the lovers is manifest on the lowest level in their endless invention of new pleasures and diversions, summed up in Antony's question: "What sport to-night?" (I.i.46–47). On the connection between creativity and nihilism in *Antony and Cleopatra*, see Terence Eagleton, *Shakespeare and Society* (New York: Schocken Books, 1967), pp. 122–23.

22. For a possible connection between beast and god in this one image, see Robert G. Hunter, "Cleopatra and the 'Oestre Junonicque,'" *Shakespeare Studies*, V (1969), 236–39.

23. Cf. Simmons, p. 18: "In Coriolanus Shakespeare discovers a hero whose fate is the abstract of a larger tragedy, the tragedy of Rome itself." See Simmons, p. 9, for a statement of the nature of this tragedy: "The pressures and the exigencies of Rome conflict with vision even as the city helps to generate aspiration."

24. T. S. Eliot is one of the few, calling *Coriolanus*, together "with *Antony and Cleopatra*, Shakespeare's most assured artistic success" (*Selected Essays* [New York: Harcourt, Brace, 1932] p. 124). As if to prove the point, Charney, p. 40, finds this a "bewildering remark."

25. Cf. Adelman, p. 159, p. 225 (note 44).

Index

Adelman, Janet, 25, 212-213, 222-223, 225
Alcibiades, 14, 211, 216-218
Aristotle, 101-102, 123, 209, 211, 213-217, 219, 225
Athens, 173, 184, 219
Auchincloss, Louis, 224

Barroll, J. Leeds, 212, 220-221, 224
Battenhouse, Roy, 214-216, 220-221, 223
Beethoven, Ludwig van, 210
Blisset, William, 221
Bloom, Allan, 211, 214, 217-218, 220, 222
Bodin, Jean, 219
Bradley, A. C., 213, 220
Brecht, Bertolt, 210
Brower, Reuben, 214, 216, 218
Browning, R., 215
Bryant, J. A., Jr., 221
Bullough, Geoffrey, 12, 210-211
Burke, Kenneth, 219

Carr, W. I., 218-219
Cecil, Lord David, 219, 222, 224
Charney, Maurice, 24, 27, 212, 217-218, 220, 222, 225
Cymbeline, 181

Daiches, David, 222
Danby, John, 224
Danson, Lawrence, 215, 217-218
Donne, John, 170, 175, 203
Dryden, John, 127-128

Eagleton, Terence, 225

Eckermann, Johann Peter, 209
Eliot, T. S., 210, 225
Enright, D. J., 217
Evans, G. Blakemore, 210, 212

Fritz, Kurt von, 209

Goddard, Harold, 12, 16, 210-211, 213-215
Goethe, Johann Wolfgang von, 209
Greville, Fulke, 17, 210

Halio, Jay, 220
Hamlet, 89, 114
Hardy, Alexandre, 210
Holloway, John, 224
Huffman, Clifford Chalmers, 210, 213, 215
Hunter, Robert G., 225

Jaffa, Harry, 213
Johnson, Samuel, 7, 8, 209
Jonas, Hans, 223
Jonson, Ben, 7, 17

Knight, G. Wilson, 136, 220
Knights, L. C., 218
Kott, Jan, 210

Lear, King, 124
Lees, F. N., 217
Levin, Harry, 218
Livy, 12, 216, 219
Lycurgus, 83-84, 215-216

Macbeth, 114, 182

MacCallum, M. W., 209, 213, 220
Machiavelli, Niccolò, 41-42, 209-210, 213, 215-217, 219-220
Mack, Maynard, 220
Mansfield, Harvey C., Jr., 217, 219
Markels, Julian, 223
Marvell, Andrew, 170
McCanles, Michael, 215-217
A Midsummer Night's Dream, 161, 172-173, 222, 224
Milton, John, 145
Montesquieu, 11, 210
Much Ado About Nothing, 159
Myers, Henry Alonzo, 222

Nicanor, 118-119, 218-219
Nietzsche, Friedrich, 53, 125, 219
Nolan, C. E., 222
North, Sir Thomas, 61, 137, 211, 218

Ortega y Gasset, José, 211

Palmer, John, 209
Petrarch, 160
Phillips, James, Jr., 209, 214
Phocion, 218-219
The Phoenix and Turtle, 223
Plato, 14, 69, 213, 217, 224
Plutarch, 12-15, 41-42, 61-62, 66-67, 97, 118, 137, 142, 209, 211, 213-214, 216-223
Poison, Rodney, 216
Polybius, 209, 215
Proser, Matthew, 224

Rabkin, Norman, 209, 214, 219, 222
Rank, Otto, 215

Riemer, A. P., 219, 222
Romeo and Juliet, 160-161, 163, 172, 177, 224
Romulus, 215-216
Rose, Paul Lawrence, 224
Rougemont, Denis de, 222

Schanzer, Ernest, 224
Schwartz, Elias, 223
Seaton, Ethel, 221
Sen, Sailendra Kuman, 218
Seng, Peter J., 220
Shapiro, Stephen, 224
Simmons, J. L., 215-217, 219-221, 224-225
Slater, Ann, 220
Socrates, 218-219
Sparta, 82-84, 117, 215
Spencer, T. J. B., 210-211, 214, 218-219
Stampfer, Judah, 214, 222
Stein, Arnold, 221, 223
Stockholder, Katherine, 215, 217-218

Thomson, James, 210
Titus Andronicus, 211
Traversi, Derek, 128, 213-214, 216, 219, 223
Tristan and Isolde, 163, 170, 177-178
Troilus, 160, 164
Troilus and Cressida, 217, 224
Twelfth Night, 224

Wagner, Richard, 170, 177
Waith, Eugene M., 217

Xenophon, 225

Shakespeare's Rome

Designed by R. E. Rosenbaum.
Composed by York Composition Company, Inc.,
in 11 point linotype Janson, 2 points leaded,
with display lines in monotype Bulmer.
Printed letterpress from type by York Composition Company
on Warren's Number 66 Antique Offset, 50 pound basis.
Bound by John H. Dekker and Sons
in Joanna book cloth
and stamped in All Purpose foil.

Library of Congress Cataloging in Publication Data
(For library cataloging purposes only)

Cantor, Paul Arthur.
  Shakespeare's Rome, Republic and Empire.

  Includes bibliographical references and index.
  1. Shakespeare, William, 1564–1616—Knowledge—
Rome. 2. Shakespeare, William, 1564–1616. Coriolanus.
3. Shakespeare, William, 1564–1616. Antony and
Cleopatra. I. Title.
PR3069.R6C3   822.3'3   75-36522
ISBN 0-8014-0967-5